THE
COMPLETE
BOOK
OF

DALLAS™

THE COMPLETE BOOK OF DALLAS™

Behind the Scenes
at the World's
Favorite Television Program

by Suzy Kalter

Introduction
by David Jacobs,
creator of Dallas.

HARRY N. ABRAMS, INC., PUBLISHERS, NEW YORK

CONTENTS

To my Texas girlhood chums,
who always make going home so much fun:

Rena Pederson Gish — Dallas
Maggie Sheerin — San Antonio
Ellen Ross Gover — Houston

Remember the Alamo;
hook 'em horns
and Bodoni Bold forever.

Project Director: Robert Morton
Editor: Beverly Fazio
Designer: Carol Robson

Library of Congress Cataloging-in-Publication Data
Kalter, Suzy.
   The complete book of Dallas.
   Includes index.
   1. Dallas (Television program)   I. Title.
PN1992.77.D3K35   1986   791.43'72   86–3573
ISBN 0–8109–0836–0

Photograph of Linda Gray on jacket supplied by Greg Gorman

Published in 1986 by Harry N. Abrams, Incorporated, New York
All rights reserved. No part of the contents of this book may be
reproduced without the written permission of the publishers

Times Mirror Books

Printed and bound by Amilcare Pizzi, S.p.A., Milan, Italy

ACKNOWLEDGMENTS

With a show that spans two of the greatest states in the union and runs as long as *Dallas* has, I could be thanking people for a very long time. All cast and crew members were warm, friendly, helpful, and always tolerant of my presence underfoot—for which I thank them. I'm particularly grateful to those who handed out coffee at 5:30 in the morning, gave me shade in 110-degree heat, put pages back in photo notebooks, and answered even my dumbest questions with kindness. Without the cooperation of Phil Capice, Jim Brown, and Leonard Katzman, it would have been difficult, if not impossible, for me to have written this book.

I must especially thank my editor, Robert Morton, who makes any project a delight, and Leonard Katzman, the creative consultant to *Dallas* and for eight years producer, director, writer, and cast guru. Uncle Lennie spent countless hours with me and is largely responsible for the accuracy of this text. So if you find any mistakes in this book, write him—not me. His assistant, Louella Caraway, also helped out in identifying pictures, looking up story lines, and keeping it all straight. This book is a tribute to their contribution to television. At Abrams I must also thank Paul Gottlieb, Beverly Fazio, Harriet Whelchel, and Carol Robson, who were all devoted to J.R.'s and my foibles.

My husband, Michael Gershman, spent a lot of time editing the episode sequences of this book, and our son, Aaron, spent at least one hour a night watching reruns of *Dallas* with me, just to be the only six-year-old in America to know who shot J.R. Thank you both for your patience and good company. And no, Aaron, Bobby isn't really dead.

At Lorimar, I must thank Danny Simon for creating this project and Pamela Harris, Linda Ritter, Terry Johnson, Tina Hampson, and Joe Whitaker for taking me under their corporate wing and finding a place for me in the Producer's Building and at the commissary. David Jacobs, creator of *Dallas*, wrote the introduction and became my good friend the minute we discovered we each have a son named Aaron—I thank him for his time, his energy, and his hard work. Mary Kay Kelly helped me through all the production phases and gets a single card credit as a reward.

Thanks and hugs are due Jim Calio, who once again proved himself a great friend.

The information within *The Complete Book of Dallas* comes from many sources. I did read each script, but owing to dictates of space and design my episode synopses could not follow through on every story line. Quotations used in this book come from the scripts and may have aired in a slightly different fashion. While I have seen just about every episode of *Dallas*, the scripts—not the tapes—have been the basis of the story information. Remarks made in these pages by cast and crew members were collected from personal interviews, press releases, and newspaper clippings. No quotes were ever borrowed from tabloid newspapers. Much of the commentary on dramatic structure comes from lessons learned in a class on story structure taught by Robert McGee of U.S.C. and from the book *Theory and Techniques of Playwriting*, as well as from the creative forces behind the show itself.

INTRODUCTION

I had lofty aims then.

It was 1977; I'd only been writing television for a year and had a good job: story editor of the dramatic series *Family*. It was a fine show, lofty in intent, critically appreciated. The only trouble was, it wasn't mine. Formerly a legitimate writer (a writer whose words are meant to be *read*, not communicated to his audience through such intermediaries as directors and actors), I was accustomed to writing stories for characters I'd invented myself; thus my uneasiness at *Family*. For if it was true—and it was and is and always will be true—that character is plot and plot character, then there was something a little shady about making up stories for characters somebody else created. The only way to make an honest man of myself would be to create a series of my own.

I talked to Mike Filerman, then a development executive with Lorimar, about developing such a series. I had, I explained, aspirations. I wanted to do something *good*, a show that mattered, insightful drama that intelligent people could watch and discuss and be moved by.

I waxed; Mike listened.

"*Scenes from a Marriage*," I said—something like that, maybe; that was the level I wanted to aim for. We screened it, loved it.

But there was another movie Mike thought we should take a look at: *No Down Payment*, a semi-sleazy 1950s potboiler. I saw the movie and got the picture. Mike knew television better than I did.

That remained the pattern of our working relationship. I wanted to do art, Mike wanted to do trash, and between us we made television.

Between the heights of *Scenes from a Marriage* and sleaze of *No Down Payment* was a midpoint level we found when we formulated *Knots Landing*—the first idea we took to CBS. CBS liked the *kind* of show we described to them, but thought *Knots Landing* a little too middle-class and tame to break into a prime-time field dominated by cops and doctors. How about something richer, they said, more sensational, easier to promote? A modern saga. We'll give it a shot, we said.

A saga—I liked that. And the best place, to my mind, for a modern saga to unfold was in modern, urban Texas. Bigger, brasher, richer, newer than the Northeast, not so trendy as California. A setting that matched Wall Street in the harboring of unfathomable wealth and equaled Tennessee Williams's South in the fostering of unrelenting decadence.

But where in urban Texas? Houston, maybe? No, too modern for a saga, too new and oil rich; deep dark secrets can't be hidden behind all those glass walls. San Antonio? Too exotic, almost Mexican. Austin? Fort Worth? Waxahachie?

We settled on Dallas, although I suppose there never was any doubt that we'd come around to it in the end: Dallas was an arena for saga, at once a big city and a redneck town, a place with right and wrong sides of the track—one side populated by barefoot bumpkins and the other side by millionaire bumpkins. Both populations, I knew, would play a part in the saga. I may have blanched when I realized I was setting a television show in the town where Kennedy had been killed, but on reflection I decided that fifteen years was long enough to hold the grudge; besides, the Dallas Cowboys had won the Super Bowl the year before and that somehow entitled the city to a fresh start.

So I went to work on *Dallas*, evoking as best I could the texture and character of this great booming metropolis where cowboys crossed paths with oilmen in the shadow of towers built by financial men, where Old West and Central Sunbelt met to form what might be New America. It felt right to me; I could feel the grit between my fingers.

Then I had a sudden inspiration: maybe I should actually *go* to Dallas.

When I told Mike I thought I should see the city I was writing about, he talked me out of it. Timing is everything. CBS is really hot for this script, he said; let's get it in as quickly as possible; don't give them a chance to cool. Go to Dallas *after*.

I said okay, but knowing I was writing about a place I'd never seen gave me a few uneasy moments—until I remembered having read that Moss Hart wrote his quintessential Hollywood play, *Once in a Lifetime*, without ever having been to Hollywood: he simply wrote the stereotype, and it checked out. The precedent was all I needed; from here on it was smooth sailing.

Half a day later and I'd constructed the network of characters that became and remained the core population of *Dallas*. Like Moss Hart, I wrote stereotypical images: my Texans were a mostly self-serving bunch, corrupt up to certain points, generous to a purpose, certainly not admirable, but kind of fun.

Indeed, in giving vent to my imagination, I was having so much fun that I was forgetting to make the piece lofty.

Back to the phone. Mike must have anticipated my call, because before I had a chance to complain he told me he was *this* close to selling another pilot script of mine, *Married*, a poignant, ambitious little piece about a couple of kids who graduate from high school and get married the next day. This news let me off the hook, gave me a Plan B: I'd write one "for them" and one "for me." Since *Married* was sufficiently artful to satisfy my lofty aspirations, I could drop all pretenses for *Dallas* and just keep on having fun with it.

(For the record: Plan B had a short life. *Married*, critically praised, flopped after four episodes. *Dallas*, critically roasted—*venomously* roasted is really more accurate—became a worldwide phenomenon. Learning my lesson, I went on to Plan C: do it for "them"; then square it for "me." Or: get it on the air any way you can; make it a hit; *then* make it good.)

The first draft of *Dallas* was dated December 10, 1977. Six weeks later we were in Dallas, filming this and four additional episodes. And in April we were on the air.

I finally got to go to Dallas, to check out my stereotypes. I didn't have to change much. Moss Hart knew what he was doing.

In 1986 I wrote and executive-produced a prequel called *Dallas: The Early Years*, a three-hour movie that told the "back story" of Digger Barnes and Jock Ewing, their partnership, and their mutual love for Ellie Southworth. We hired a linguist-dialectician from a Dallas college to help the non-Texans in the cast with the regional accent. When we met, she complimented me on the dialogue in my script. "You've got Texas in your rhythms and Texas in your heart," she told me in her own, lovely idiosyncratic Dallasese; "I bet you've also got Texas in your blood."

"Why not?" I replied. "I've been here two or three times."

If the truth be told, though, *Dallas* is in my blood, and I suppose it is there to stay. It made me a few dollars, thrust my career forward by light-years, and provided a kind of sixteenth-level celebrity I never aimed for or wanted but enjoyed when it came. *Dallas* became one of the most successful television dramas ever and a worldwide hit of unprecedented scale. I was the guy who'd created it. It was impossible for me not to be affected by that.

To millions of fans the world over the *Dallas* logo
has come to mean an evening of glamour,
greed, and intrigue.

Dallasites consider *Dallas* their show, and often turn out to watch the filming. The producers sometimes advertise for extras in the newspapers.

And yet, for a long while, I distanced myself from *Dallas*. When people asked how I felt about being the creator of this phenomenon, I generally used words like "delighted," "amused," "surprised"; never "wow!"

There were reasons for this. When *Dallas* was launched, I was still working on *Family*; I had no authority over the ongoing development of *Dallas*. When I left *Family*, I went to work producing *Married*. *Married* was where my heart was. After *Married* flopped loftily, I produced—thanks to the rising success of *Dallas*—*Knots Landing*, the idea that started it all. While *Knots* was not a flop, it struggled for the first few years, and I couldn't help but feel sensitive about the lack of attention it got compared to its monster-hit brother. And finally, I knew that while I had created *Dallas*, I wasn't responsible for its evolution. As executive producer Phil Capice had supplanted development executive Mike Filerman as the executive authority behind the show, *Dallas*'s indefatigable producer Leonard Katzman had replaced me as the "consciousness" of *Dallas*.

So when people asked me how I felt about the success of my baby, I used gentle words to describe small emotions, as if embarrassed to say, "Wow."

It was that prequel that restored my proprietary feelings about *Dallas*. Writing it I was immersed again in the characters that gave life to the series. Here was the triangle that started it all: Jock Ewing, Digger Barnes, and Ellie Southworth, younger than we'd ever seen them, acting out the drama from which later drama would emerge, creating the feud their offspring would share and challenge, giving birth to passions and conflicts that festered and grew and became the stuff of a story that keeps going on and on and on.

They wanted a saga; I gave them a saga. Jock, Ellie, Digger, and I bred J. R., Gary, Bobby, Ray, Pam, Cliff, Val, Lucy, Sue Ellen, and their offspring. Their faces and those of the characters drawn into the saga by their loves and machinations are known in scores of countries; they speak dozens of languages—and, obviously, some universal language that keeps *Dallas* alive and thriving all over the Earth.

Don't ask me to analyze the universal appeal of *Dallas*; I've tried and never bought my answers. The appeal is there, though, and it's enduring. At this writing the story started by Jock and Digger and Ellie is more than two hundred hours long and still going strong.

Wow.

Chapter One

SOAP OPERA GOES PRIME TIME

Amerika has known how to spell "Dallas" since 1956, when Frank Loesser wrote the Broadway play *The Most Happy Fella*: "Big D, little A, double L, A-S."

Thirty years later, America has changed its tune, but it still knows how to spell *Dallas*. The bold and brassy theme song of America's most popular television show blares from 30 million television sets on a weekly basis. Nearly one-half of the country—over 100 million people—tune in to view the weekly *sturm und drang* of the Ewing clan, where love, hate, murder, mayhem, infidelity, greed, and mental cruelty are inflicted on the family members—by each other—at regular intervals.

"It's not really Dallas we're talking about, it could be Tulsa, Kansas City, or anyplace else," says former producer and current creative consultant Leonard Katzman. "The name has mythic qualities, that's why we picked it—but this isn't a show about Texas. It's about a family."

Indeed . . . a very unusual family. The Ewings of Texas all manage to live under one roof—a ranch house called Southfork, which their mother, one Miss Ellie Southworth Ewing Farlow, inherited from her father, Aaron. Although Southfork is only an 8,500-square-foot dwelling, it houses anywhere from eight to twelve adults and two or three children, all in merry conflict. Conflict, after all, is what drama is all about. And while more and more Americans may be moving back home to save on the rent, the Ewings do not live together to save money. In fact, individually each Ewing is rumored to be worth over $10 million, or about as much as a Kennedy. They live together because they like it; they live together because they represent the old-fashioned family that all of us remember and to which few of us now belong; they live together because there wouldn't be a television show if they didn't.

They pretend to be a normal, all-American family that just happened to strike it rich. But they are hardly normal. Most of the main characters have been to jail—on murder charges, no less; almost all have been kidnapped; several of them have or have had addictive problems, and the head of the family—a middle-aged quasi-villain named J.R.—is guilty of at least five of the seven deadly sins each week. This is the story of a family, but it is not a family like the one that lives next door to you.

"Don't you think all this would happen in any family that lives under the same roof?" asked Jim Davis, who played the family patriarch—Miss Ellie's husband, Jock Ewing. "Why we're all under the same roof is a mystery to me—except it's in the script. It's an unusual situation. We're supposed to have a big spread and so much money that we all want to stay together, I guess. That's TV for you."

Or soap opera, anyway.

Soap Opera and Television

Soap opera began on television in the early 1960s as a daytime formula to capture women viewers who were otherwise occupied with childcare, home care, and volunteer work. Actually, it was a spin-off of television's predecessor, radio. The pace was slow, the drama was heady, and the story lines were, well, addictive. The sponsors were generally corporations that made household-cleaning products, including cleansers and detergents—hence the name "soap opera." Soap operas, whose only competition was game shows, became a valued part of network programming when marketing statistics proved just how many millions of people were home, glued to the set. By the mid-1970s major league ballplayers, celebrities, and blue bloods admitted their addictions to certain shows. From that point on, soaps were taken seriously.

In conception, the soap opera was never ending—that way the sponsors could be assured that viewers would tune in each day to learn the newest plot developments and thus to incidentally hear more commercial messages. Indeed, serialized plots had kept a generation of early moviegoers coming to the theater each Saturday to see what would happen in next week's thrilling episode. Soap opera as television fare merely adapted the concept to the audience—largely female, as it was in radio days—and the times. By definition, a melodramatic presentation of reality, the soap opera allowed viewers to see, among other things, that money doesn't buy happiness, that everyone has problems, and that the good die young. It personified and personalized life's biggest clichés so that in time soap opera itself became synonymous with cliché, and as such was considered anathema for serious television, for prime-time viewing.

Television executives and program producers did not believe the audience would stay tuned to serialized stories in prime time. Their perceptions changed in 1975, when Leon Uris's novel *QB VII* was introduced as the first mini-series; it provided the industry with a real shock—viewers loved it. Irwin Shaw's *Rich Man, Poor Man* and Alex

The Ewing living room at Southfork—
where many a family crisis occurs—is
an exact replica of a private home in
Dallas, Texas, built to scale on a soundstage at MGM Studios.

Haley's novel *Roots* followed, and Americans stayed home in astounding numbers to watch the week-long, continuing sagas. Startled executives came to believe that people would stay tuned over a period of time, but only for special occasions such as big-time, big-name, big-budget, and usually big-book-based mini-series.

It took *Dallas* to make TV history.

Dallas was not, however, initially produced as a serial. It was conceived as a noncontinuing drama. "I had hoped we'd be able to serialize after we got a hold," says David Jacobs, *Dallas*'s creator. Indeed, the show changed to its present serialized form after about ten episodes of its first official season, in the fall of 1978. As a result, the early episodes of *Dallas* presented story lines that had no relationship to each other—one week Bobby is kidnapped and shot, yet the next week he has no bandages. "My favorite one of those," says executive producer Philip Capice, "is the one where suddenly Pam has an ex-husband who just shows up and says, 'Hi, we used to be married,' and then by the end of the show he sort of disappears."

Indeed, the passage of time is one of the trickiest elements to deal with in a nonserialized show. Time passes much more easily in serialization, because almost anything can be made to make sense when it is written in perspective. Yet the main difference between prime-time soap and daytime soap is the passage of time and story line. In daytime television, the story moves very slowly and is highly repetitious, mainly because studies show that the average viewer watches only three out of five episodes a week, but if she misses too much of the action she will feel lost and may then quit the show. The story therefore constantly reviews what has already passed so the viewer can easily be brought up to date. *Dallas* producers assume that their viewer is a regular who has either seen all the episodes or has caught up on the news through a friend. There is no reviewing of the situation in a new episode (in syndication, a narrator explains the previous episode with one minute of flashbacks).

"We move a lot faster than a daytime soap," says Capice. "In the course of twenty-five or twenty-six shows a season, we did the same amount of material that a daytime serial does in two hundred and fifty shows. Now we're doing thirty or thirty-one shows a season."

Serialized and continuing plot lines are not the only factors that make *Dallas* a fancy soap. At the time the show was first broadcast— five episodes aired in spring 1978 to test the waters—there were no big, splashy family dramas dealing with larger-than-life "real people." One-hour dramas in prime time were primarily doctor shows, detective shows, or family shows in the *Eight Is Enough* mold. (*Family*, the one serious family drama of the time, was so serious it was canceled.)

Dallas was the first show to combine the scope of a mini-series with the big ideas of life—themes such as good *vs*. evil and brother *vs*. brother. Set in the big state of Texas—where life is lived in the fast lane, where everything is bigger and badder than anywhere else—the breadth of the show made viewers realize that *Romeo and Juliet* had at long last come to *Giant*.

Lucy was snatched from her mother, Valene, during infancy and raised at Southfork. When she was sixteen she successfully located her mother and secretly began to see her. In "Reunion," she brings Val back to Southfork.

"In its form, *Dallas* is a kind of soap opera," says Larry Hagman, known the world over as "J.R." "But let me tell you something. Soap opera is damn good. I worked almost three years on *The Edge of Night*. It was done live and provided marvelous training for actors. Soap operas provide fine acting performances, and they're damned hard too. I consider *Dallas* drama—turgid drama, sometimes, but it's always interesting with the major characters bouncing around. The show's fine when it revolves around several themes. People say that it's sexy and trashy. If you call screwing your wife's sister sexy, then perhaps it is. To me, it's just all in the family."

Soap opera has traditionally taken a set of very human characters and given them a set of very real problems. Anything that *can* happen to a character, does. Each character in a soap opera will have enough problems for any viewer to identify with at least some of them. (It would be extraordinary for a real person to endure what a television character is forced to endure.) But people are people and characters are creations whose very actions are governed by the dramatic needs of a story.

The man viewers
love to hate—
J.R. Ewing.

Bobby James Ewing, Daddy's favorite son.

The Elements of Soap

All dramatic action demands the same structure to make it effective. Soap opera is merely effectiveness gone effusive. A soap opera is so dramatic that it is melodramatic; its edge on reality borders the comic. Good soap opera is as enticing as a finely crafted novel; at its worst soap opera is simply funny.

Dallas is soap at its best. If all the pages of all the scripts—222 at this writing—were written in running prose and bound in hard cover, *Dallas* would be a best-seller. It has plot and character aplenty. All it lacks now is a sizzling ending.

Conflict

Dallas works because it delves into layer after layer of conflict. No drama can exist without conflict; there is no serious drama without inner conflict. To say *Dallas* is the story of good *vs*. evil is an oversimplification. Well-developed characters—and the *Dallas* characters are among the best ever developed on television—have conflicts within themselves, just like real people. J.R. wouldn't be as compelling as he is were he all bad; Sue Ellen is most interesting because she seems to be her own worst enemy. Even Miss Ellie, who personifies strength and virtue, increases in depth when we discover her offscreen history, or "back story."

The essential conflict in *Dallas* was originally to be between J.R. and Pamela. "The idea was that a poor girl from the wrong side of the tracks marries into a rich Texas oil family," according to David Jacobs. Beginning episodes tilted toward Pam's ability to tackle the world. The balance of power shifted in the first year when it appeared that her character was being oversimplified: "In the beginning, we called it 'Pammy Solves All,'" says Katzman.

Thereafter, Pamela and her husband, Bobby, were together to represent "good" while J.R. stood for "evil." Each character subsequently added to the story line was brought in to set off more conflict. After all, if everybody got along fine, there would be no show. While some weekly dramas reach outside the core cast for added conflict, it has been *Dallas* policy to keep the main interaction between the family members. Of course, there are layers of secondary conflicts in *Dallas*'s subsidiary story lines, and new characters are brought into the show periodically to multiply the tensions, but this is not the kind of show that solves a crime a week or inserts a guest star a week to keep the excitement moving.

The Inciting Incident

All conflict stems from one action, something that starts the avalanche. That something is called the inciting incident. The inciting incident is the first major event of the main plot and is the cause of everything that follows. Each action thereafter becomes a complicating incident.

Whether *Dallas* had run for only five shows and been canceled or continues to three hundred episodes, the inciting incident would still be the same. The inciting incident in *Dallas* occurs when Bobby Ewing marries Pamela Barnes. Boy has met girl, married her in a quickie ceremony in New Orleans, and is now taking her home to live happily ever after with his family, pretending that fifty years of animosity between the Ewings and the Barneses will not affect their relationship.

The protagonist is developed from the inciting incident. The protagonist can be an ordinary, undramatic person, until *whammy!* he encounters the inciting incident. Thereafter, life will never be the same. The protagonist always reacts profoundly to the inciting incident; it is the driving force behind his actions. Out of the inciting incident, the protagonist must declare himself; his goals must begin to crystallize. Something happens to him with the inciting incident, something that never happened before, and from here on in, he must pursue a certain path. He believes that path will be easy and is always surprised at the complications that get in the way. But he keeps on going forward, even when complications temporarily set him back. No matter what happens, Bobby will love Pam.

In traditional feature films, the inciting incident happens on screen within the first half-hour of the film so that the viewer can see it and feel it. In *Dallas*, the inciting incident happens off screen—before the series even started.

Dallas begins with the complicating incident, when Pam says to Bobby, "Your family's gonna throw me off the ranch."

Maybe they will; maybe they won't.

Complicating Incidents

The complicating incidents in the story line move the action along; they are the backbone of good story-telling, and out of them grows the much-needed conflict. Each complicating incident in *Dallas* is a result of the inciting incident, Pam and Bobby's marriage. To ensure the conflict, two immediate complicating incidents set up the rest of the action.

The Back Story Complication

Pam and Bobby's marriage is particularly significant because their fathers had been business partners but wound up sworn enemies. Pam's father, Digger, had even tried to kill Bobby's father, Jock.

Once Pam and Bobby get married, Pam convinces him to give up his "public relations" work (a euphemism for his job of traveling, partying, and bribing Ewing family friends) and join his brother J.R. in the corporate offices of Ewing Oil. Because J.R. is threatened by Bobby's arrival, the resulting complication is rich in potential conflict. J.R.— who heretofore had Ewing Oil all to himself—must get rid of Bobby, and therefore Pam. His hatred for Pam is twofold: not only is she the daughter of Digger Barnes, but she has infringed on J.R.'s absolute power in the company.

J.R. Ewing is not the kind of man who tolerates this kind of thing easily.

In traditional drama, the complicating incidents build to a crisis which must then be resolved. In serial television, a small story thread may be resolved on a weekly basis, but greater story lines are only resolved over a whole season—a thirty-week time period—with a potent series of complicating incidents firmly planted into the last ten weeks to provide the proper backdrop for a cliffhanger.

The Resulting
Complication

The cliffhanger is a device borrowed from serials in the days of silent movies, when the heroine was literally left dangling from a cliff. The viewer had to come back next week to see how she was saved. Serialization relies on a suspenseful cliffhanger to bring the original viewers back the next week (or the next season) and to stimulate speculation— word of mouth—which, it is hoped, will increase the number of viewers for the next episode. A successful cliffhanger is one that everyone has to talk about, one that infects a large segment of the population with the need to know the outcome. Even if the cliffhanger itself does not attract many nonregular viewers, the heightened, much-advertised suspense may bring in hordes of nonregulars for the beginning of the next season.

"I think the original cliffhanger goes back to *1001 Arabian Nights*," says Capice. "Wasn't it Scheherazade who was sentenced to death but kept telling gripping, suspenseful tales to the sultan, night after night? She was never beheaded because the sultan always wanted to hear the next installment of her story. *There* was a woman adept at building a cliffhanger."

Dallas writers proved themselves just as adept with their first official cliffhanger, at the end of the first season, in spring 1979. "We made a conscious effort to do what no one had ever done before," says Katzman, "to leave an audience hanging in the air for an entire summer. Having run away from the sanitarium, J.R.'s wife, Sue Ellen— eight months pregnant—got in an automobile accident and was left in

The Cliffhanger

Cliffhanger for 1981: whose body is floating in the pool? To avoid leaks to the press and simultaneously make sure even the cast didn't know, the producers had Sue Ellen, Pam, and Kristin all take a dunk. Here, Sue Ellen does the Dead Woman's Float for Cliff.

a coma. Her baby, born prematurely, was barely alive. It could go either way. We wanted people to have something to think about over the summer.

"No show had ever gone off and left us wondering about something very important. We got a tremendous number of letters after the first year saying, 'How could you let us go on worrying about that baby?' The reaction to that last show was very strong. The next year we decided to go for something even stronger, and we ended up with the mystery of 'Who Shot J.R.?'"

The most famous cliffhanger, probably in television history, was indeed "Who Shot J.R.?" But it was not what producers had originally planned. The second season was to end with Digger's death, Pam's discovery that Digger was not her real father, and a shot of Cliff—who the audience knows has a gun—standing over Digger's grave pledging revenge: "I'm going to get him, Daddy, I swear I will!"

Look out, J.R. Ewing.

Then CBS requested two more shows in order to extend the season. A new cliffhanger had to be created instantly.

"We were all sitting around and someone said, 'Let's have J.R. get his,'" says Katzman. "We started with the last scene and built backward. We built two entire scripts backward. We really didn't know who shot him when we created the whole thing. We said, 'To hell with it, let's shoot him and figure out who did it later.' Someone had to do it. Then we started eliminating and eliminating until we found the person we wanted. Kristin did it by process of elimination."

"As *Dallas* was developing, there seemed to be a special audience fascination with J.R., this guy they hated and loved," recalls Capice. "We kept getting letters asking, 'When is J.R. going to get his?' It seemed like a good idea to explore. We never really considered killing him, but we talked about several ways in which near death could occur and make sense."

Capice admits that they considered other possibilities before the shooting was settled on. Someone suggested that Sue Ellen decide to kill herself. In this scenario she would dissolve a quantity of sleeping pills in a glass of water and go into the nursery to say good-bye to her baby, leaving the glass on the bedtable. In the meantime, J.R. comes in and drinks the water. Sue Ellen sees him drink it but doesn't try to stop him; she just retreats to the nursery to rock the baby. The story was rejected because "it wasn't as stylish as establishing five or six suspects," says Capice. "We wanted an opportunity to bring four or five story lines together. The shooting was also a way to tie up plot threads. We established a motive in each of the plot lines and the public went wild."

Now Capice and other show executives find themselves burdened by the cliffhanger. "'Who Shot?' was the greatest cliffhanger of all time and created a nightmare for us. We don't try to top that time after time because we can't. That period of television history will never come again, and timing was as responsible as anything else. We were all more unsophisticated then; the viewer hadn't been bombarded with all sorts of cliffhangers, many of which have become letdowns. Back then, it was for the fun of it. Now audiences have a 'show me' attitude, or they've totally lost interest because there have been so many cheats. It's almost cliffhanger abuse out there in TV land. We're leaning more and more away from the sensational cliffhanger. You don't have to have physical drama to have a good cliffhanger. Emotional drama has much more impact."

Since that time cliffhangers have not been built backward. Stories are structured in one of three basic strategy sessions, at each of which approximately twelve episodes are discussed. The cliffhanger is only begun in earnest in November, as the last group of stories is organized. "It's ridiculous to think we would have our best idea a full six months ahead of time and then be locked into it," says Katzman.

Plot Twists Plot twists must lead to each cliffhanger and unite the characters in an overriding master goal. But each twist and turning point must still serve to develop the characters and promote the story threads in an individual manner. On *Dallas*, the plot twists can be conventional, controversial, or both.

"I think from the middle of the first year *Dallas* made it clear that this was not a show where you could expect the expected," says David Jacobs. "In a rather early show J.R. leaves Sue Ellen at Southfork to go out on his own and she follows him to the car and very bitterly shows her frustration. After J.R. angrily leaves, Sue Ellen bumps into Ray and says something to him that could be interpreted as provocative. We go to a commercial break. In any other show, the implications would have been left in the air. In *Dallas*, we went back and picked up Ray and Sue Ellen. We made it obvious what had gone on. From then on, *Dallas* became a show on which anything could happen."

A good bit of what happens is based on the producers' ability to weave reality, coincidence, and fantasy into a believable bundle, yet the viewer brings to the show each week a set of rules that define what he or she is willing to accept of the characters. If what is shown on the screen is not believable, the viewer is lost—possibly forever.

Reality for the Ewings, of course, is not reality for the real world, but the basic problems that plague all Americans also surface in the Ewing family, so plot twists hinge on recognized values and familiar problems. Consider these few: Sue Ellen is an alcoholic; J.R. plays around; Lucy is confused and angry and needs to find herself; Ray and Donna discover their unborn child suffers from Down's Syndrome, a risk that every almost-forty mother runs; Bobby and Pam have problems in their relationship that prevent them from living happily ever after. It is therefore only natural that Sue Ellen gets drunk at critical moments and has had to be hospitalized several times; that J.R. would go to bed with anyone; that Lucy's marriage fails and that she falls heir to several nonproductive relationships; that Ray and Donna face the agonizing consideration of abortion; that Pam and Bobby finally divorce. No matter how unique, a plot twist cannot work if it does not make sense.

J.R. will use any means to gain his ends. Here, he tries to charm Pam into selling her son's birthright.

Pam's welcome to the family is icy. Sister-in-law Sue Ellen considers her a tramp and makes deprecating remarks for at least two seasons.

(*above right*)
Characters often provide information essential to the story line in telephone conversations. The exposition might seem boring in regular dialogue.

Traditionally, the plot twist functions to place the character in a new situation so that the audience can gain from his or her behavior further insight into the character's personality. Plot twists grow out of complications, and they can be external or internal. No character would be believable if at least some of his or her conflicts didn't come from within. Thus Sue Ellen's alcoholism is an internal problem and Jenna's incarceration for murder is an external matter.

Dallas takes its plot twists from current issues—rape, abortion, homosexuality, murder, babynapping—and fashions them according to the standards of drama. Reality comes from the fact that these things do happen; the unreality of television is that all these things happen to the Ewings.

J.R.'s telephone talk is peppered with phrases like "Yep," "Well now," and "You just leave this to me"—all positioned to help him project an image of power.

Reality and Coincidence

Cast and crew alike are fond of quipping, "This isn't real life, it's *Dallas*." What happens on *Dallas* is the difference between truth and believability. Many true-life events that are reported by the media are too strange to ever be used in fiction for the very reason that readers, or viewers, just wouldn't accept them. This has nothing to do with factual evidence. "Believing reality is always a tremendous problem," as William Goldman says in his book *Adventures in the Screen Trade*, "because the screenwriter runs dead into the problem of audience expectation and what they will and won't accept. The reality of a script has almost nothing to do with the reality of the world which we, as humans, inhabit."

An example of this can be seen in a very early story in which a hurricane hit Dallas. Texans were quick to point out that Dallas is too far inland to get hurricanes; it gets tornadoes. But no one is concerned by this bit of Hollywood hokum when the story works.

A larger example of dramatic fudging lies in the very core of the story. There is no oil whatsoever in Dallas County, but the show doesn't work unless the Ewings are in the oil business and actually have oil under their property. Therefore Braddock County was invented. Because it works, no one cares about the truth.

Coincidence

Coincidence is a method used to move plot along and add a sharp twist to the story. In the basic structure of a television script, every scene counts and every apparent coincidence is manufactured. To the viewer, however, a coincidence provides a dramatic surprise and a renewal of attention with a light-handed touch.

When Bobby bumps into Jenna Wade after putting Pam on the airplane for Paris, it appears to be a coincidence. Jenna's return allows the story to take a new twist that it otherwise could not take. Coincidence is best used in the early development of a new plot twist: the audience considers itself cheated if the coincidence happens too late in the story and throws them off course, just as in a murder mystery the murderer has to be introduced in some way in the first act. A coincidence only works if it can be accepted while it pushes the story further along. The coincidence of Jack Ewing resembling Dimitri Marinos took *Dallas* through almost twenty weeks of solidly built episodes, even though much of the time the audience did not know what the coincidence was or how it would pay off.

The Payoff

The payoff is the emotional jackpot at the end of a story line. The viewer can say, "Aha, that's why she began wearing that engagement ring when she hadn't had it on for years; now I understand." The payoff in a serial is a continuing series of rewards that makes the viewer glad to have stuck around and kept watching. The payoff is most satisfying when it has been developed slowly over a period of time yet still comes as a surprise. Usually, the payoff involves a sympathetic character or the protagonist.

The Protagonist and the Antagonist

In simple terms, the protagonist is the good guy and the antagonist is the bad guy. The good guy tries to reach a victorious conclusion, the bad guy tries to stop him. In *Dallas*, the characters are so complex that it is not always clear who the protagonist and the antagonist actually are.

"When I originally created the story," says Jacobs, "Pamela was the protagonist and J.R. was the antagonist. I saw Bobby as a playboy type. Bobby paid the bribes, Bobby got the girls, Bobby took the clients to Las Vegas. He was a bad boy who always got in trouble and whose father bailed him out and laughed about it. He was like Brick in *Cat on a Hot Tin Roof.* Then he married Pam, who said, 'Be a *mensch.*' He didn't want to go into the office, but he did it for her. This screwed up J.R. I wanted to kill off Bobby at the end of the pilot and leave Pam to fight J.R.

"When we finally got down to it, everyone wanted a hero in the story. The network and Patrick [Patrick Duffy, the actor cast as Bobby] both wanted Bobby to be a nice guy, a sympathetic character. In addition, if I killed off Bobby, Pam would get the life insurance and maybe wouldn't want to stay around to fight J.R. So when the pilot aired, Bobby became another protagonist. That deprived me of a lot of the conflict I wanted between Pam and Bobby. Yes, the conflict came early but it was manufactured over soapy issues. I wanted the conflict built in between the two of them. It's hard to make things happen when there are too many good people around.

"Larry [Hagman] began as the antagonist, but structurally he became a kind of protagonist in the sense that he's the one who makes things happen. Other people react to him. Bobby is so virtuous that things have to happen to him. Traditionally, the villain thwarts the action with a counteraction. In *Dallas*, the villain—J.R.—initiates the action and everyone else is forced to react."

"We never think of J.R. as the bad guy," says Capice. "If you had to name a protagonist and an antagonist, I guess in the broadest sense Bobby is the protagonist and J.R. is the antagonist, but J.R. is too complex to simply be the antagonist. We've seen enough sides of him so that if he's not always likable, at least he's understandable. Sometimes he is even the protagonist and the world is the antagonist. I think it was Sam Goldwyn who once said, 'It's a dog-eat-dog world and nobody's gonna eat me.' J.R. would say the same thing. We have tremendous empathy or sympathy for him. I think that part of what made this show so startling was that we always showed all sides of our characters. There are no traditional heroes. There isn't a good guy and a bad guy. We have maintained an unusual level of honesty about our characters. We try to show not only their black-and-white sides, but also the gray areas in between. Our characters are multidimensional and flawed. Just like real people."

Seven years after creator David Jacobs originally planned it, Bobby died, setting up Pam and J.R. as protagonist and antagonist and leaving the rest of the Ewings to mourn.

That the show's success did not hinge on Bobby became abundantly clear at the end of the 1984–85 season, when Bobby was killed. Many people interpreted Bobby's death as an elaborate scheme by the network to boost the number of viewers. Some thought that Patrick Duffy was demanding too much money. Actually Bobby's death was a way of writing Patrick out of the story (money was never the issue), solving the cliffhanger dilemma without having a real cliffhanger, and still providing an emotional blockbuster and moving forward a story that had been all but beaten to death anyway. Bobby's death freed the show to go in a new direction—which would not have been possible if Bobby Ewing were the sole protagonist.

The Turning Point

The turning point of the story is also called the crisis climax. Any story with a beginning, a middle, and an end has a crisis climax. The crisis climax comes when the protagonist is forced to make a final decision that makes his march to the climax irrevocable.

A serial does not have a crisis climax because it has no end. When producers decide to take *Dallas* off the air, look for the turning point to be placed approximately ten episodes before the last show. The crisis will offer a leading character, probably J.R., a choice. Once he makes that choice, the problems are resolved.

Soap Opera Goes Prime

With its dramatic elements securely in place, *Dallas* was introduced as the first prime-time soap opera. It was classified as a soap opera because of the high drama and the belief that it would appeal more to women than to men.

"I don't think even a soap opera is what a soap opera is supposed to be," admits Capice. "Daytime television now deals with many subjects we wouldn't think of tackling in prime time. If you watch the nighttime soaps, you'll see that each one has its own personality and that they are all different from daytime soaps. Our show is much more concerned with character and emotional drama than with sexual situations contrived to titillate; we don't do sequences designed to show off series of costumes. I'm not criticizing other shows, it's just not our strength. Our strength is developing characters."

"I don't think night soaps are really soaps," says Jacobs. "We don't use the same conventions. We don't have to review the show every Monday; our pacing is enormously different; we use film rather than videotape; and we take seven days to make one hour. Daytime soap is shot on tape and they shoot one show every day. We have the time to develop a story and introduce some fancy plot twists that might not work on daytime. *Dallas* was not created simply by someone at a network saying, 'Hey, let's do a prime-time soap opera and see if we can change the face of television.' "

Jacobs and his partner, Michael Filerman, had what is called a "development deal" at Lorimar. Lorimar paid them to sit around and work on new ideas which might or might not be approved by the network and might or might not be made into a pilot episode, much less a series. The first idea Jacobs came up with was *Knots Landing*, the story of four American couples. When he took it to CBS, the network liked it, but the executives told Jacobs that they would prefer a family drama with a little more glitz to it, something a little more sensational. They did not suggest he revamp *Knots Landing* to fit, so he started on a new show. Jacobs's assignment was to create a star vehicle for an actress CBS had under contract, so various shows that he devised were called "Untitled Linda Evans Project." Jacobs's original intention was for Linda Evans to portray Pam, but as *Dallas* evolved, it was soon obvious that the part would not be big enough for Evans. Eventually, Evans left CBS and became Krystle in *Dynasty*.

"*Dallas* was really Richard Berger's [then head of drama program development at CBS] idea," says Jacobs. "It filled the network's need at the moment. Cop shows weren't working, especially with all the curbs on violence. The networks were having trouble developing dra-

Crew members work in over 100° heat while some of the cast cool their heels for a run-through.

mas; only one or two were emerging each season. Doing an upscale, bigger-than-life drama could be highly profitable if it worked. And it could work as a character-based drama, rather than one based on plot."

Jacobs's decision to set his family drama in Texas was partly due to Berger's suggestion that the Southwest was virgin territory in TV land and partly because he was reading Tommy Thompson's best-seller *Blood and Money*. Although Jacobs had never been to Texas, he liked the idea of a state with its own personality. Jacobs also had fond memories of an old friend named Pamela Hynds Daley, originally from Waco.

On the day he and Jacobs were to present the story idea to the network gurus, Filerman balked at the already outdated nontitle. "I'm not sending that presentation in with 'Untitled Linda Evans Project' written across the top—it doesn't have enough class." He then substituted "Dallas" as the show's title, remarking that it could always be changed later.

Dallas as Mini-series

The network liked *Dallas* so much that they agreed to put some money behind it. Deciding that a one-hour pilot would not "show well," CBS ordered five episodes to give *Dallas* a chance to attract some viewers and win a spot in the fall 1978 lineup.

"It was not really a series yet, it was a five-part pilot," says Jacobs. Jacobs himself wrote the first and last of the five shows and contracted other writers for the other three. In the original setup, Bobby was to be killed in episode five to launch the series. It is not unusual for a principal character to be killed in a pilot. The producers decided that they wouldn't have a show without Bobby, though, so they convinced Jacobs to keep the youngest Ewing alive. Jacobs never liked the idea, but he agreed to it.

Although the first five shows were indeed pilot episodes, the myth has persisted that *Dallas* began as a mini-series. Cast and crew alike now refer to those first five episodes as "the mini-series." Still, it was not created as a mini-series and never aired as one. It was simply a heavily promoted pilot aired during the traditional replacement part of the calendar.

The first episode, "Digger's Daughter," which began with the infamous first line "Your family's gonna throw me off the ranch," then went on to set up Pamela and J.R. as the central conflicting characters. The three subsequent scripts served merely as three additional stories, which, although they developed the characters somewhat, bore no relation to any master plot. The fifth story, "Barbecue," was the one in which Bobby was supposed to be killed and which would end with Pam's resolution to stay on and fight J.R. In the rewritten version of the story, J.R. and Pam have an altercation in the barn and Pam falls from a hayloft. She suffers a miscarriage as a result, and the couple decide that they will leave Southfork and start over again—on their own. Jock convinces Pam to stay on the ranch, and thus the stage is set for the continuing saga.

Casting the Pilot

Producers like to cast pilots with actors who will be able to reprise the role if the show goes to series. Larry Hagman made two pilots, *Dallas* and *Three's Company* (no relation to the ABC comedy). Patrick Duffy, hot off *The Man from Atlantis*, was considered the biggest star name in the show when the first five episodes were shot. In fact, when The *Dallas Morning News* reported that *Dallas* was in town filming (in a one-inch story), it did not even mention Larry Hagman.

"No one was looking for big-name actors when we cast the pilot," says Katzman. "We just wanted the best ensemble cast we could come up with." Barbara Bel Geddes, a big name in the theater, was the first cast, then Jim Davis, as her husband, Jock. The only parts for which there was some contest between actors were Sue Ellen, which almost went to Mary Frann (of *The Newhart Show*) and Pam, which was between Victoria Principal and Judith Chapman. Ken Kercheval originally came in to read for the part of Ray Krebbs and Steve Kanaly read for the part of Bobby.

The part of J.R. was first discussed with Robert Foxworth, who later went on to star in *Falcon Crest*. Foxworth thought that J.R.'s character should be softened. Larry Hagman loved J.R. just the way he was, and got the part based on his enthusiasm. "What Larry brought to the part that was never written is his joy in everything he does. Larry brought this wonderful, wicked smile and an enjoyment of everything that J.R. did, no matter how horrible."

Getting Started

The show was shot in Dallas in the winter of 1977–78 with the intention of making everything look real; no Hollywood look-alikes or substitutes would be tolerated. Among other things, it is practically impossible to shoot outdoors in Los Angeles and not get a palm tree in the frame.

Len Katzman and a scout scoured the countryside, from Fort Worth to Denton, looking for appropriate locations. They used real homes rather than sets; some of the wardrobe actually belonged to cast members. Although it rarely snows in Dallas, it snowed during the first week of production of *Dallas*. For five weeks, cast and crew worked twelve or more hours a day, six days a week, huddling together to keep warm. Jacobs was on location too, and often sat up until 3:00 A.M. in the North Park Inn, rewriting scenes and plotting Sue Ellen's revenge—which would not come until the show was a hit.

When the shooting was over, the cast returned to Los Angeles for other jobs or a period of intense waiting. There began the postproduction phase of cutting and looping sound; Jacobs began work on another show he created called *Married: The First Year*; Hagman did everything but dream of Jeannie.

The five episodes aired on consecutive Sunday nights beginning April 2, 1978. Three of the five shows scored exceedingly well in the A. C. Nielsen ratings, with over "30" shares, proving that a more than respectable number of television viewers were watching; the last episode ranked in the top ten of the week's most watched shows. The two less popular shows were up against stiff competition—*Holocaust* one week and a Helen Hayes–Fred Astaire made-for-television movie the next. On the basis of the impressive numbers, CBS gave the go-ahead for thirteen more scripts, and "Year One" officially began the next fall season.

The Bible

Daytime soaps have always used a "bible"—a notebook filled with information about the characters and the directions in which they grow—but *Dallas* was the first nighttime television show to have one. All continuing dramas now use a bible, since it is virtually the only way the show can be solidly built.

"What the bible does," explains Katzman, "is enable you to build a well-crafted story. Look at the example of when Sue Ellen had the baby; J.R. never touched that baby until fifteen episodes after that, when he finally found out it was his son. When he does pick up the baby it becomes a big, important moment. The only way to properly build to something like that is to have it written down in the recipe so all the writers for the show know that they build their scenes with J.R. and the baby specifically to show that J.R. refuses to touch the baby—until the big payoff."

The *Dallas* bible is actually a three-parter that will total four hundred pages by the end of the season. It is written in novel form and includes story lines as well as a character-by-character breakdown of how each one interacts with all the others. Only top executives working on the creation of *Dallas* even see the bible, and each keeps his copy hidden away.

Each season the *Dallas* bible is hashed out in three story sessions, each one concerned with roughly twelve episodes. (A season can run as long as the network says—the average is twenty-six episodes, but the 1985–86 season ran thirty-one episodes.) The hardest session is the first one; the easiest is the last. The first session for a new season begins in April; the creative team reconvenes in July, and again in late November, when the cliffhanger is decided. Stories on a show may be adjusted backward with rewriting. Not every detail that solidifies the puzzle is in the bible. As shooting progresses the writers may juggle scenes, props (which often serve as clues), and foreshadowing in order to make the fabric of the larger story fit together like a master spider web. "The bible is a road map," explains Katzman. "As we go along, we write in the towns, the cities. Like all roads, it twists and turns and takes unexpected little bends."

Willard Barnes got the nickname "Digger" because he had a second sense: wildcatters used to say he could smell oil and always knew just where to dig.

John Ross Ewing the First.

She married him to save her daddy's ranch, then she fell in love with him: Ellie and Jock.

The Back Story

Every story has a back story—that part of the story which the teller knows but never verbalizes. This is true in television, stage, and even novels. The back story, or past history, allows the characters to do what they do, since every action must have a reason—and a purpose. In a long-running series, the back story is revealed in bits and pieces as needed.

"I always start with the back story," says Jacobs, "because as a novelist I know that the reader has to know where everybody came from. The original back story wasn't that detailed. Digger and Jock had been partners; Jock had the business sense and Digger knew where to dig. Digger was totally self-destructive—a drunk. He grew up on the ranch and was in love with Miss Ellie, but she married Jock to save the ranch." Subsequent back stories were created as needed and worked into scripts when appropriate.

The Network

"The network was always friendly and supportive, except for one incident," reports Katzman. "They've given us less interference than I've had with any other show I've ever been on, but they did move us around a good bit the first year. The mini-series ran on Sunday at 10:00 P.M. We opened our first year on Saturday at 10:00 P.M., then we moved to Sunday at 10:00 P.M., then Friday at 10:00 P.M. All of that happened in the first season. Otherwise, it went well. Everything that could go right, went right. The cast became friendly early on; the network was supportive.

"The network did not meddle much in the show. They were against serialization at first, but so was Lorimar. The network's big concern was for Pam and Bobby. They always saw Bobby as the hero. When Bobby and Pam started having marital problems, the network insisted that they remain chaste until the story worked it out. They felt that Pam and Bobby couldn't sleep with anyone else or the audience would lose sympathy for them."

One of the reasons for the lack of problems with the network was the great experience of the writers and producers. When they did "issue shows" dealing with homosexuality, abortion, or other social concerns, they already knew that Standards and Practices (a division of every network) would insist that both sides of the issue be aired. Shows were never rejected or rewritten due to network pressure because the scripts were so carefully constructed in the first place.

"We have been careful with language," says Katzman. "Jim Davis had a habit of saying his lines and throwing in extra swear words— there were a lot of 'hells' and 'damns' in his natural speech pattern. We have a pretty strict count of four or five 'cuss words' per show, and Jim could get us off count easily. The network let us say 'bastard' under certain circumstances. 'Tramp' is okay but 'whore' is not. Mostly, the network has always said we could do or say whatever we wanted, as long as we were discreet about it."

Serialized Stories

It was one thing to bring soap opera to prime time, but quite another to serialize a story in prime time. Aside from the mini-series format, serialization had never even been attempted. Furthermore, there was a big financial reason not to serialize the stories. While networks air episodes in consecutive order and could use continuing drama effectively, stations that buy shows for airing in hours other than prime time do not like to be forced to release those shows in any order. Lorimar, as provider of the series, had to accept the fact that if they allowed *Dallas* to use serialization, they could lose millions of dollars of revenue from syndication. Nonetheless, Lorimar gave the go-ahead in the late fall of 1978.

Soap Spins

While daytime soap operas move at a slow crawl and characters come and go, successful prime-time soap opera characters are often likely to earn their own shows or their own places in a second time slot if the fans—or sponsors—are devoted enough. Charlene Tilton claims that there was early talk of spinning off her character, Lucy, and giving her a series of her own, but the idea came to naught.

David Jacobs had better luck. With the huge success of *Dallas*, CBS was anxious to get more Jacobs-inspired product on the air. "Remember that show *Knots Landing* you first created?" they asked him as *Married: The First Year* folded. "Could you adapt that original concept into a spin-off of *Dallas*?"

Indeed, the original *Knots Landing* was the story of four couples, so Jacobs merely made one of the couples be Gary and Val Ewing. Thus Ellie and Jock's middle son, the one who seemed to be such a loser, who was just too sensitive and couldn't take the pressure of living under the Southfork roof, remarried his childhood sweetheart—at Southfork, in prime time, of course—and moved with his bride to California, where they lived quite high in the ratings ever after.

And the soap keeps spinning.

Romeo and Juliet. Bobby James Ewing marries Pamela Jean Barnes, and a new classic love story is launched.

Mark Graison, played by John Beck, fills the gap in Pam's life.

Chapter Two

VIRTUES AND VICES

Love and Soap

Love makes the world go round. It also keeps the pot boiling on a soap opera. In fact, it's virtually impossible to keep a continuing drama continuing if there isn't a lot of love and loving going around. *Dallas* would never have survived at the top of the heap if it did not feature several concurrent love stories.

The very heart of the show is a love story. The inciting incident is built on love, sweet love: the marriage of Pam and Bobby. Even when Pam and Bobby separate and divorce, their love story surfaces in the subtext and subplot of continuing episodes, right down to the painful final scenes of the last episode of the 1984–85 season when Bobby asks Pam to remarry him. She accepts joyfully ("I thought I had lost you forever"); Bobby spends the night; the next morning Bobby is killed in front of Pam's house while saving her life. If that's not a love story, what is?

Pam and Bobby's love story is the stuff of fantasy. From the beginning, Bobby always represented Prince Charming; Pam was sweet and good and deserved the best. Bobby's "substitute," Mark Graison, is the least well-drawn character in *Dallas*. Graison's only quirk is having a terminal illness that might claim him at any minute. Other than that, he is even more perfect than Bobby. "That's what the audience demands for Pam," explains Leonard Katzman, who created the Graison character. "He may be more one-dimensional than the other characters but it's only because everyone thinks Pam deserves nothing less."

If Pam is full of pure, true love, there are plenty of other people around her who have more difficult love relationships. Sue Ellen and J.R. have a love-hate relationship of enormous proportions; J.R. continues to find false love with his many tootsies—Kristin, Sue Ellen's sister; Holly Harwood, who framed him with Sue Ellen; Leslie Stewart, his P.R. lady; and Mandy Winger, who thought she was different from the others until she discovered that J.R. had betrayed her with Angelica Nero.

(left)

Plots twist and untwist on Dallas, but beneath them is a constant on which the show's heartbeat pumps—Sue Ellen and J.R. are embroiled in an intense love-hate relationship.

There is unrequited love, mostly suffered by Cliff Barnes. Cliff fell in love with Sue Ellen, lost her back to her husband, and then stood by in pain to discover that the child he was certain was his was actually J.R.'s.

Cliff's love life is such that he mostly gets girlfriends on the rebound. Mandy Winger was Cliff's girlfriend before she turned to J.R., but usually J.R. gets them first and Cliff gets the leftovers: Julie Grey, Sue Ellen, Afton Cooper. Cliff dated Donna Culver once when she was on the rebound from Ray but was dumped when Donna and Ray got back together. Cliff never really even had a love interest of his own until Jamie came along.

Then there's triangular love. Pam's half sister, Katherine, loves Bobby so much that she is willing to do anything—including murder—to get him for herself. If she can't have him for herself, no one can have him, she reasons when she tries to kill Pam. Bobby makes it clear to Katherine that he's not interested in anything but a brotherly relationship with her. After all, Bobby has his own problems. He finds himself in love with two different women at the same time and spends years in unresolved conflict. As much as he loves Pam, he can never quite make the relationship go as smoothly as it should—as smoothly as life with Jenna.

"Bobby is the love of Jenna's life," says Priscilla Beaulieu Presley, who has played Jenna since she became a regular character. "Bobby is her childhood sweetheart, her one and only. She has carried the torch for him since childhood. Yes, she married Naldo, but that was because she was so young. I think Jenna grew up with Bobby and his family but was not able to quite face the prospect of living with the Ewings and being one of them. It was all very small town and she had to get away. At that point, she didn't understand her love for him. She was very much her own person and she felt he should be his own person, that he should get away from the family. He couldn't do that, so she got away by marrying Naldo. But she carried the torch. She's very passionate and very romantic. She gives a lot and expects a lot in return.

"When Bobby is killed, Jenna just can't believe she has lost him again. For a long time she doesn't know he had proposed to Pam, so she lives in a dream, that life could have been perfect for them. She doesn't think anyone can ever replace Bobby and feels his death is a betrayal.

"Except Charlie. Charlie is her life force, that's why she goes on. Jenna's a smart girl but she needs someone to love. Her daughter keeps her going.

Bobby taught Pam how to ride the day after he married her.

Jenna Wade was Bobby's first love. The proverbial girl next door, she grew up on the ranch behind Southfork. Morgan Fairchild once played Jenna, but when the character became a regular, the part went to Priscilla Beaulieu Presley.

(above right)
Bobby and Pam shared a love so true that it withstood family pressure, blackmail, divorce, and treachery. Here Bobby denies his own feelings to give Pam a chance at happiness with Mark.

(left)
Bobby didn't have to teach Katherine (Morgan Brittany) how to ride. His sister-in-law just didn't know the meaning of "nay."

"Jenna never saw Pam as a real threat. It's quite a shock for her to find out that Bobby was going to remarry Pam. Jenna believed she was the only one for Bobby. To Jenna, Pam was merely a rebound love. Bobby married her in a quickie ceremony only after Jenna ran off with Naldo. They were only married for about three years, not very long. Then Bobby went back to Jenna right away. Jenna and Bobby were together at Southfork for three years, as long as he was married to Pam. That's a marriage in itself. Jenna had known Bobby forever; she knows his family; she knows that she belongs in his life, not Pam. In fact, her problem, as she sees it, is with Pam and Bobby's adopted son, Christopher—not with Pam. And she's fighting the hold Southfork has on Bobby. Most women can't believe that the other woman in a man's life was the one that was forever. Jenna will always believe that she was number one with Bobby but that things just got in the way.

Jenna returned to Texas with a divorce
and a daughter, Charlotte—called
Charlie—played by Shalane McCall.

When Jack Ewing discovered he was in love with Jenna, Ray warned him to hold back—Jenna still needed time to recover from Bobby's death.

"After Bobby dies, Jenna stays because she really is part of the Ewing family. She wasn't the outsider Pam Barnes was. She was literally the girl next door. She and Bobby used to ride their horses together. They went to school together. With her family dead, she is as much a part of the Ewing family as anything else. And Bobby is Charlie's emotional father.

"Jenna certainly isn't ready to love another man. Jack is very attractive, but she never meant to get involved with him. She has feelings, but she can't let go of Bobby. When things heat up with Jack, she's torn between the two loves—one dead and one alive—and the very fact that she had other feelings of love for someone else. This makes her feel more confused and guilty. She's totally tormented by her feelings for Jack.

"Of all the family, Jenna is the most sensitive one. She's very aware of the manipulations J.R. uses—she's known his number since childhood. But J.R.'s always been on her side; she's never had to deal with his wrath the way Pam did. Jenna is a survivor. She came back to Dallas and then she lived in Fort Worth and was working as a waitress. She's got a real strength of character. She wouldn't let Bobby give her the boutique, she wanted to pay him for it. She very much wants to make it on her own and if she can ever get over Bobby, I think she will."

Miss Ellie, like all grandmothers,
serves up comfort, advice, and recipes
from her favorite room in the house.

Only a big man could fill Jock Ewing's shoes: Howard Keel, at 6'4", size 13, fits the bill as Miss Ellie's second husband.

The second most important virtue in a soap opera is strength, emotional strength. The characters must have the strength to endure what comes their way, they must be someone the audience can look up to. Courage on a soap is the ability to keep on "keeping on" without being too self-indulgent.

Although Bobby's principal part in the drama was to serve as a kind of idealized hero, a Prince Charming, one of the virtues that emerged from him was a calm strength. "When I took the part," says Patrick Duffy, "I really had to fight for my life. My character had all the forcefulness and panache of a three-day-old piece of lettuce.

"I bemoaned my fate every day, but they told me Bobby had to be the way he was to maintain some sort of equilibrium with the others. I asked, 'Couldn't he do something—anything—interesting?' They told me he had to be the epitome of all that was ethical and nice. I've joked before that, basically, Bobby has two lines: 'It's all right, Mom, I'll take care of it,' and 'Okay, Mom, I took care of it.'"

Bobby's strength of character has somewhat been replaced by Mark Graison's. While Graison doesn't get into the ethical scrapes that the younger Ewing did, he still provides the protective shoulder that spells safety, at least for Pam.

Strength is a fantasy that plays particularly well on television, where each action is controlled by the script and life is never so awful that it can't be handled well by someone. As Mark Graison, John Beck steps into the role of Mr. Perfect with ease. Who else would Pam turn to when her true love (Bobby Ewing) had just been killed? Even when Pam admits her ambivalence to Graison, he takes it like a man; he says the strong thing, the perfect thing: "It's okay, I understand."

In the first five episodes of *Dallas*, the pilot run, it is Pam who appears to have the strength in the family. But J.R. seems to crush Pam's spirit in "Barbecue," when he knocks her from the hayloft and causes her to have a miscarriage. As the series evolves, it is Miss Ellie who is the predominantly strong character, backed up by her husbands—first Jock, then Clayton Farlow. It's a strong person who will cheerfully live through divorce, arson, near bankruptcy, cancer, kidnapping, missing family members, and assorted mini-disasters. Yet Miss Ellie, as the matriarch of the Ewings, has lived through this and much more.

"I think that Ellie spends a lot of time in the kitchen making cocoa," says Howard Keel, who plays Clayton, "and while she is undeniably a strong woman, I think she gets her strength from the men around her.

Jim Davis, who died during the 1981 season, was the irrepressible Jock Ewing— wildcatter who made good.

Jock was a tough man. Actually, he was a reprobate. Jock was a tough old wildcatter who made good, but money and success don't change what a person is inside. He taught J.R. everything he knows; he liked for him to play dirty. Clayton's entirely different. I sometimes wish he were more of an s.o.b. He'd be more interesting to play.

"Clayton came from money. He's old Texas. Jock was a street fighter. Clayton could have gone to Harvard. Have you ever noticed that he doesn't speak with a Texas accent? That's important to me. Not all Texans have accents. He's a well-educated man, a brilliant man. He's well traveled. They don't bring this out in the story, but he's been out of San Angelo and Texas. One of the reasons he married Miss Ellie is that he acts as her adviser, helps take care of her. He has a great need to give, and to help people.

"He's so unlike me, it tests my intellect to find out where the hell he is. Oh, Ellie's very strong. But she needs strength right beside her. She'd have a hard time to stand by herself. Clayton is a rock and she really needs someone like that. I've kind of patterned the part after a friend of mine—a very rich man, handsome and big and with a great sense of humor about himself. He was flamboyant and loved fast cars but was also kind and gentle. He was a real man in all the senses of the word and you knew it.

"Ellie is a real Texas mama. She makes Southfork so warm that no one ever wants to leave it. My wife makes my home like that, so it's something I understand. I just love being with her. And that's what Miss Ellie is all about. It's an earthiness; her feet are in Texas, in that ranch. That's what the show is really all about. Whatever strength Ellie has is what she gets from the ranch, from the earth beneath her, and that's what makes Texans so different. They understand how important the land is. Clayton understands that too. He doesn't have to be verbally strong, or to take on J.R. too often. It's hard for Clayton to be in that house with J.R. But the truth is, Clayton's strength comes from his intellect, his experience, his feelings about the land, his understanding of Miss Ellie and J.R. There are a lot of times Clayton doesn't do anything, he's just there and his very presence and understanding are what give balance to many of the other characters. Now that's strength."

Greed and Soap

Soap opera wouldn't be any fun it was all about love and strength. In fact, love and strength wouldn't be worth anything if they weren't tempered by the seven sins. On *Dallas*, most of the sins are enacted as regular rituals. The characters are themselves defined by the number of sins they commit. Few of them are so simple as to be guilty of only one thing. A character may have only one virtue (J.R., for example, is a wonderful father), but to be truly meaningful, he must have several sins.

J.R. has always looked up to his daddy.

J.R.'s biggest sin, no doubt, is greed. He wants everything. And his appetite is not limited to financial greed. While he wants the best that money can buy—fancy cars, fine clothes, diamonds and furs for his ladies—he is not tied to material wealth. His greed runs much deeper; it is tied to his childhood need for his father's attention and affection. Because Bobby was his father's favorite, J.R. could never get enough—of anything. His immature need to make Daddy proud has kept him trapped in greed. Even though his father is dead, J.R. still inwardly plays to that audience of one. He sublimates his childhood hunger into an insatiable quest for power.

"I admire old J.R. Ewing," says Larry Hagman. "He's the most unmitigated s.o.b. on TV. Nobody calls him Junior except his pappy. He cheats on his wife at every opportunity. In our first twenty-seven weeks on the air he had six different mistresses. He keeps ladies in New York, Houston, Austin, and a couple in Dallas.

"He's got two hundred million bucks. Nobody gets the best of him in a business deal and survives. The guy's a bounder, but he's protecting his empire as any good businessman would. J.R. isn't an evil man; he thinks he's doing the right thing. He's no more ruthless than the TV executives who moved our series around from one night of the week to another.

J.R. reads the fine print. Always.

"Some people think I'm giving a false impression of Texas oil people. Others are convinced I'm cleaning up the image. If I played J.R. truthfully, he'd be a lot worse than he is. Some Texans say I don't know what I'm talking about. But I know all about the oil business. I worked for an oil tool factory and I've seen what those big shots do to one another. If we told the real story, they'd blow up CBS.

"I've pretty much played J.R. against the obvious from the beginning. I do get my comeuppance every five episodes. My character is the evil focal point for the show. I'm as much onstage when I'm offstage. It's like Iago in *Othello*. Everybody's worried about him all the time.

"I don't know why, but I think maybe people are sick of good guys. I am so tired of everybody being so nice and warm and cuddly to each other. J.R. is totally amoral, with plenty of money and a lot of beautiful women and I think lots of people want to be that way these days.

"If they ever make me nice, well, there goes the show."

Envy and Soap

Jealousy, it's been said, is a triangle. Envy, on the other hand, is a private matter. Envy consumes the one who envies far more than anyone else. Jenna envies Pam for having been married to Bobby; but Katherine was jealous of her sister because she couldn't get Bobby to take her own affections seriously. Her jealousy consumed her and drove her to try to kill Pam—and to kill herself.

Cliff Barnes is also consumed, but not, according to Ken Kercheval, with jealousy. Cliff's envy was primarily directed toward Bobby Ewing when he was growing up—"I always liked Bobby Ewing. I even liked him back in college when I was waiting on his table"—but his focus has shifted away from direct envy of any one Ewing to simple scorekeeping. Once he inherited a share of Barnes–Wentworth from his mother, Cliff changed dramatically. Yet the deprivations of his early life, emotional as well as physical, still show in his personality.

"I don't think envy fits Cliff Barnes that well," says Kercheval. "You have to understand him better than that. The motivating factor with him has always been that he's felt that he would be in a position similar to J.R.'s if Jock hadn't cheated his father. The issue I'm talking about is justice. In the story line there is the scene that reveals testimony that Jock had bought Digger's share of their oil company legally. Digger was a drunk, though, and you can't in good conscience buy anything from a drunk unless you're certain he's sober. Jock couldn't prove that to me. I think that in this particular episode they were trying to make Jock look honorable, after he was dead. But it doesn't cut it with me, because Jock knew he was buying a deed from a drunk. It doesn't negate the fact that Digger had his faults. Perhaps Cliff is shortsighted about that, but we're talking about morality here, about right and wrong, and that's what Cliff is so angry about all these years. It's not envy. If you're talking about Cliff Barnes, you're talking about one of the few honorable people on this show.

"I read the pilot series scripts on an airplane and sat there thinking about them, and I said to myself, 'There's not one redeemable character in this show except Cliff.' Cliff is the only one with a sense of morality. Initially, Miss Ellie was not the source of strength that she is now. She was off in the kitchen frying chicken. All this stuff would come down and she'd just want to feed everybody.

"J.R. was always out to screw his brother. J.R. is sensitive and yet unfeeling at the same time. The characters are so complex.

"You want to talk about complex? There was a scene that Art Lewis wrote when I, as Cliff, finally agreed to see my mother. She came to my apartment and we talked and I found out that she had lived two

In early, early episodes, Cliff's character was loosely modeled on the spirit of John and Bobby Kennedy, but by the middle of the first year the concept was abandoned.

Will the real antagonist please stand up?

hundred miles away from me for my entire life. I flew into a rage at her and she got up to leave. As she reached the doorway I picked up a bowl of licorice, which I had gone out and bought for this visit, and said, 'You didn't even have any licorice.' It was a pathetically poignant scene. Then Cliff falls into his mother's arms and starts to cry. Now that's a complex scene.

"J.R. and Cliff Barnes are alter egos. If anything, Cliff is a classic character. He always picks himself up, dusts himself off, and is back again. That's not the characteristic of a loser.

"I get a lot of questions from people asking me about Cliff being a loser. I take great exception to that. If you feel Cliff is a loser then obviously you are shortsighted. If he were a loser, he wouldn't be on the show anymore, would he? J.R. has had adversaries come and go, coming at him from all different angles. Cliff Barnes is the only one that J.R. keeps having to worry about. No matter how he gets Cliff down, he can be assured that he'll turn around and Cliff Barnes will be there. To be able to go up against J.R. as a foe time after time denotes courage. Cliff's got tenacity—and he never holds back. He hasn't got any reserve—it's all out in front. I have contended all along, as an observer of Cliff Barnes and a heavy participant in his life, that Cliff unfortunately is looking for an outside fix on his life. But it never works out that way. Being content and happy and successful is being a success at life and that's an inside job. If I view him like that, from where I am in my life, then I can come to him with compassion."

The Barnes-Wentworth
family—Rebecca,
Pam, and Katherine
flank Cliff.

Sue Ellen Shepard Ewing,
Miss Texas 1968.

Steven "Dusty" Farlow (played by
Jared Martin) appeared to be
Sue Ellen's knight in shining chaps,
until he rode off into the sunset
with someone else.

Gluttony and Soap

Gluttony may be everyone's favorite sin, although it is barely even
considered a flaw in soap opera characters. These people must have
voracious appetites that drive them to all sorts of excesses. A soap opera wouldn't be a soap opera if there weren't a lot of sex and abundant
drinking. Smoking and overeating aren't prime-time bad habits, so
gluttony has to be placed in a more sophisticated surrounding. Sue
Ellen Ewing, as coached by her mother—the consummate glutton—
has shown us an addictive personality that, before her final drying-out
period in the 1985–86 season, all but drove her to ruin.

"The first thing you have to know about characters," says Katzman,
"is what drives them. As despicable as J.R. is, we know that what
drives him is his need for his daddy's approval. Sue Ellen is searching
desperately for someone who loves her."

Naturally, Sue Ellen can't find what she seeks because she doesn't love herself. It takes Sue Ellen eight years to learn that and then a few weeks to get straight. Before the lesson hits home, she will have a one-nighter with Ray Krebbs, become so entangled with Cliff Barnes that she cannot determine the father of her child for over a year, and leave J.R. and return to him many times—almost as many times as she returns to the bottle. Some people overeat to find solace; Sue Ellen drinks too much. Often people don't blame her. Linda Gray has frequently been approached by fans who tell her, "Honey, I'd drink and have affairs if I were married to that man too."

"Sue Ellen is the most interesting female running character on television today," says Gray. "What's fascinating about her is that people don't know what she's going to do. It's like the old radio days. My God, she doesn't even like her baby when he's first born. She drinks. She has affairs. The quality that has emerged is vulnerability. As an actress, I really fight to keep that edge.

"I feel that most of us are going through growth problems. Should we work? Stay at home? Would we want to have lovers? What would we be like as single parents? These things are coming out all over the country. There are women out there who have the same problems as Sue Ellen. This is a show that respects that. There are a lot of men out there who would like to put their wives in a sanitarium. This show does it. The character of Sue Ellen says it's okay not to be perfect."

"Sue Ellen barely had a part in the beginning," says David Jacobs. "I had to write an audition scene for Sue Ellen. But I always planned Sue Ellen's revenge. The first two years, the conflicts between the Barneses and the Ewings gave us a lot of mileage. The essential ingredient of the first five episodes centered around the question of whether the marriage of Pam and Bobby would last. The biggest development of that whole time period was Sue Ellen's role getting bigger."

"I have always acted with my eyes," says Gray. "At one point, the camera moved in for close-ups of each member of the family. I thought, 'I'm going to give them a look to kill.' I said to myself: 'Watch this.' Venom came out. They saw the dailies in Los Angeles and a phone call came saying do something with that part. So I began hanging out in Dallas in a lot of beauty shops. I got my nails done a lot and listened. My character was a former Miss Texas. I got her down, picked out all her clothes, and she started emerging. When we went from the mini-series to the fall pickup, I decided she was an incredible person in conflict, going about the search to find out who she was. She was born and raised to be socially acceptable, to go to charity fundraisers, and to marry rich. But Mom forgot one thing—the emotional part of her life."

Ray fell in love with Donna McCullum Culver (Susan Howard) while she was still married. She broke off the adulterous affair when she discovered that her husband was dying of cancer.

Pride and Soap

All the characters in *Dallas* have a good bit of pride built into them—pride in their families, pride in their work and their success, even pride in the state of Texas. But the sin of pride is a little different. By being too proud, a person may not take advantage of a situation and may well suffer the consequences. Jenna is guilty of pride in her actions toward Bobby; Jamie is guilty of pride when she first comes to Dallas and refuses to show the legal papers she brought with her; Clayton suffers from hurt pride when Ellie bails him out of financial difficulty; Jack's pride is hurt when Jenna rejects him.

But it is Ray who is most guilty of the sin of pride.

"That's the way we portray him, all right," says Steve Kanaly. "Ray's hardheaded, and sometimes he lets his pride get in the way. It's his only character flaw, though. And if this is his biggest problem, well, the guy's in pretty good shape. Remember what happened when he needed money to go into a business? He took some of his wife's money and lost it—that made him feel awful and led to adultery. But then Donna and Ray got back together. I don't think he'll make that mistake twice.

"Of course, you have to look at the other kind of pride. Ray came to that ranch when he was fifteen years old. He ran away from his past and grew up on that ranch, gradually growing into prominence. There's pride in that, in doing a good job and gaining acceptance from Jock.

"Larry [Hagman] and I cooked up the fourth son idea. Think of having all that pride in Southfork and being the foreman and doing all that hard work and then finding out Jock was your daddy and it was all part of you when you didn't know it. It got to be a hard part to play without being a family member. I felt like I always had to say, 'Okay Jock, I'll wait outside for you.' I had this mark in the living room and I never got beyond that point until Jock recognized me as his son.

Ray found a soul-mate in Jack Ewing (played by Dack Rambo)—they are two outsiders related by blood but not really part of the inner family.

"Standards and Practices said, 'What's going on with Ray and Lucy if Ray is really Jock's illegitimate son?' so we waited for the Lucy bit to die down. I thought we'd do it in the second year, but it was the third year before Ray was acknowledged as Jock's son. I'm the long-distance runner in this show. I think the Ray–Donna relationship is one of the strongest on the show. We're not involved in the search for greed or power. There's no greed in Ray at all, he couldn't care less about money. Hell, he must be worth a hundred million dollars, to say nothing of what his wife is worth, and he's just a real simple, nice guy. He drives a truck. He doesn't care about jewels or furs or trips to Europe. He provides a real good contrast to the Ewings. Ray just wants to do a good job and not care about the rest.

"Ray's my hero. I grew up with Hopalong Cassidy on TV and I think Ray Krebbs is the only good cowboy on television now."

Lust and Soap

While a large number of the characters in *Dallas* have traded sleeping partners, the show has its own morality. Despite early warnings that the show would be sexily titillating, it has not proved so. Sue Ellen seems to have traded lust for self-esteem; Ray and Donna are happily married; Clayton and Ellie are kept in the nonsexual atmosphere reserved for all characters over sixty. Even J.R. seems to have tired of bedding one gorgeous girl after the next and had all but given his heart to Mandy Winger before he discovered she betrayed him. Certainly the most lust *Dallas* has seen lately is the gleam in Angelica Nero's eye—the look that proves her lust is not only for sex, but for money and power.

"She's dreadfully ambitious," explains Barbara Carrera. "Greed and a lust for power are the keys to her personality. I think that J.R. and Angelica have very similar personalities—they are a good match to watch. They think alike in many ways. To put it in a nutshell, with

Dial M for murder—Angelica Nero, played by Barbara Carrera.

those two the real question is who is the bigger bullshitter. They are experts in the con game; they are pros at deception—Angelica maybe more so than J.R. For her, this comes from being so beautiful and having a taste of power. Power conquers everyone; she wants to keep it. After all, she is CEO of a shipping company. That's not bad for such a young woman. If you had a taste of a lifestyle like that, you would do anything to get more and more power, to ensure that no one could take anything away from you, that you were safe and protected. She wants to own things on her own. She wants to be her own boss. Whatever she goes after, she wants to get. And she positively doesn't take no for an answer.

"I think we attract what we are; that's why J.R. and Angelica are attracted to each other. It's their karma. But you pay for your actions. She's ruthless, and she will complete her mission, but she has no qualms about using anyone in order to secure her goal. She uses J.R. and he uses her. This is not only the basis of Greek tragedy but of the universal human condition. We all want to believe we could behave like J.R. or Angelica. Vicariously, we love the villain. We, the audience, are forced by society to be goody-goodies. On the screen we want people who can act out our fantasies.

"Angelica has more to prove than J.R. but she also has more to lose. She's a woman in the 1980s—she's attractive, she's sexy, and she has a brain. She's terribly intimidating. Any man who is insecure could not be around her. But J.R. doesn't have that much to prove. He's simply greedy for oil money and more power. His way of life is guaranteed him; he was born rich. Angelica created everything for herself. She's not near forty and look at her. I'm not a feminist, but look at Angelica. She has gifts. Let's give credit where credit is due. She's a cunning, clever female."

J.R. openly flaunts his mistress, Mandy Winger (Deborah Shelton), at the 1985 Ewing Rodeo.

Wrath and Soap

As the antagonist of the show, J.R. has taken the most wrath. Indeed, when he was shot, there were half a dozen strong suspects. Just about everyone in town has a reason to hate J.R. Ewing. For the most part, J.R. takes wrath from women. Although he's ruined several men and continues to con and swindle Cliff Barnes, he is usually only hurt by the women he has loved . . . or made love to. It's questionable if J.R. could love anyone, except maybe John Ross. But he suffers a good bit of wrath.

Lois Chiles as the irresistible Holly Harwood: business was never so sweet.

Jack Ewing drifted into Dallas as a man without a future; a few weeks later he was a man of considerable fortune.

Kristin, his sister-in-law, tried to murder him.

Holly Harwood, a former business associate, framed him.

Leslie Stewart, his public relations expert, dumped him when he was down and out.

Even Julie Grey, his secretary, sold him out to Cliff Barnes.

Mandy Winger has proved no different from the others. Her hurt feelings and jealousy sent her after revenge.

"J.R. was really crazy about Mandy," explains Deborah Shelton. "But once he got her securely in his pocket, he didn't seem the same. He needs to run after something he can't attain. That's how it's always been with him. He likes the challenge.

"Jealousy is what drove Mandy to her wrath. When she found out about Angelica, she thought, 'He's playing me for a fool.' Whatever morality Mandy has, she really is a nice person. You might not approve of her having an affair with a married man, but she left J.R. once because he was married. She came back to him, but that was hard for her. She really loves him. She thinks she's different from all the others. She has a strong personality and she is very dignified. I hated it when she had to come back to J.R. at the Oil Baron's Ball and tell him she'd be anything to him.

"Mandy really hates spying on J.R. for Cliff. She tells J.R. and he forgives her. He understands that she did it from anger and jealousy, it wasn't business to her. She's very impulsive. Once she threw champagne in J.R.'s face. I know she couldn't shoot him the way Kristin did. She's too good a person. But when you're good and you care and you get hurt, anger can make you do a lot of things. Many of them J.R. actually deserves."

Sloth and Soap

Sloth and soap don't really mix.

If you think of sloth as not caring about appearances, it's hard to even imagine a character who fits the bill. Even when characters are having mental breakdowns and terrible emotional problems, they never let themselves go the way a normal person might.

"I think the real sloth of *Dallas*," says David Jacobs, "was Digger. He was a drunk, but beyond that he was totally self-destructive."

Digger had his good sides, of course. He was devoted to Ellie until the day he died, and he tried to be supportive of his children. He just lacked social skills. And he was lazy.

If you think of sloth as laziness, then sloth becomes a somewhat enviable characteristic. Rarely do the lazy pay the price.

Jack Ewing has his own streak of laziness in him—he certainly made his millions the quick and painless way. Blackmail always seems to be the easiest of crimes. Jack works hard in the physical sense and is no stranger to labor, but he seems lazy in a bigger, intellectual way.

"I don't think you can say Jack is lazy," says Dack Rambo. "He was mysterious when he first arrived and rather undefined. But he's quick-witted and has lived by his wits all his life. He left home at an early age. He traveled a lot, working along the way. He wasn't a gigolo, which might be the easy way out. He just happened to luck into an opportunity and felt he had to grab it. I think that's part of the American dream.

"At first we didn't know if Jack was a good guy or a bad guy, but I think he's a good guy. There can be only one bad guy in a show like this and J.R. does that brilliantly. Jack really isn't the con man one might have thought. He lives by his wits, yes; he's not good at office hours or big business. But he knows hard work, and I think he could do anything he sets his mind to. Maybe he saw a need for family and that's why he pushed his luck with the Texas branch. He does an honest day's work; he's no slouch about that.

"Maybe that laziness is just part of the fantasy, part of the allure. We all wish we could walk into a fortune like that and not have to work for it. But if push came to shove, and J.R. asked Jack to be part of a dirty deal in order to keep his money, Jack would have the strength of character not to do it. Jack's not greedy, he's not envious of anyone else. He's his own man. He doesn't envy the Ewing lifestyle. You have to remember that working in the oil fields in Alaska, he made good money. This man might not have had the wealth of, say, the Carringtons or the Ewings before he moved to Dallas, but he's not ready to sell out to it either. He has strong, solid values.

"If you think he's a bit lazy, well, I disagree. You have to judge him by his values, and his values are A-okay."

Dallas premiered with a sexy full slip scene, but
Pam was rarely shown not fully dressed again—
except in bathing suits.

Pam and Bobby's marriage starts out on the wrong foot as Ray leaps into an icy pond carrying his ex-sweetheart.

Pam, wet and naked under an Indian blanket, stands back while Bobby confronts Ray and J.R. Pam wins this first showdown with J.R. and sets up the rest of the series for repeated conflicts.

Chapter Three

SYNOPSES OF EPISODES

The Pilot Season 1977–78

DIGGER'S DAUGHTER
by David Jacobs

"Your family's gonna throw me off the ranch," Pamela Barnes Ewing laughs nervously in her soft Texas drawl as her husband of two hours, Bobby James Ewing, propels his red Mercedes-Benz 450 SL north toward Dallas.

Bobby tries to reassure his wife, but deep inside he knows it's not going to be easy. After all, he's a Ewing. And no one in the Ewing family had spoken to a Barnes in about forty years.

"If we had planned it, Mama," Bobby explains to his mother, "if we told everybody first, there would have been a lot of animosity and we'd have gotten married anyway. . . . Everybody'll come around a lot quicker this way."

Bobby is wrong. Real wrong. None of the Ewings much take to the notion of the youngest son of their oil and cattle family marrying the daughter of Digger Barnes, a man who has mostly wasted his life on a love affair with the bottle and who raised his children on the wrong side of the tracks.

The Barneses have sworn to destroy the Ewings ever since 1930, when Digger and Jock Ewing, Bobby's father, were partners in an oil stake. Digger had found the site and Jock had drilled it. When he struck black gold, he registered the stake in the Ewing name only. Jock Ewing became a multimillionaire; Digger became a serious drunk.

Their feud simmered over the years. Pamela's brother Cliff blamed everything that went wrong in his life on Jock Ewing and his sons. For the most part, the Ewing boys weren't too fond of Cliff Barnes either. Barnes was a self-righteous do-gooder bent on "cleaning up" the oil industry and there wasn't much in that the Ewings could take kindly to.

But when Bobby and Pam ran off and got married, the feud went from cool to hot in just as long as it takes to say, "Congratulations, Mrs. Ewing." J.R.—Bobby's big brother—first tries to buy Pam out of the family. When that doesn't work, he sets up a rendezvous between Pam and ranch foreman Ray Krebbs, who had been her beau before she met Bobby. Ray had lost Pam to Bobby at one of the annual Ewing barbecues and had subsequently begun a secret liaison with Lucy Ewing, J.R. and Bobby's teen-aged niece. After choreographing a seduction scene, J.R. drives Bobby to a ranch shack—expecting to catch Ray and Pamela in a compromising position and thus end their marriage.

But Pam has too much spunk to be intimidated. She threatens Ray that she will reveal his affair with Lucy, for which J.R. would fire him—and possibly kill him—if he doesn't back up her story. Together, they face down J.R., and Pam makes it clear that she will be one of the few people in the family, possibly in all of Texas, who is willing to stand up to John Ross Ewing, Jr.

LESSONS
by Virginia Aldridge

Lucy prefers getting her education in the barn with Ray to attending school. She steals warning letters from the school and burns them before anyone can find out she's in jeopardy of not graduating. Nevertheless, the family is concerned with her attitude, and Miss Ellie, her grandmother, does not want to be forced to send her to a private boarding school.

When the school calls Southfork about Lucy's grades, Pam takes the call. She knows just what to do; she goes back to the shack where Ray had tried to seduce her. Catching Ray and Lucy red-handed, Pam blackmails Lucy into attending class.

But Lucy is too much of a Ewing to be defeated by Pam's simple threats. At school the next day she fakes a sexual assault by her student counselor.

"I'll have Lucy here on Monday to tell the truth,"says Pam. "Maybe this is a practical joke." But before the confrontation, Pamela discovers a student who had seen Lucy take off her sweater to reveal a torn blouse, proving her "attack" was a fraud.

Pam brings Lucy to school in an attempt to set the young girl straight. The purpose of this show was to change Lucy's feelings toward Pam from resentment to friendship.

Lucy pretends she's been attacked to gain revenge and power, just like her uncle J.R.

SPY IN THE HOUSE
by Arthur Bernard Lewis

Cliff Barnes, legal counsel to a state senate committee on corruption, discovers documents that link the Ewings to questionable financial dealings with Senator Orloff. When J.R. learns this he repeats his original accusation that Pam has married Bobby just to spy on the family.

No one in the family likes Pam, let alone defends her—except for the adoring Bobby—but Pam goes to see Cliff to find out his source. Cliff not only gives her no information, he frightens her. "He's just so intense," Pam tells Bobby.

By doing a little sleuthing of their own, Bobby and Pam discover that Julie Grey—J.R.'s secretary—has been having an affair with Cliff and had also over the years been one of J.R.'s many extramarital flings. Bobby threatens to blow the whistle on J.R. and Julie if his big brother doesn't leave Pam alone, and he announces to the family that it was J.R.'s trusted secretary who was the traitor.

"I'm glad this damned thing is cleared up, but as far as I'm concerned, my wife has been done a terrible disservice."

"Of course she has," agrees Lucy, "we all thought she was guilty as hell."

Julie Grey (played by actress Tina Louise) in bed with Cliff—a former beau who reintroduces himself into her life when he discovers that she is J.R.'s trusted secretary.

Dinner time at the Ewing home: Pam is accused of revealing family secrets. The setting is "Swiss House," used only during the first five episodes.

Luther Frick (played by Brian Dennehy) leers as
Sue Ellen whimpers in "Winds of Vengeance."

Sue Ellen is forced to don her Miss Texas swimsuit
in a humiliating confrontation.

WINDS OF VENGEANCE
by Camille Marchetta

When Luther Frick finds his wife—and one of J.R. Ewing's business cards—in a Waco motel, he plans revenge on the Ewing women. An approaching hurricane takes all the men from Southfork except J.R. and Ray Krebbs, who are forced to watch what Frick and his friend Payton Allen have in mind as "justice"—the group rape of the Ewing wives.

"It was awful," Pam tells Bobby when the ordeal is over, "but we came through as a family. For the first time, we've been one."

BARBECUE
by David Jacobs

Old Jock Ewing made the prediction to J.R. right from the beginning, telling his older son that if he and Sue Ellen didn't get busy, Pam and Bobby would present him with a Ewing grandchild first. When Pam discovers she's pregnant, she is thrilled, certain that the birth of a

A bitter Sue Ellen tells J.R. the facts of life—that
Pam is pregnant and will bear a Ewing heir before
she does.

Actor David Wayne as Digger Barnes, who makes a
drunken appearance at the annual Ewing barbecue.
It was at such a barbecue in 1953—so goes the
back story—that Digger took a shot at Jock.

grandchild will end the long-standing feud between Jock
and Digger.

She invites her father to the Ewing's annual family barbecue, where she makes her announcement. But the
news is met with bitter envy and hatred by Sue Ellen,
who has been unable to conceive throughout her eight
years of marriage to J.R.

Sue Ellen corners her husband at the cookout: "It's apparent from your good humor that you don't know the
news of the hour."

"I've *heard* about the Alamo!"

"Waterloo's more like it," counters Sue Ellen. "Yours.
I'm talking about your brother Bobby, the apple of Jock
Ewing's eye, and his wife and their marriage. Their boun-
tiful marriage . . . not like ours."

"Sue Ellen. . . ."

"There's nothing in this world Jock wants more than a
grandson; I haven't given him one because of your disin-
terest in me. She's pregnant. Little brother Bobby and
that Barnes girl are going to have a baby named Ewing.
Maybe a boy! Think about that!"

J.R. does—and he doesn't like it.

Family may be the theme of the show,
but some characters just came and went—
like Cousin Jimmy (foreground),
seen only in "Barbecue."

He picks a fight with Bobby, insinuating that the baby is actually Ray's. Then he follows Pam up to the hayloft of the barn, and approaches her angrily; she fights back, loses her balance, and falls to the loft below.

"She lost the baby," Bobby announces to the family after the barbecue.

When Pam regains strength, Bobby promises her that they will move out of Southfork and get away from his meddling family.

Jock begs them to stay on. Miss Ellie adds, "We weren't ready for any of this, for our Bobby and Digger's daughter and everything that's come since. . . . I've worked hard to keep us as a family. It hasn't been easy with these Ewing men. Sometimes I've failed. But if I fail this time, I've failed for good. I want to keep my family together. I need your help, Pamela, please."

J.R. tries to give Pam a hand to stop her fall.
She recovers, but loses her baby.

1978–79 Season

REUNION, PART ONE
by David Jacobs

In his bachelor days, Bobby did a good bit of entertaining for Ewing interests in Las Vegas. On a return to Las Vegas he hits a different kind of jackpot when he runs into Gary Ewing, his long-missing brother and the father of Lucy. Bobby convinces Gary to come back to Southfork.

Meanwhile, at the ranch, Lucy has a surprise of her own. She has secretly been seeing her mother, Valene, and reunites her parents.

Not everyone is thrilled about the discovery of the long-lost kin; J.R. considers Gary's return yet another threat to his power at Ewing Oil.

"Lucy wants you to come back to the ranch with us," Gary tells Val.

"No way, sorry. He'd kill me."

Bobby begins to strongarm a pushy waiter in Las Vegas until he realizes the man is his long-lost brother Gary, first played by David Ackroyd. Gary was named for Ellie's older brother, Garrison, who was believed to be drowned at sea.

With Gary back at Southfork, Lucy plans another reunion; she brings her father to meet her mother, Valene, whom he hasn't seen in sixteen years.

Val remembers how J.R. had hired thugs to track her down in Virginia and take away baby Lucy, leaving Val terrified for her life.

"Momma and Daddy keep him in line," Gary promises her, so Valene agrees.

REUNION, PART TWO
by David Jacobs

J.R. often does the opposite of what's expected of him. Everyone thinks he wants to make trouble for Gary, so he decides to act friendly. He boldly pressures Gary into assuming business responsibilities that are way over his head.

"You know, I was thinking about your staying here and got an idea that was so exciting I just couldn't wait until we got back to the ranch to tell you about it.

"Not too long ago, Ewing Oil acquired a little company that's turned out to be a jewel. It distributes petroleum by-products—all that gook that's left when we finish doing what we have to do to the crude. It's running at about five or ten percent efficiency. Even at that rate, it's turning a nice steady profit. I thought it would be a great project for you. It's a can't-miss operation. A little common sense and some capital and you're gonna turn that nice steady profit into a big fat profit in months, and you don't have to learn hardly anything, just a little tender loving care. You run the company mostly like it's been run and you have it made. And I don't have to tell you that Daddy and I will be one hundred percent behind you."

Valene knows this is just another J.R. trick that is actually designed to drive Gary away again by setting him up for failure.

J.R. schemes to get Gary off the ranch for good, but his plan backfires: Val and Gary remarry and move to Knots Landing, and their own television show.

Pam tries to help Digger out of another drunken stupor.

Val isn't the only Ewing wife having trouble with her men. As Digger recovers from one of his more serious binges, he decides to disown Pamela because she has married a Ewing.

OLD ACQUAINTANCE
by Camille Marchetta

Jenna Wade, Bobby's old girlfriend, comes back into his life as a woman with a problem; she and Charlie, her seven-year-old daughter, need a place to live. Jenna has been forced out of her more than comfortable Dallas life-style because the man who had been keeping her is due to get a political appointment, and his wife threatened to ruin his chances by revealing that he has a mistress if he didn't dump Jenna.

"I was so young, Bobby, and I was having the time of my life—champagne and caviar and colored lights, private planes to Paris and golden yachts to Rio. I couldn't come back to you after running off with my Italian count.

And then there was Charlie. I couldn't let her suffer because my daddy had spent all the money and I had been so wild."

"So now you're out on the street with two hundred dollars in your pocket. And you come to me."

Bobby agrees to help Jenna and becomes more and more involved with her as he slowly comes to realize that her daughter, Charlie, could be his.

J.R. sees in the situation just the kind of dynamite he likes to play with. He believes he can use Jenna and Charlie to drive a wedge between Pam and Bobby. Jenna needs very little encouragement from J.R.; she decides to win back Bobby on her own.

But Pam won't let go of Bobby quite so easily. She forces a showdown at Jenna's apartment, where both women declare that they want him; Jenna refuses to reveal whether Bobby is indeed Charlie's father.

Bobby walks out, leaving behind the deed to the apartment and a sizable check, which he had written before Pam even came for the showdown. He had already chosen Pam; she just didn't know it.

After arguing with J.R. about Bobby's involvement in Ewing Oil, Jock suffers a heart attack on the patio at Southfork.

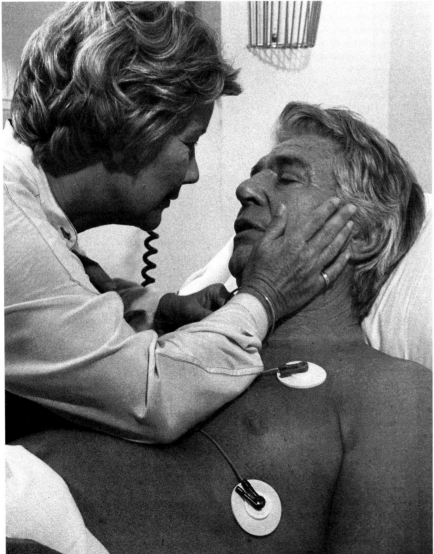

Ellie checks in on Jock at Dallas Memorial Hospital after he has undergone successful bypass surgery.

BYPASS
by Arthur Bernard Lewis

Bobby and J.R.'s constant bickering is such an irritant to their father that he brings the matter up with J.R. In the middle of the discussion Jock has a heart attack and collapses at his son's feet.

To remain close to the family, Bobby leaves Ewing Oil. He goes to work instead at the ranch with Ray, doing the work his father used to do.

"Maybe that's the way to solve the whole problem," says Miss Ellie.

But a bedside chat in the hospital puts Bobby straight.

"Bobby, I do not want you leaving Ewing Oil Company. Do you hear?" Jock says strongly. "J.R.'s doing fine. I'd like to have you there too. I get the feeling sometimes that your brother's not telling me everything."

Further tests show that Jock needs open-heart surgery, a bypass graft, to detour the blockage in his ticker.

The family stands by tensely as the surgery is performed. Only J.R. is missing from the hospital waiting room; he's out making deals on the assumption that his father will die in surgery.

But Jock comes through the operation just fine. His first question is whether or not Bobby is still planning to leave the oil company. When Bobby gives an evasive answer, Jock shakes his head and tells his eldest son, "Well, J.R., it looks like you'll have that office all to yourself."

BLACK MARKET BABY
by Darlene Craviotto

Terrified that Pam will become pregnant again in the near future and produce a Ewing heir before her, Sue Ellen decides to adopt a baby. When she finds out how difficult it is to get a healthy white baby and how long the waiting period can be, she decides on a "black market" baby. Believing that J.R. wouldn't allow her to do anything illegal, Sue Ellen decides to keep the whole thing a secret from her husband.

When she found out the transaction would cost fifteen thousand dollars, Sue Ellen insisted on meeting the mother. Enter one Rita Briggs.

"Friend! You want to be friends? I don't like you! I don't like any of this. If I weren't so dumb, I could be home now." Rita begins the relationship bitterly, but soon warms up to Sue Ellen.

On a shopping spree for baby things with Rita, Sue Ellen bumps into Pam, who is trying to get back her old job in retailing. Sue Ellen is worried that Pam will spill the beans. Instead, Pam just asks Sue Ellen why she thinks it's a contest to have the first baby.

Pam does not tell J.R. what she has learned, but he finds out through his own means. After he ships Rita to California, he confronts Sue Ellen.

"Don't you think I want a baby as bad as you do? But it's got to be our child, not somebody else's."

Sue Ellen goes shopping for a layette for the child she plans to buy from unwed mother Rita.

Spiteful because Jock will not allow Valene
to come to Southfork for her 17th birthday party,
Lucy steals the keys to J.R.'s car and goes on
a joy ride. Stopping at a coffee shop,
she is kidnapped by a drifter.

At gunpoint, Willie Gust,
the kidnapper, forces Lucy
to become an accessory to
a robbery.

DOUBLE WEDDING
by Jim Inman and Arthur Bernard Lewis

Pam's first husband, Ed Haynes, comes back from the past to haunt her. He loosens up Digger's tongue with a few double bourbons, then goes to The Store, where Pam is working, to see the woman he claims is still his wife. She is horrified.

"I'm not your wife!" she says emphatically.

While Ed was in Vietnam—he was shipped out the day after they married—Pam had their Mexican quickie marriage annulled and shipped him the papers.

Then Ed shows up at Ewing Oil to announce he wants Pam back, ten years later but with marriage license in hand. "Mail's not too regular in a North Vietnam prison camp." J.R. is thrilled. Certain he can use Haynes to destroy the Pam-Bobby match, he encourages Haynes to go ahead.

"I'm the wrong Mr. Ewing. My brother Bobby is married to Pamela, but I assure you, I'll help you see that justice is done. The Ewings would never turn their backs on a veteran."

J.R. quickly spreads the word around that Pam is a bigamist. Pam assures Bobby that her first marriage had been annulled, but she can't find the papers to prove it. To make matters worse, Digger has lost his copy, and Digger's attorney has died.

Then Bobby and Pam realize they are being tricked. So Pam tells Haynes she's been kicked out of the Ewing family—without a dime—and is so glad he can protect her. At the same time, Bobby tracks down Haynes's partner in the con job and gets a copy of the annulment papers. Haynes skips town, and his partner follows quickly.

RUNAWAY
by Worley Thorne

Lucy runs away from home when Jock refuses to let her invite her mother to her seventeenth birthday party.

"You can't buy my present, Grandaddy; nobody can. I want my mama invited to my party."

"The way Valene left here last time, I won't allow her in this house."

"J.R.'s a liar, Grandaddy. He lied about the money . . . everything."

J.R. never even denies his lies. He just smiles. "Well, she's a female," he shrugs. "Sometimes their emotions get in the way of their common sense. It's her birthday. Nobody can predict how a woman's gonna react to that."

In escaping the ranch to find Valene, Lucy hitches a ride with a man named Willie Gust, a psychotic thief who can't believe his good luck in meeting Miss Lucy Ewing.

He takes Lucy with him as he robs the cafe where her mother used to work, then makes her work with him on a few more stick-up jobs. Next Gust forces Lucy to get up onstage to sing at a club, in order to distract the patrons while he robs the bartender. When the police discover his intentions, Gust takes Lucy hostage.

Meanwhile, Bobby, who has been tracking Lucy down, forces a showdown with Gust and helps turn him over to the waiting police. Then he brings Lucy safely back to Southfork.

She's still sad she didn't get to see her mother.

"It's not the last birthday you're gonna have," Bobby reminds her.

"It almost was. Thanks," she replies.

ELECTION
by Rena Down

Cliff Barnes's race for state senator places Pam in an awkward position. She decides to help her brother—even though the Ewing family is firmly committed to another candidate. Cliff asks her to host a benefit fashion show just as Bobby signs on to do fundraising for the Ewing-backed candidate.

"Well, well, we'll have to see who raises the most money for their candidate—Bobby or Pam," says J.R. with his wicked smile.

When Pam mentions at the dinner table that the media specialist Cliff has hired from New York is donating his time and talent because the two men were roommates in college, J.R. immediately begins to hint at an unnatural relationship between the two.

"I just think it's strange—a man past thirty—never been married . . . ."

"It just so happens he was engaged to a girl in New York. He's just never gotten over her. She died."

J.R. has found the dirt he needs to start digging a grave for his enemy. He decides to find out if Cliff is gay and also to learn what happened to his girlfriend. When he discovers that she died after an illegal abortion, he implicates the candidate in her death and spreads the word to the media.

"How could you have done that?" Pam asks J.R.

"Politics is politics," replies Jock.

"That's your excuse for taking a fine man and destroying him for your own self-serving entertainment."

"Now hold on, Pamela," counters J.R. "We understand you love your brother. But you do have a slightly prejudiced view of him. And despite what you consider his sterling qualifications, the man apparently doesn't hesitate to do what's illegal, whenever it suits him."

"I want to tell you something," says Pam through clenched teeth. "I don't know how to play by your rules, but someday I will and you're going to pay for what you did to my brother."

Cliff Barnes runs for Congress on an anti-oil, anti-big business platform.

On a rare business trip together, J.R. and Bobby crash land in a small plane.

SURVIVAL
by D.C. Fontana and Richard Fontana

A severe thunderstorm forces the Ewing plane, with Bobby and J.R. on board, to crash in a swamp. When the plane goes off their radar, air traffic control reports the news to Miss Ellie, who orders a search to begin as soon as helicopters can go out.

As the Ewing women await news of the overdue flight, they try to keep their fears from Jock—afraid that any shock may cause another heart attack.

"Miss Ellie wants you to act like nothing's wrong," Ray tells Pam when he gives her the news. "She's afraid the shock could kill Jock."

While Pam worries about the possibility of life without Bobby, Sue Ellen worries about her future without a Ewing heir. Lucy taunts her with the truth:

"If J.R. is dead, without a child, you'll never have Southfork."

Sue Ellen begins to drink.

A reporter sneaks onto the ranch through an abandoned culvert and confronts Miss Ellie about the crash. Jock overhears and takes charge of the waiting and watching. Finally word comes that the boys have survived.

"J.R. did it," reports Bobby. "After we crashed, Johnnie was too hurt to help and I was out cold for three hours. J.R. pulled us out of the plane, got us to shelter, set up some signals . . . everything."

"I'm proud of you," Jock says to J.R., sincerely.

ACT OF LOVE
by Leonard Katzman

Sue Ellen had been out flirting with Cliff Barnes the day her husband was in a plane crash. After all, he treats her like a lady—unlike J.R. He tells her she is beautiful and desirable—things J.R. rarely mentions.

When J.R. goes out of town, Sue Ellen continues her relationship with Cliff, which has by now become more than a flirtation. In fact, when Sue Ellen discovers that she is pregnant, she is not sure who the baby's father is.

"Sue Ellen," says J.R., "something is wrong here. Even if I did remember the time you're talking about, it still seems mighty peculiar that after over seven years of marriage one night would get you pregnant."

"Well, stranger things have happened."

"Not to me, they haven't."

"What are you suggesting, J.R.? That you're not the father of my child?"

Sue Ellen knows that the best way to get back at her philandering husband is to go to bed with his worst enemy—Cliff Barnes.

TRIANGLE
by Camille Marchetta

Ray Krebbs falls in love with a would-be country and western singer named Garnet McGee, whose fingernails are probably still weak from clawing her way up. She has learned to take advantage of the opportunities that come her way, and when the Ewings catch her act, she hears opportunity knocking.

"When you grow up like we did, dirt poor, always hungry, never one thing of your own, not a blanket, not a dollar toy, it's not easy to be satisfied. You're lucky," she tells Ray, "you learned how. For me, the wanting's like a disease. Nothing ever cures it. Nothing's ever enough."

Ray proposes to her, but Garnet does not accept. She has found an even more exciting prospect—J.R. Ewing.

To win Garnet for himself, J.R. agrees to use his wealth and influence. "I introduce you around, you get a recording contract. I use Ewing money to back you all the way to stardom."

"And in return?"

Lucy tries to resume her affair with Ray, who insists that it's over between them.

Bobby returns to executive life at Ewing Oil after Jock makes it clear that he does not trust J.R. to run the business without a watchdog.

"I get twenty-five percent of your earnings from all sources—and the exclusive use of your services for as long as I want them." Garnet bargains him down on the percentage.

When Lucy finds out about their deal, she tells Ray, who has pushed her aside for Garnet.

Ray heads right out after J.R. Bobby, urged by Pam to stop the fight before Ray and J.R. kill each other, follows him, and manages to break them up after each man has bruised the other's face and ego.

KIDNAPPED
by Camille Marchetta

Although they've planned it carefully, the kidnappers just can't do anything right. Their target is J.R.—worth $100 million—but one day when the brothers switch cars they end up snatching Bobby by accident.

"If this is some kind of hold-up, I've got a couple of hundred on me," says Bobby at gunpoint.

"Couple of hundred! You kidding? You're worth millions, mister."

Cliff Barnes is chosen by the kidnappers to act as the go-between. J.R., who has never much liked Cliff—and likes even less to do things someone else's way—proceeds on his own.

"You just do what you're told, Barnes. Leave the thinking to me," says J.R.

But J.R. blows the swap, and Bobby's escape attempt fails, putting Cliff back on the case. When J.R. overhears Cliff set up the rendezvous for the exchange he sets out with Ray to trap the kidnappers. He shoots them, but not without almost hitting Cliff.

"It was me you wanted to get, wasn't it, J.R.? Put me out of your hair. For good!"

FALLEN IDOL
by Arthur Bernard Lewis

Bobby has dabbled in the construction business since returning to executive life at Ewing Oil, so when his best buddy, Taylor "Guzzler" Bennett, comes back to town after a stint in Venezuela, the two men have a good old time of a reunion and decide to go into business together—the construction business.

Guzzler's hot idea is to build a shopping center. Not a bad idea, but there's one big hitch: the land he has in mind is part of the Ewing ranch, and neither Miss Ellie nor J.R. wants to let go of the parcel.

To Miss Ellie, the ranch is to be preserved just the way her father left it. She never let Jock drill for oil, and she certainly won't allow a shopping center to be built.

J.R. is more practical. Section 40 can't possibly be turned into a shopping center because the day after Jock dies J.R. will be out there drilling for oil. He's had his eye on that section of the ranch for years and is certain that oil lies beneath the pasture.

HOME AGAIN
by Arthur Bernard Lewis

When Miss Ellie mysteriously receives a painting of Southfork as it looked in the old days, she is surprised almost to the point of shock. When her brother, Garrison Southworth, who she thought was dead, turns up quite alive, she has even more of a shock.

She gathers the children together to make her announcement. "This is very hard for me because you know how I love Southfork and all of you, but my brother was named heir to Southfork in my Daddy's will. When he was lost at sea, your father and I had him declared dead and claimed the ranch. Now that he's back, I have to do what's right and honorable. Southfork must be given back to Garrison."

Naturally, everyone is opposed to Miss Ellie's idea—including Garrison. But before he can explain himself, J.R. insults him, and the older man for the sake of his pride is forced to fight back. Finally, Garrison's nurse calls Miss Ellie to explain the situation. Her brother had just come home to die.

FOR LOVE OR MONEY
by Leonard Katzman

Sue Ellen, deciding she has finally had enough of J.R.'s unfaithfulness, seeks comfort from Cliff Barnes and from her sister, Kristin, and her mother, Patricia Shepard, who have just moved to Dallas.

"I saw you today, J.R. I was in Fort Worth with some friends having lunch. I'd just finished telling them you were in Austin when you came parading off that elevator with your tramp."

"Now, Sue Ellen, you know I wouldn't associate with that kind of woman. She happened to be a most charming lady... not a tramp at all."

When J.R. discovers that his wife has been involved with Barnes and, furthermore, wants to leave him for his rival, he decides that there is nothing he wants more in this world than to stay married to Sue Ellen—whether the baby she is carrying is his or not.

JULIE'S RETURN
by Rena Down

Ever since his bypass surgery, Jock Ewing has been treated like an invalid, and he doesn't like it one bit. J.R. uses the illness to keep his father even farther away from the business than before; Miss Ellie tries to keep any upsetting news from her husband lest he have another attack.

When Julie Grey, J.R.'s former secretary and part-time girlfriend, comes back to town, she and Jock strike up a friendship. Jock soon forgets the mess she created for the Ewings with Cliff Barnes, and he spends more and more time with the lady, enjoying himself as he hasn't in years. He's even late for a business appointment because of her—for the first time in his career.

Anxious about his father's affair with Julie, J.R. tells him that the girl is just trash, but Jock will hear none of it. Not knowing how else to break the couple up, J.R. tells his mother the whole story. When Miss Ellie tries to step in, Jock skips dinner and seeks comfort with Julie.

Still, Jock knows he won't leave Miss Ellie. He presents Julie with a gold necklace, a gift he had bought her to cement their friendship, but now given as a going-away present. No sooner has Jock left for home than J.R. arrives at Julie's door.

"I caused you a lot of trouble," says Julie with a half-satisfied smile on her lips.

J.R. nods.

"Well, I'm gonna cause you more," Julie promises.

"Don't count on it," replies J.R.

THE RED FILE, PART ONE
by Arthur Bernard Lewis

J.R. suggests to Julie that she renew her friendship with Cliff Barnes and have an affair with him so she can spy for J.R. Julie vows she is finished being used, and she decides to tell Cliff Barnes everything she knows.

Julie leaves a message on Barnes's answering machine, telling him she knows where all the Ewing skeletons are buried and is ready to spill the beans—for a price, of course. She invites him to her apartment to show just how serious she is.

When Cliff arrives at her apartment Julie is not there—which is not surprising since she has already fallen from the roof.

A few hours later, and with J.R.'s help, Cliff Barnes is booked for the murder of Julie Grey.

Julie steals some Ewing secrets and gives them to Cliff to use against J.R. (one of many times that J.R. will be hurt by vengeful former lovers).

Garrison proves that he really is Ellie's younger brother by giving her a painting of Southfork as it looked when they were children.

Kidnappers meant to snatch J.R. but settled for his younger brother and sent the family all over Dallas to deliver the ransom money.

THE RED FILE, PART TWO
by Arthur Bernard Lewis

Pam is so certain that J.R. has framed her brother that she moves out of Southfork, leaving Bobby hurt, confused, and still living on the ranch.

Bobby is certain that J.R. is trying to get rid of Pam once more. "You've tried all these months and now you've finally succeeded in driving Pam away," he shouts.

Bobby goes to see Cliff to ask what he can do to help. At first, Cliff is not interested in seeing another Ewing—ever. Then he tells Bobby that if he really wants to help, he can. All he has to do is find out who really killed Julie.

Bobby's first big clue comes when he collects Cliff's mail for him and discovers a pawn ticket sent him by Julie. When Bobby redeems the ticket, what he gets is not what he expected—the gold necklace that Jock had given Julie—but instead, an attaché case that includes secret Ewing Oil files and Jock Ewing's will.

Bobby confronts J.R. with his discovery that there is an apparently forged codicil to the will, but J.R. explains it away as "a business maneuver." Bobby further accuses J.R. of killing Julie to prevent her from turning the papers over to Cliff.

"Bobby, I'm not a killer. I never killed anyone in my life. Not even in the war."

Out of fear that Bobby will tell Jock about the doctored will, J.R. reveals to Bobby the name of the man who tapped Julie's phone. Through him, the identities of the killers are discovered and Cliff is exonerated.

Even though Bobby gets her brother off the hook, Pam is not ready to come back to Southfork.

"It's the lousy Barnes-Ewing feud, isn't it? Well, Pam, you knew I was a Ewing when you married me, and I'm going to be a Ewing until I die. If you can live with that, then call me, because I love you and I want you back."

SUE ELLEN'S SISTER
by Camille Marchetta

With Pam away from Southfork to think things over, Sue Ellen's sister, Kristin, decides it's a good time to see if another Ewing man might be interested in another Shepard woman's obvious charms. J.R. encourages the possibility of a match with Bobby.

"You've had a remarkable effect on my brother. He's been more cheerful than I've seen him in weeks. You know, he hasn't wanted to admit it, but his marriage is over. Finished. I think he just finally accepted that fact."

While J.R. uses Kristin to gain more power over Bobby, Cliff tries to use Sue Ellen to get some information on

J.R. sends his henchmen to Julie Grey's apartment
one night to find the evidence she has sequestered.
Hearing the men approach, Julie races to the roof
to hide but ends up in a struggle, during which she
plunges to her death.

J.R. and his dirty dealings. When that doesn't work he goes to Pam for help—even if it means widening the rift between Pam and Bobby.

"You've been trying to destroy my marriage," Pam says angrily to her brother.

"Only partially," he admits.

"Knowing what you've become should make a difference. Now, instead of just not wanting to be a Ewing, I don't want to be a Barnes either."

CALL GIRL
by Rena Down

Pam, still separated from Bobby, makes friends with a model named Leanne Rees.

When J.R. sees the two women together, it doesn't take long for him to come up with the perfect scheme to kill two birds with one stone; he can ruin both Pam and Ben Maxwell—one of the biggest political supporters of Cliff Barnes—with just the teeniest bit of blackmail.

J.R. tries to hire Leanne, who he knows has been a call girl named Amber, to "entertain some friends," but Leanne tells him that she no longer sells her services. Miffed, J.R. has her busted, just to show her what power really is. To keep her record clean, Leanne agrees to help J.R. by setting up a little threesome among herself, Maxwell, and Pam—"just like we did to that congressman and his wife."

After Pam becomes Leanne's roommate, Leanne persuades Maxwell to come up to the apartment for a nightcap. As she maneuvers the inebriated Maxwell into the bedroom, Pam wakes up, and a photographer jumps out of the closet to catch all the action. The pictures are printed in the newspaper the next day.

Maxwell resigns, and Pam decides to leave Dallas. But Bobby comes after her. "It's only over if you want it to be, Pam. It's only over if you want to stop fighting. J.R. has been trying to do this to you and me ever since I brought you to Southfork. You leave now, you run, and J.R. wins, finally, completely. I thought you were a fighter. Are you ready to let J.R. win? Or, Pam, do we face this together? Together, we can beat him, Pam. I know it. And I want you with me."

ROYAL MARRIAGE
by Camille Marchetta

Lucy Ewing had been madly in love with Kit Mainwaring III from the moment she met him. Kit's feelings were a lot more doubtful, but that never stopped Lucy from pushing for what she wanted—and she wanted to marry him.

Sue Ellen's baby sister—Kristin Shepard, played by Mary Crosby, daughter of the late Bing.

J.R. thought that would be fine, since Kit was from another oil-rich, powerful, old Texas family. He saw the marriage of his niece as the best possible way to join the two families together into an independent oil dynasty.

Kit's family is equally impressed. "You've made a fine choice," Kit's mother praises him, with a voice that reminds him there is no other choice.

"I don't know what kind of a husband I'll be. I've always thought a pretty lousy one. But I love you. I really do," Kit tells Lucy as a proposal.

When Lucy discovers that Kit really only has eyes for his former college roommate, Gary Gates, she begins to realize that there could be trouble in paradise.

Then Kit reveals himself to Bobby.

"I'm a homosexual, Bobby. I'm a queer, a faggot, or if you prefer, gay. Though I'm not feeling very gay at this moment."

J.R. has known all along. "C'mon, Bobby," he admonishes his brother, "women marry faggots all the time. Seems to suit a lot of them. Lucy loves Kit; she'll be just fine."

But Kit can't go through with it. When J.R. hears that he plans to call off the wedding, he decides to blackmail the young man into carrying out the plans. Kit still can't do it. When he finally tells Lucy the truth, she thinks of a way to help them out of the mess.

She returns home and announces to her family that she will not marry Kit, because he flew into a jealous rage at a restaurant. Her story is convincing, and Jock agrees that she doesn't have to marry.

"That was quite a performance," Bobby tells her later. "Kit has a lot to be grateful to you for."

THE OUTSIDERS
by Leonard Katzman

Ray Krebbs falls in love again, this time with Donna McCullum, a woman he meets in a bar. Despite their obvious attraction for one another, it becomes apparent that Donna is not revealing all there is to know about herself. She is already married.

It turns out that she's married to Sam Culver, former governor of Texas and a powerful politician whom J.R. has been courting in the hopes that some of Culver's connections may help keep Cliff Barnes away from Ewing Oil.

When Sam Culver tells the Ewings that he's concerned about ecology and is not quick to take sides on these issues, he implies that his wife, Donna, helps him make a lot of his decisions these days. J.R. can't wait to come up with some way to enlist Donna's aid.

Pam and Bobby happen to enter a bar and see the Southfork ranch foreman Ray with his new lady love—none other than Donna McCullum Culver. Pam is terribly upset; first she herself had thrown him over, then

Garnet McGee broke his heart. She tells her husband, "I can't stand the thought of Ray being hurt again."

But Pam and Bobby aren't the only ones who know. J.R. has followed the couple. He tells Donna that he knows her guilty little secret and tries to get her to influence her husband on the matter of the Office of Land Management—the organization that Cliff Barnes has been using to try to get at Ewing Oil.

For one of the few times in his life, J.R.'s plan backfires. Donna decides to tell her husband everything—about Ray and about J.R.'s blackmail. She leaves Sam so that she can sort things out for herself, and Sam calls J.R. to tell him that the O.L.M. and Cliff Barnes have his full support.

"Well, sir, I think I could get you to change your mind," says J.R.

"There's nothing you could tell me that Donna hasn't."

JOHN EWING III, PART ONE
by Camille Marchetta

Sue Ellen's alcoholism has developed to the point that Jock and Miss Ellie can no longer ignore it. Sue Ellen has continued to drink heavily even though she is pregnant; and the Daughters of the Alamo have politely asked her to resign. But still she does not let up on the booze.

"I am what you made me," Sue Ellen tells J.R.

She is not the only Ewing woman with an addiction problem. To get over the hurt of her broken engagement to Kit, Lucy has become addicted to pills—a secret that

Attendants from the Fletcher Sanitarium
drag a reluctant Sue Ellen off for treatment.

Bobby comforts his heartbroken niece after her broken engagement.

Bobby is determined not to let his family discover. Instead, he enlists Ray's aid and together they force Lucy to go straight. J.R. commits his wife—for her own safety, of course—to a sanitarium. Once again, the Ewings have made a decision for her, and there is nothing she can do.

"But there's nothing wrong with me," she pleads.

JOHN EWING III, PART TWO
by Arthur Bernard Lewis

Sue Ellen is sent to the Fletcher Sanitarium, one of those fancy retreats where the rich dry out but never dry up—the rooms look more like a hotel than a hospital, the furnishings are tasteful and expensive. Mrs. Ewing is not looking much like Miss Texas any more. She may wear a peignoir and pearls, but she's obviously having a hard time getting over her alcohol dependency.

"She seemed to be a reasonably happy woman before she got pregnant," Jock says, still amazed that Sue Ellen could have such a serious problem.

"Daddy," said J.R., "you know how women are. Sometimes their hormones get all jumbled up."

So do Sue Ellen's emotions. She tells Bobby of her misery. "Oh Bobby, the doctors aren't going to cure what's wrong with me. How can I explain it to you? For you, life is so simple; you have Pam. You love her. J.R. doesn't love me. I love him, and I wanted his baby, for a long time....Then I went out and got pregnant. At first I thought maybe I would hurt J.R., but I hurt myself and the baby and the baby's father."

"What are you talking about? Who is the father?"

"Cliff Barnes."

Although she is obviously distraught, Sue Ellen keeps talking about leaving the sanitarium. Bobby tries to convince her to give it a chance.

When J.R. visits and shows her a newspaper photograph of Cliff Barnes with a new girlfriend, Sue Ellen has a relapse. She bribes her nurse to sneak her booze in mouthwash bottles. The liquor makes her brave, so she attempts an escape—which leads to an automobile accident. Luckily she is pulled from the wreckage just as the car goes up in flames. An announcement airs on the late news: "Mrs. J.R. Ewing, wife of the president of Ewing Oil, has been involved in a serious accident. At the moment, she is undergoing emergency surgery at Dallas Memorial in an attempt to save her life and the life of her unborn child."

Although it is a full eight weeks until Sue Ellen's baby is due, doctors have no choice but to perform an emergency Caesarean section. When Cliff hears the news broadcast he rushes to the hospital, certain that it is his child who is in danger. While Sue Ellen struggles toward stability, hooked up to a battery of fancy machines, her baby fights for his own life.

"Oh my God, will he live?" Cliff anxiously asks Pam.

"They don't know."

Sue Ellen and J.R. learn from the press
that their infant son has been kidnapped.

WHATEVER HAPPENED TO BABY JOHN, PART ONE
by Camille Marchetta

Sue Ellen makes a physical recovery from the accident and the early birth of her son, but remains emotionally weak. Standing at the window of the hospital nursery looking at the boy, it is clear that she has lost her zest. J.R. tells her not to worry, that the baby will soon be home. Cliff Barnes is also anxious; he wants Sue Ellen and John Ross III home with *him*.

"I know how you feel," Pam tells her brother. "I don't like what's happened, but I can still sympathize with you. Only there's not only the baby to consider, there's Sue Ellen. Emotionally, she's a mess. It's as if she's walking a tightrope. Any distraction or disturbance, and she'll fall. You'll help her right back on the bottle if you're not careful."

Settled back at Southfork, Sue Ellen is remote and refuses to return to the hospital to see the baby. Her rest is more important, she claims.

"You wanted a child so much. Don't you care for him at all?" J.R. asks his wife, presenting her with a maternity ring as a baby gift.

"You bought me once, J.R. But you can't anymore. I'm no longer for sale," Sue Ellen tells him—loud enough that the whole family can hear.

Pam and Bobby also feel the tension. Cliff's struggle to get Sue Ellen and the baby affects their relationship as well. Often torn apart on family issues, the couple this time agree that Cliff has to leave Sue Ellen alone.

J.R. and Sue Ellen finally go to the hospital to pick up the baby, where they are confronted by a group of reporters. The reporters ask if they have any leads, or if the police have any suspects—J.R. and Sue Ellen's first notice that their son has been kidnapped.

WHATEVER HAPPENED TO BABY JOHN, PART TWO
by Camille Marchetta

The shock of the baby's kidnapping brings the Ewing family together as they seek various ways to recover the child.

"We should have learned our lessons last time," Jock says bitterly, referring to Lucy's kidnapping.

Bobby believes that Cliff took the baby as a way to get Sue Ellen back.

"Cliff wouldn't do something like this," Pam says adamantly.

When he learns that a ransom has been demanded, J.R. reasons that the kidnapping may be the handiwork of some of his one-time friends who have since become criminals—the same ones who caused Julie Grey to fall from the roof. It appears that they have just been released from prison.

One of the ex-cons, Willy Ames, gloats: "What a stroke of luck somebody took that kid. Looks like we're going to get a million bucks for nothing."

But it is Pam who solves the mystery. She remembers that a woman called Priscilla Duncan had spent a great deal of time at the hospital nursery window. When she goes to talk to Priscilla, Pam hears a baby cry and she comes to the realization that the child that Priscilla claims is hers is actually John Ross III.

"What will happen to Priscilla?" Pam asks Bobby after it's all over.

"She'll probably be remanded for psychiatric care, poor kid. Husband running out on her, baby dying... she's had a rough time."

THE SILENT KILLER
by Arthur Bernard Lewis

Cliff brings his father, the infamous Digger Barnes, to Dallas to show him how he's getting even with the Ewings. Digger arrives wearing a cheap, rumpled suit and a too-narrow tie, and carrying a small battered suitcase.

He doesn't look at all well, but, with Digger, it could always be the booze. Then he develops a serious medical problem, totally unrelated to his drinking.

"I haven't seen a doctor in thirty years and I don't intend to start now; just give me a couple of aspirin," Digger protests.

Testing shows that Digger has neurofibromatosis, a fatal genetic disorder that has probably been passed on to Pam and Cliff, and even to baby John Ross—if Cliff is indeed the father. Cliff remembers that he and Pam had another brother and sister who had died mysteriously in childhood; the doctor confirms that they probably died of neurofibromatosis.

"Are you saying that any child of mine could die at six months?" Cliff asks the doctor, incredulously.

"To be blunt...yes."

Pam discovers she is pregnant again—and she is anything but thrilled. The first time she was happy, and seeing little John Ross has again made her want a child of her own, but now that she knows about Digger's disease, which she and Cliff have doubtless inherited, she can't

Keenan Wynn became the second actor to play Digger Barnes in a recurring role that ended with Digger's death at the close of the 1979–80 season. Digger had been drifting around for years, living in Corpus Christi before Cliff flew him home to Dallas.

decide if she should tell Bobby her terrible secret or have an abortion before anyone finds out.

"What do I do," Pam asks her doctor, "carry a baby for nine months and then sit back and watch him die by the time he's a year old?"

"You know I can't answer that," says Dr. Holliston. "That's between you and your husband."

"No! I don't want my husband to know anything about this."

Pam uses a pay phone for her private conversations because Southfork offers little privacy to a woman trying to keep a secret.

J.R. keeps it "all in the family" in his affair with Kristin.

THE KRISTIN AFFAIR
by Worley Thorne

Kristin returns to Dallas with her mother to visit Sue Ellen's new baby and convinces J.R. to give her a summer job in his office, where she openly flirts with him. When her mother heads back to California, Kristin is left on her own. "J.R. is such a fine man, the way he stands behind Sue Ellen," says Patricia Shepard, with pride. "Someday, Kris, you're going to find a man like that yourself."

"I think that's possible, Mama. Quite possible."

"When I leave tomorrow, you'll be entirely on your own. I know I can trust you to remember the things I taught you about watching for the right opportunity.

"Mama," Kristin says, "I remember *everything* you taught me."

Pam can't seem to find the right moment to tell Bobby her terrible news, and he learns about her pregnancy before she can make a decision about having an abortion. Once Bobby has proudly made the announcement to the family, she's in even more of a quandary.

Sue Ellen catches her sister and husband
on their way from a lunchtime tryst
and senses that they are doing something
more than discussing crude oil prices.

Ellie decorates the nursery
as she prepares for
the arrival of the next
generation of Ewings.

Upon learning that her grandson was kidnapped,
Ellie, in an unusual release of emotion, vents her
tears.

Pam is horrified to learn that she may transmit a deadly hereditary disease to her unborn child.

Digger hugs John Ross warmly,
mistakenly believing that
Cliff is the baby's true father.

THE DOVE HUNT
by D.C. Fontana and Richard Fontana

On a hunting trip in Louisiana, Jock finds himself a target for revenge from a man he doesn't even remember, when he and J.R. are wounded by a sniper's bullets. Ray and Bobby walk to town for help, leaving the two wounded men alone. Afraid that he won't pull through, Jock reveals all his secrets to J.R., including everything he has been hiding from Miss Ellie since their wedding.

"I was married, J.R. She's still alive. Her name's Amanda Lewis. She was a pretty little thing, too fragile for me . . . kind you have to protect . . . you know. I was wildcatting—those were rough times—men were shooting each other, just like today. There were accidents.

"She had a hard time living with all that. All that strain, everything just got to her. Two years after we were married she had a breakdown . . . lost touch with reality. Had to be confined to a state mental hospital. Her doctor told me to get a divorce, that she'd never be well again. I never told anyone about her."

While out hunting with Bobby and Ray, Jock and
J.R. are wounded by snipers.

THE LOST CHILD
by Rena Down

Sue Ellen decides to see a psychiatrist to pull her life together again, but does it on the sly. Her secret meetings lead J.R. to believe that she's having another affair or has reunited with Cliff Barnes. He hires a detective to keep tabs on her. At the same time Pam is having her own secret meetings with her brother—to discuss her fears for the unborn child. Bobby is so excited by the impending arrival of their child that Pam has been unable to break the news of her inherited disease to him.

One morning she takes a horse out on the prairie to meet Bobby for a ride. A rattlesnake slithers out from under a rock into her path. Pam's horse shies, she is thrown, and she suffers her second miscarriage.

RODEO
by Camille Marchetta

Sue Ellen takes up with cowboy Dusty Farlow at the annual rodeo sponsored by the Ewings. The new romance puts a little of the old spark back into Sue Ellen, and ignites a flame of jealousy in J.R.

Digger wants to attend the rodeo to get a look at baby John Ross, thinking that he's the child's grandfather. Pam expects trouble if her Dad turns up, but Miss Ellie is convinced that Digger wants to end the feud and to see her new grandson.

Kristin, taken in by all the glamour of the big-time rodeo event and the surrounding party, rashly speaks out against Sue Ellen and J.R. quickly puts the girl in her place.

"However I spend my play time, sugar, I never forget my first loyalty is to my family, my wife and my child. If you're smart, you won't forget it either."

Lucy stirs up several hornet's nests. She asks Kristin, "Are you really trying to take J.R. away from Sue Ellen?" And she confronts Ray with some letters from Donna that he had hidden away but never read. She drops a bombshell concerning Donna and Sam Culver that Ray was never ready to hear: "She only went back to him because Sam's dying of cancer. She had to go back to be with him at the end."

MASTECTOMY, PART ONE
by Arthur Bernard Lewis

When Ellie found the lump in her breast, she meant to tell Jock about it. Then she learned the long-hidden secret about Jock's first wife, who had become mentally ill.

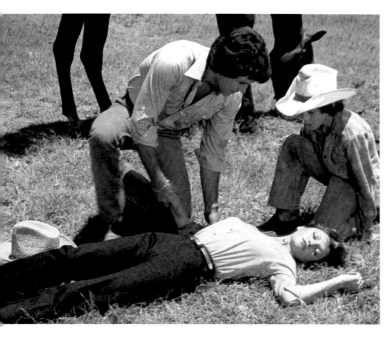

Pam is thrown from her horse and suffers a miscarriage.

Digger and Cliff visit Pam at Dallas Memorial.

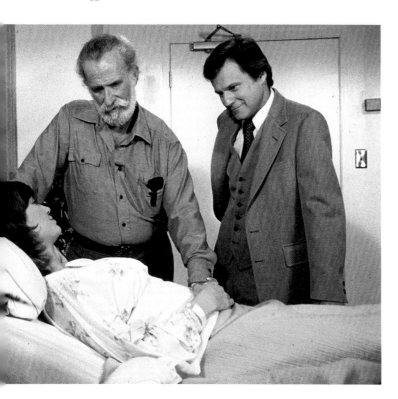

Afraid that Jock would also divorce her if she were to have a mastectomy, Ellie decides not to tell her husband about her health problems. "The man gets better looking as he gets older . . . tall, lean, not an ounce of fat on him. And he admires beauty," Ellie says to Pam. "He still has an eye for a good-looking woman. How can I tell him I may need a mastectomy?"

Keeping their secrets causes friction between Ellie and Jock and when they fight, the other Ewings worry that the two may actually split up. After one particularly bitter spat, Ellie goes into the hospital without ever reconciling with Jock.

"Can you imagine that woman checking into the hospital for surgery and not even telling me?" he muses to J.R. over coffee in the waiting room.

When the surgery is over the doctor talks to Jock.

"Ellie was right. Her breast was full of cysts, and there was also a small cancer. It never registered on the mammogram. We had to perform a mastectomy. Jock, when Ellie wakes up, we're going to have to tell her we had to take her breast."

MASTECTOMY, PART TWO
by Arthur Bernard Lewis

After her mastectomy, Miss Ellie has to face up to the future. She and Jock seem to be drifting apart as she struggles with the anger she feels over the forty-year-old secret that he had been unable to reveal to her. It's not the fact that Jock was married before that bothers her, but that he kept it from her. And, to aggravate the issue, he appears to have rejected his first wife because of illness. Now, with her own medical problems, Ellie fears the same rejection.

In addition to her own health worries, Ellie has her hands full with Lucy, who fears that she too may have a similar problem someday.

"Lucy, because this happened to me doesn't mean it's inevitable that it will happen to you. But I don't want you to avoid regular examinations or learning about your own body just because you're frightened. We all have to live with fears sometimes, Lucy, but you have to learn to deal with it and get on with the business of living."

THE HEIRESS
by Loraine Despres

When Lucy sees attorney Alan Beam stand up to J.R. she decides that he is the man for her. What she doesn't know is that she has witnessed a setup: the fight at the rodeo was staged to convince Cliff Barnes of Beam's loyalty so that Beam could become a double agent for the Ewings.

Lucy makes a play for Alan at the end of the rodeo, and his eyes light up with delight—not only at the idea of winning little Miss Ewing but also at having her as his pawn.

"Sometimes," Alan tells Lucy, "I get the feeling that my main attraction for you is J.R.'s dislike."

"Oh no," Lucy counters. "It's just that I'm with the one man who isn't afraid to stand up to him. That makes you pretty rare in this town."

"I don't want you ever to get hurt because of me," Alan tells her, stringing her along. "If you think you'll get in trouble because of seeing me, and you'd rather not, I'll understand."

Lucy becomes certain Alan is madly in love with her.

ELLIE SAVES THE DAY
by Arthur Bernard Lewis and E. Michael

J.R. is in big trouble when a devastating typhoon delays oil drilling in Asia. His bank loan is due, he has mortgaged Southfork to finance his Asian deals, and now the family stands to lose everything.

When the efforts of all the Ewing men seem to have failed, Ellie decides, against her father's last wishes, to allow drilling on the ranch itself to raise the capital to save the homestead.

MOTHER OF THE YEAR
by Rena Down

Despite getting psychiatric help, Sue Ellen still avoids her baby; Pamela, on the other hand, dotes on him. In fact, Pam and Bobby have practically come to think of the baby as their own, which creates tremendous conflict with Sue Ellen and J.R. When the baby cries, for example, Pam rushes in to him as Sue Ellen stands by waiting for Mrs. Reeves, the nurse, to go to him.

"Why didn't you pick him up?" Pam demands of her sister-in-law.

"It's bad to pick up a baby every time he cries."

"He's your baby. How can you bear to hear him cry?"

Lucy also gets into the act and criticizes Sue Ellen as well. "What is it about the Ewings that makes kids unwelcome? Is it a curse or something? Is every child in this family meant to grow up without parents?"

Ultimately all the speeches work, and Sue Ellen finally takes her child to her heart.

Sue Ellen, whose maternal feeling had been blocked, after working with a psychiatrist to break through her fear, finally picks up her son to mother him.

Dusty Farlow sweeps Sue Ellen off her feet and proves himself the opposite of J.R.: he's kind, loving, and crazy about her. It'll never work.

The conniving attorney Alan Beam (played by actor Randy Powell) sets his sights on Lucy Ewing's fortune with the understanding that if he marries her, J.R. will set him up in business—outside of Texas.

Pam becomes more and more involved with her work at The Store, modeled on Neiman-Marcus.

RETURN ENGAGEMENT
by David Jacobs

Miss Ellie is usually sad on the birthday of Gary, her only son who does not live at Southfork. But, this year, her pain turns to pleasure when Gary announces that he and Valene are back in Dallas and plan to remarry. Ellie wants to keep the wedding a secret from J.R.—out of town on a business trip—who she fears will try to ruin the match again. But Sue Ellen takes great pleasure in passing the news on to her husband.

J.R. rushes back from Austin to stop the wedding, but he is fifteen minutes too late. Seeing that he's lost, J.R. kisses the bride and shakes his brother's hand.

"Congratulations, Gary. I sure do wish I'd been here in time."

LOVE AND MARRIAGE
by Leonard Katzman

J.R. decides that bringing Bobby back into Ewing Oil from his duties on the ranch is the best way to keep Jock out of the office.

Pam becomes a workaholic to cover her pain over the loss of her own child and the additional hurt of not being able to look after baby John Ross any longer. Her additional work strains her marriage even further. This doesn't upset J.R. at all. In fact, he goes to Pam's boss to get her a promotion so that her schedule is even heavier. Bobby is not happy.

"This isn't a start, it's a finish. You don't want to have a baby? Fine. You don't want to adopt a baby? Fine. I can live without a child. But I can't live like this. I want you to quit your job and come back to being a wife."

POWER PLAY
by Jeff Young

Kristin, getting more and more like J.R. every day, finds out about Lucy and Alan Beam and decides to squeal on them, certain that J.R. will fire Alan once he finds out about his ambitious plans to use Lucy to better himself.

Instead, J.R. plays true to form and does exactly the opposite of what anyone expects. Instead of breaking them up, he *encourages* their affair and urges Alan to marry Lucy.

"Lucy's a Ewing," J.R. advises Beam. "We all want what we think we can't get. You just tell her things are off between you two and leave the rest to me."

PATERNITY SUIT
by Loraine Despres

Alan Beam's insidious work on "behalf" of Cliff Barnes has paid off, and Barnes is forced out of the race for congress. A reporter goes to Cliff's house for the inside story.

When Digger answers the door, she gets a bigger story than she planned on: Digger goes on a drunken binge and tells her his whole tale of woe, all about the feud with the Ewings. He also tells her that Cliff is really the father of Sue Ellen's baby.

Sue Ellen reads the news in the headlines while she's enjoying a sojourn in a Fort Worth hotel with Dusty Farlow; she rushes home to Southfork.

Jock wants to sue Cliff. Barnes wants to countersue for custody. The battle for the baby forces both J.R. and Cliff to submit to blood tests so the real father can finally be identified.

"There's no doubt about it, J.R., you're the daddy."

JENNA'S RETURN
by Camille Marchetta

Pam's work at The Store has paid off—too well. Her boss is so impressed with her that he decides to take her to Paris for the collections. At first Pam is a little afraid of the idea, but she decides that a few days away from Southfork will give her time to sort out her thoughts.

Although Bobby asks Pam not to go, she goes anyway. Just as Pam walks out the airport gate, Bobby bumps into his old girlfriend Jenna Wade. Pam turns to wave goodbye to her husband, and sees him in Jenna's arms.

Conveniently, Jenna has put her daughter on a plane to Rome, to spend time with her ex-husband, the girl's father, Renaldo Marchetta. "You know," Jenna confides, "Naldo's turning out to be a pretty good father." Charlie is now ten, and Jenna has become an independent, modern woman—fashion editor of *High Style* magazine.

While Pam is away, Jenna and Bobby spend time together, doing many of the things they did as teenagers. Bobby decides to spend the night with Jenna.

"If we do this, Bobby," she warns him, "it can't be just this once and no more. I've regretted losing you for too long to settle for that. I want more from you, Bobby. A lot more."

SUE ELLEN'S CHOICE
by Camille Marchetta

The Ewing women are having trouble staying married. Sue Ellen, under pressure from Dusty, finally asks J.R. for a divorce.

"You don't have the guts to leave me and head out on your own. Who is he?" J.R. asks her.

Sue Ellen refuses to name names, but J.R. agrees to a divorce and tells Sue Ellen she can leave anytime—without the baby.

Pam returns from Paris and is shocked to find Jenna so clear in her intentions about Bobby. Bobby makes one last attempt to save their marriage.

"I almost slept with Jenna last night. I didn't. I wanted to."

"What stopped you?"

"I love you, Pam, and she knows it. Please. I want to save our marriage, but I can't do it by myself. Help me...."

"I don't think I can, Bobby."

Pam and Jenna talk it over, woman to woman, and Jenna lays it on the line: "I'd like to know if you want Bobby. Because if you don't, I do."

Pam explains her situation to Bobby, "I feel so inadequate, Bobby. I feel, all the time, as if I'm failing you. And I can't stand it. It makes me pull away from you. It's so crazy. Sometimes I want you to leave. And sometimes, I think I'll die if you go."

Both Pam and Sue Ellen decide to stay and try to work things out—one more time.

SECOND THOUGHTS
by Linda B. Elstad

J.R. wants to move Alan Beam to Chicago and get Lucy out of his way in the bargain, so he pressures the attorney to get Lucy to set a wedding date.

"We have a deal," J.R. reminds Beam. "You get Lucy and a law practice in Chicago. I get her and her scheming parents out of my hair . . . and if it's not that way, the wedding's off!"

But Jock wants Lucy to stay in the Dallas area, so he gets Alan a partnership in a local law firm—without consulting J.R.

"I've taken care of Lucy all her life," Jock explains. "Habits like that are hard to break."

Kristin's bad habits are also hard to break. She tells Lucy that Alan has another girlfriend—Betty Lou.

Lucy doesn't care. She finally sets the date: June 14th. But a chat with Bobby helps Lucy to realize that she doesn't love Alan and is only marrying him to spite J.R. She breaks off the engagement and returns to Southfork.

DIVORCE—EWING STYLE
by Leonard Katzman

Sue Ellen, that famous chameleon, has changed again. Now she is the perfect wife and mother. Her act impresses everyone at Southfork, except J.R., who figures that Sue Ellen is probably just setting him up for a divorce.

Tensions in Pam and Bobby's marriage implode before they explode.

J.R. is questioned about an old pistol, which may have been the murder weapon in the 25-year-old case of Hutch McKinney.

Dusty's disappearance sends Sue Ellen to her only other friend—the bottle. When Sue Ellen discovers that Dusty never turned up because his plane had crashed, she is filled with guilt and self-loathing.

This time she works slowly and cautiously to build up her case. No one will be able to call her a drunkard or an unfit mother. To gather even more evidence, she hires a detective to follow J.R.

Furious with her tactics, J.R. decides that the only way to keep his son at Southfork is to prove that Sue Ellen is drinking again. He forces her into a showdown with his family. In retaliation, Sue Ellen reveals her detective reports to Ellie and Jock. But J.R. has already found them and switched them, so Sue Ellen merely looks like a fool.

JOCK'S TRIAL, PART ONE
by Arthur Bernard Lewis

A human skeleton is found at Southfork and the district attorney surmises that his new assistant—Cliff Barnes—would just love to work on the case. Since the corpse has a bullet hole in it, there is a mysterious murder to unravel. And, if it can incriminate a Ewing, Cliff is all for it.

He calls in an anthropology professor to examine the evidence and becomes obsessed with building a case. Since the remains—of a male adult—are twenty-five to thirty years old, Barnes must identify them by using old ledgers and interviewing old-timers who worked on the ranch back then. By the process of elimination, he decides that the dead man was Hutch McKinney, a one-time foreman who disappeared the day Jock fired him.

J.R. isn't impressed. "Some old derelict's body is found on Southfork, and Barnes is gonna make it look like the biggest case since Bonnie and Clyde."

When a metal detector finds the murder weapon, Jock tells Ray and J.R. that the gun is his and asks their help in getting the case dismissed.

But the investigation cannot be called off or fixed and Jock is arrested for the murder of Hutchison McKinney.

JOCK'S TRIAL, PART TWO
by Arthur Bernard Lewis

The news at Southfork is bad. Reporters swarm around the ranch after Jock is arrested for murder.

Sue Ellen leaves home, expecting to be rescued by Dusty, but turns to the bottle when he doesn't show up. Later, when she finds out that his plane crashed and he is dead, she blames herself.

As the legal investigations progress, Jock looks more and more guilty; he seems to have had both motive and opportunity. Bail is set at half a million dollars.

Bobby confronts Digger Barnes, who is now dying, and urges him to tell anything he knows about McKinney's

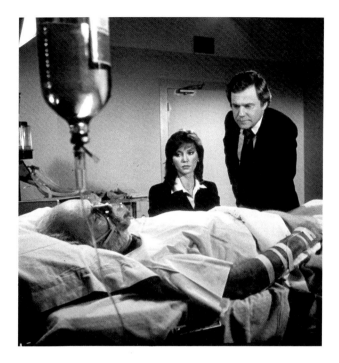

On his deathbed, Digger confesses that he killed Hutch McKinney because the man was having an affair with his wife. Without the confession, Jock may have been convicted.

With his dying words, Digger told Pam he was not her biological father.

death so that Jock can be cleared. Digger is overwhelmed that Jock might be convicted of the murder.

As he dies, Digger confesses that he killed Hutch McKinney because the man had had an affair with his wife. And everyone learns that Hutch McKinney was Pam's real father.

WHEELER DEALER
by Barbara Searles

J.R. finally succeeds in tracking down Amanda Lewis, Jock's first wife, who is in a sanitarium in Colorado. Jock used to visit her every now and then, but had stopped some years ago. Ellie suggests that they all go see her in an effort to make peace with their pasts.

Pam, too, needs to find her roots. Upset by the news that Digger was not her biological father, she becomes obsessed with finding out more about her mother, who has been presumed dead. She may be alive, too, Pam reasons, and she means to find her.

While most of the Ewings are consumed with thoughts of their past, J.R. is looking to the family's future—his in particular. One of his flunkies flies in from Asia to give him the word that a certain government is unsteady, and a revolution is brewing. J.R. decides to sell the family share of the Asian deal—without telling anyone—before there's any trouble.

A HOUSE DIVIDED
by Rena Down

J.R. sells the Asian oil leases just before the fields are nationalized. He comes out richer than ever. His former business partners are wiped out, and havoc reigns throughout the small world of independent oilmen. The Ewings are reluctant to help their old friends—the same men who had denied them a helping hand when they were about to lose Southfork. But Bobby doesn't like the way things have turned out one bit.

"What did you do, consult a psychic?" he asks J.R. angrily—not believing that J.R. could have had the foresight to sell without having an "in."

Jock also needs to know that J.R. has handled this like a gentleman. He asks: "Did you know the oil fields were going to be nationalized?"

"No, Daddy, I swear it. You know I wouldn't have done that to my friends."

J.R.'s doings so disgust Pam and Bobby that they decide to move out of Southfork.

Sue Ellen makes one more attempt to beat the booze so that J.R. doesn't send her back to the sanitarium or take the baby away from her. But J.R. is intent on committing her.

"You know, Sue Ellen, I do believe you're going ninety miles an hour toward a nervous breakdown. We're going to have to do something about your ravings."

"Bobby won't let you put me away."

"Don't count on it, sweetheart. I always get what I want."

Cliff Barnes also plans to get what he wants—revenge against J.R. In his father's safety deposit box, Barnes has found the original contract, dated 1938, that made Jock Ewing and Digger Barnes partners in their drilling.

Meanwhile, Alan Beam brings over to Kristin's place a briefcase that he knows isn't safe from J.R. in his possession. J.R.'s spies are everywhere. Beam not only has important information in the case, he has a gun. While he is with Kristin, she is arrested for prostitution. The sheriff says he'll hold the warrant for twenty-four hours if she promises to get out of town.

"I'll kill him," Kristin murmurs.

"Take a number," suggests Alan Beam. "There are a few ahead of you."

That night J.R., working late at his Ewing Oil office, is shot twice by a mysterious assailant.

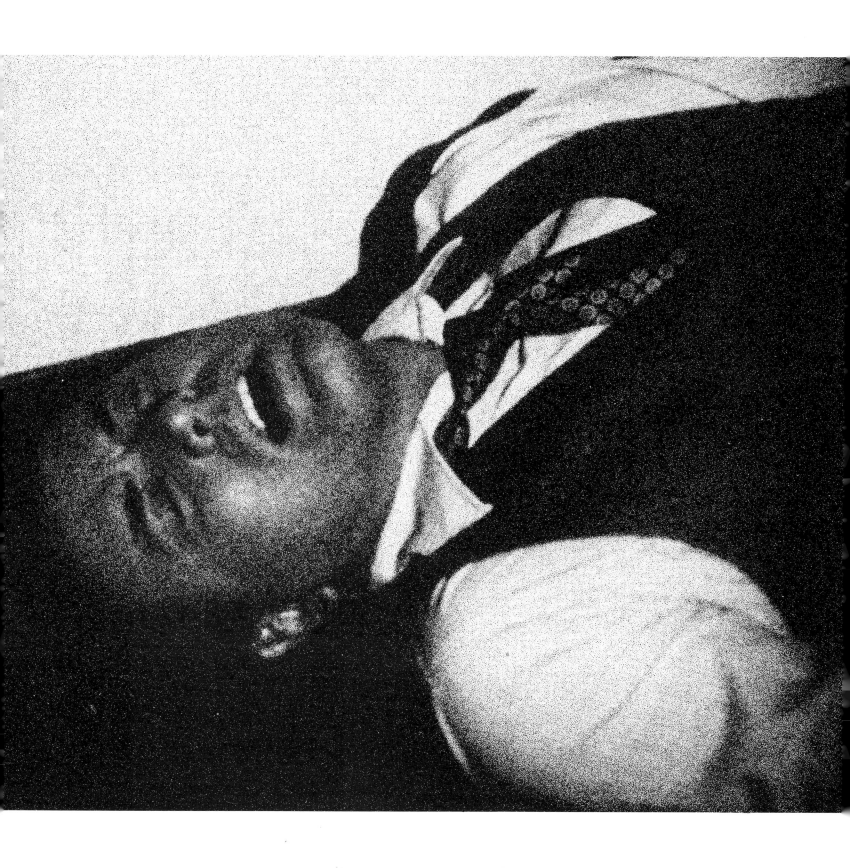

Who shot J.R.?

NO MORE MR. NICE GUY
by Arthur Bernard Lewis

The cleaning woman at Ewing Oil discovers J.R.'s body sprawled across his beige carpet. Close to death, J.R. is rushed to Dallas Memorial Hospital.

The family stands at J.R.'s bedside, awaiting news of whether he will live or die. He is attached to life-support equipment. Sue Ellen, however, is nowhere to be found: she has spent the night in her car at the airport, so drunk that when she wakes up she has no idea where she is or how she got there.

In his fight for life, J.R. undergoes a second operation. Bobby takes over Ewing Oil. Sue Ellen tries to combat her guilt: she is terrified that, in her drunken stupor, she could have shot J.R.

The Sisters Shepard—did one of these lovely ladies shoot J.R.?

(left)
Clinging to life, J.R. is rushed to Dallas Memorial. The actor on the stretcher is not Larry Hagman; Hagman was in England at the time.

Pam and Ellie stoically wait it out in the hospital as J.R. hovers between life and death. Both women will replay this scene with Bobby.

J.R. recuperates.

NIGHTMARE
by Linda B. Elstad

J.R. emerges from surgery and gains strength every day, but is paralyzed and confined to a wheelchair. The chair does not, however, restrict him to the business of getting well. Determined to run Ewing Oil from the hospital and not to let his baby brother unseat him, J.R. wrestles to regain control of the empire.

Sue Ellen dotes on J.R. and tries to help him, although he rejects her efforts. The shooting has become a pivotal point in their relationship. It has brought her back to him both because he is no longer dangerous and because she fears that she was the one who pulled the trigger. She sees it all clearly in her recurring dreams, but tells them only to her psychiatrist.

Sue Ellen's nightmare deepens when Jock discovers the gun that was used to shoot J.R.—in J.R.'s boots in his own closet. Jock turns the gun over to police, who run the usual tests.

Detective Horton comes to Southfork with the news. Sue Ellen's prints were clearly found on the gun.

"Then I must have done it! I must have shot J.R.!"

WHO DONE IT?
by Loraine Despres

Sue Ellen is booked for the attempted murder of J.R. The family refuses to put up the $100,000 bail money for fear that if she were released from jail, Sue Ellen would make another attempt on J.R.'s life.

Bail is posted, but no one seems to know who paid it.

Turning for help to Dr. Elby, her psychiatrist, Sue Ellen submits to hypnosis to explain the missing hours that she can't remember.

As J.R. recovers his strength, Sue Ellen helps him plot how he will regain control of Ewing Oil from his brother.

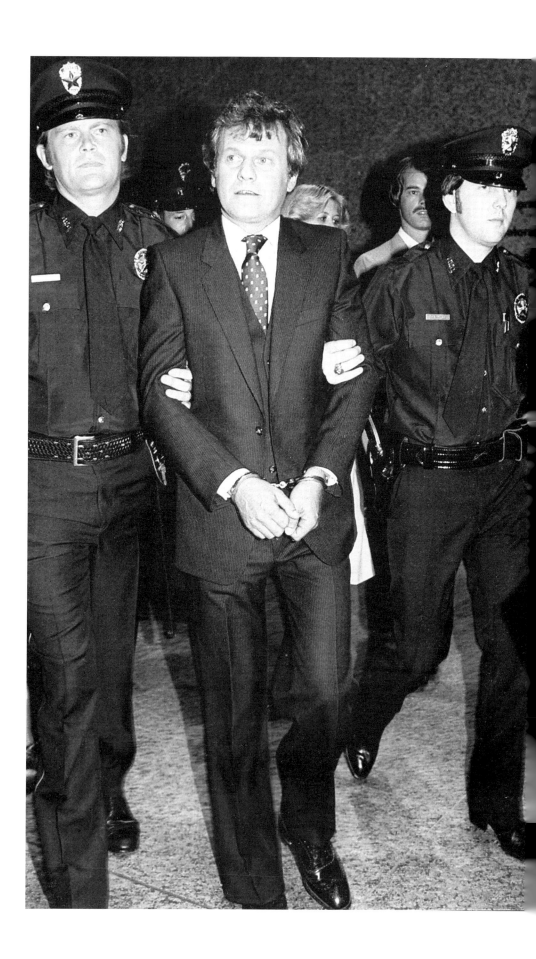

Cliff Barnes is arrested for J.R.'s
attempted murder.

Sue Ellen finds J.R. a new man now that he needs her.

Sue Ellen is booked for the attempted murder of her husband.

"You left one thing out," Dr. Elby explains, "putting the gun in the closet. When did you do that?"

Sue Ellen thinks about it. Then she remembers.

"I didn't have the gun. I changed purses. The gun was in the other purse. I would remember if I had it. I didn't have the gun!"

It all comes together, and Sue Ellen realizes that not only must her sister, Kristin, have shot J.R., but that Kristin was also clearly framing her. She asks J.R. to call the police.

But Kristin—with a trump card of her own—says, "I wouldn't do that if I were you, J.R. Unless you want your child to be born in prison. Now that would be a real scandal, wouldn't it? Jock Ewing's grandson a jail baby. I think I'll write my memoirs there."

"I'm not going to jail for her!" Sue Ellen shouts.

"Nobody's going to jail," says J.R. "I'll handle Kristin in my own way."

TASTE OF SUCCESS
by Robert J. Shaw

J.R. stages a little private hearing at Southfork for Kristin to tell her pitiful tale of a woman scorned. She gives an admirable performance. J.R. publicly forgives her and the charges are dropped.

"You're lucky J.R.'s got such a soft heart," Jock tells her. "I'd have you behind bars right now."

Sue Ellen and J.R. take Kristin to the airport so she can return to California, where she will receive payoff checks from J.R. to keep her comfortable during her pregnancy, and to keep quiet.

Bobby finds that being president of Ewing Oil is much more fun than he ever dreamed; the power is intoxicating. He works 16 hours a day, wheeling, dealing, and urgently trying to buy a refinery—something his brother could never do.

J.R. is totally dismayed by his brother's success.

"I am going to bring my little brother down. I'll get Bobby out of the company if I have to destroy Ewing Oil to do it."

THE VENEZUELAN CONNECTION
by Leah Markus

J.R. fights Bobby to regain his old job as president of Ewing Oil. Jock finds himself caught between his two sons.

Bobby negotiates a Venezuelan oil deal with Eugene Bullock and his wife, who turn out to be quite as slippery as the oil they ship.

"Well, Bobby," says Eugene, "your call last night sure put a burr in my tail. I said to my lovely Sally here, 'I've always done business with J.R. What could young Bobby Ewing be up to?'"

To ruin Bobby's credibility, J.R. arranged for a Venezuelan tanker to sink and convinced everyone that a fortune in Ewing Oil went down with it. Behind that newspaper, J.R. Ewing is smiling his famous smile.

Jock with Ray Krebbs, his fourth son, at the Fort Worth Cattle Auction.

Bobby steps in as president of Ewing Oil.

Sally, who runs the business for her husband, agrees to broker oil for the Ewings, and makes the deal with Bobby. Bobby has no idea that the Bullocks have a previous and devious arrangement with J.R.

Jock looks at the evidence—diary pages left behind by his World War II sweetheart—and talks it over with Miss Ellie. It appears that she knew all about the long-dead affair and now urges Jock to accept Ray as his son.

THE FOURTH SON
by Howard Lakin

Ray Krebbs is surprised by a visitor who claims to be his father. Amos Krebbs appears from nowhere to ask Ray for a handout. Ray lets him have it: "Let me tell you something, 'Daddy.' I came here when I was fifteen. Mama dead . . . no place else to go. Just with the clothes on my back and a note from Mama to Jock Ewing, begging him to help me out. He didn't have to take me in, but he did. And with his help, I've pulled myself up . . . made something of my life. Jock Ewing has been more of a father to me than you've ever been."

The point is not lost on Amos, who maneuvers Jock into meeting him privately and offers proof that Ray is really Jock's own son.

TROUBLE AT EWING 23
by Louis Elias

J.R. frets that Bobby's successes at Ewing Oil will leave him out in the cold. When Sue Ellen suggests that he start his own business, J.R. insists, "Ewing Oil is mine and I intend to get it back."

Then, an extortionist threatens to blow up Ewing oil field number 23 if he's not paid $5 million. J.R. takes over. Bobby is all for paying the money, a small amount compared to the income that comes from the field. But J.R. pushes the extortionist to the limit, and, in a violent showdown, the oil field is blown up and left roaring in flames.

"There was no other way," J.R. tells Bobby.

"You wanted it to happen."

Haunted by the lie that she is not Pam's mother, Rebecca Wentworth (Priscilla Pointer) finally explains her reasons for the 30-year charade.

Amos Krebbs (William Windom) introduces himself to his "son" Ray with the news that Ray actually is Jock's son. The old man provides his wife's diary as proof.

THE PRODIGAL MOTHER
by David Paulsen

The detective that Pam has hired to find her mother hits pay dirt and Pam flies to Houston to meet the woman who could be her mother.

To Pam's total surprise, the woman turns out to be a Houston socialite—and she denies ever having been married before.

"Mrs. Ewing, this is going to be difficult for you to hear, but I'd better say it now, before you go any further. My name is Rebecca Wentworth. I have never been married before. I am not your mother."

But later, after seeing Pam and then Cliff, Rebecca searches out Pam and admits to being her mother. She explains that she has been denying her past for many years, because since she never divorced Digger, she could never admit to a life before marrying Herbert Wentworth. Furthermore, she doesn't want to rock the boat now.

"Try to understand, Pamela," she begs.

EXECUTIVE WIFE
by Rena Down

J.R. pushes Jock toward a business deal that will conflict with a venture Bobby is planning. If it goes through, there would be cash problems at Ewing Oil that would

J.R. and Sue Ellen emerge from the jewelry store after J.R. buys his wife a large emerald. They bump into Cliff and Donna Culver, who has temporarily broken up with Ray.

Sue Ellen bumps into her old beau, Clint Ogden—
played by Monte Markham—at Lucy's wedding.

The ever-lovin' J.R. has already cast his ever-lovin' eye
on his new relative, Afton Cooper (Audrey Landers).
Afton is Lucy's new sister-in-law.

reflect poorly on Bobby, which is exactly the way J.R. has it planned.

J.R. is so pleased with his schemes that he takes Sue Ellen into Dallas and buys her a large emerald ring to celebrate.

It seems that Jock was right all along when he told Bobby just how power works: "If I gave it to you, you got nothing. Nobody can give you power. Real power is something you take."

END OF THE ROAD, PART ONE
by Leonard Katzman

Lucy's announcement that she will marry Mitch Cooper, an impoverished medical student, does not thrill the family, but they hope this one will go the way of her other marriage announcements. Lucy, however, means to go through with it.

When Mitch's mother and sister arrive for the festivities, J.R. takes an immediate interest in Mitch's sister, Afton. Bobby finds himself in a tricky position after he has negotiated a drilling agreement which will, theoretically, put the company back in the good graces of the cartel.

Lucy shows off her beau—and her bathing suit.

Unfortunately for Bobby, J.R. has carefully sabotaged the deal so that his younger brother looks incompetent.

"He took the deal," J.R.'s henchman reports of Bobby. "We sign contracts in a week."

"Who was that?" Jock asks when J.R. hangs up the phone.

"Just a man about some oil."

"Anything I should know about?" father asks son.

"Oh, you will, Daddy . . . and it won't be long."

Lucy convinces Mitch Cooper (played by Leigh McCloskey) that it's going to be okay—heiresses always marry poor medical students and live happily ever after.

Although he had little to do with raising his daughter,
Gary (Ted Shackelford) gives the bride away when
Lucy marries Mitch in a traditional Southfork wedding.

END OF THE ROAD, PART TWO
by Leonard Katzman

Lucy's marriage to Mitch seems doomed not to happen
after all. His family prepares to return home. They don't
understand why he has broken off the engagement. Is it
because the Ewings have offered to help him out with a
job at Ewing Oil?

"I'd rather starve than take it!" Mitch tells Lucy.

Lucy understands the problems of being a Ewing, and
the two agree to go ahead with the ceremony as planned.

Gary and Valene arrive at Southfork for the wedding,
and Ellie accuses Jock of loving Ray more than Gary,
even before he knew that Ray was his son. Tension rises
in the family; Bobby struggles with business; J.R. continues to scheme; and the family welcomes the California
Ewings from Knots Landing.

The wedding is an old-fashioned Southfork affair.
Afterward, at the reception, there is rather less of a happy
mood than at other weddings: Sue Ellen has found out

about J.R. and Afton; Bobby resigns as president of Ewing Oil when he discovers that J.R. has laid a trap for him
in the big deal he almost signed. Furthermore, Ellie is
distraught that Gary is not staying at the ranch. She
blames Jock and Ray for driving him away.

"I'll never forgive you for what you've done to him—
and to me," she says sorrowfully.

MAKING OF A PRESIDENT
by Arthur Bernard Lewis

J.R. returns to Ewing Oil as president. "You had total
control of Ewing Oil," he tells Bobby. "You were on top.
Now, you're settling for just one small slice of the pie.
Why'd you back off? Sometimes I don't understand how
your mind works."

"Different from yours, J.R."

Leslie Stewart (played by Susan Flannery) begins her formidable campaign to get good press for J.R.; she's an expert in both public and private relations.

Once he takes over, J.R. feels better than he has since the shooting. He hires a public relations woman to improve the image of Ewing Oil, which J.R. feels that Bobby had tarnished. He also wants her to create an attractive persona for J.R. as the all-American businessman.

They toast their partnership.

"To my biggest challenge," says Leslie Stewart. "I know where you stand in Dallas, J.R. No one wants to do business with you. They're saying it's over for J.R. Ewing. When I'm finished, you'll be number one again."

START THE REVOLUTION WITH ME
by Rena Down

J.R. begins to reshape history as he campaigns for power and recognition. Leslie Stewart manages to manage J.R. but still keep him at arm's length. His secretary Louella notices: "You shouldn't let Miss Stewart get to you like that. After all, you can have any woman you want."

While Leslie is doing everything she can to keep up a good front for J.R., the man himself is doing everything he can to keep his real doings out of the press. He decides, for example, to go after the revolutionaries who caused the Asian coup that resulted in nationalization of the foreign oil fields. J.R. is warned by an advisor that he is violating U.S. federal law by attempting to overthrow a foreign government. J.R. has made up his mind, however, and plans on taking the gamble—no matter what.

THE QUEST
by Robert J. Shaw

J.R.'s scheming affects everyone in the family. He ignores Sue Ellen more and more, refusing even to acknowledge her complaints that she is being followed by someone and is frightened and angry.

"J.R., please. All I want is a straight answer. Are you having me followed or aren't you?"

"Woman, I swear, you are a raving neurotic. If you imagine somebody's following you, tell your quack doctor about it."

Donna Culver decides that Cliff should not run for office. Insults are added to Cliff's injured feelings when Donna asks Bobby to run for the vacant seat instead of him. When Bobby accepts, J.R. delights that his little brother may become a state senator. Cliff is outraged.

Pam is hurt that Bobby hasn't even consulted her about his decision. Documenting his neglect, she tells him how close she has come to having an affair, but reminds him, "I love only you, Bobby."

Sue Ellen gives up trying to convince the family that she is really being followed and takes matters into her own hands. With the help of a lawyer, she tracks down the man who has been following her, and he reveals that he doesn't even know who he is working for. He merely mails reports to a post office box in Denton. Sue Ellen goes to Denton to stake out the post box and discover who picks up the reports. When she sees who it is, she cries out in shock, "Dear God! It can't be!"

LOVER COME BACK
by Leonard Katzman

J.R. is lucky again; the coup he finances in Asia is successful, and Ewing Oil is back in favor with the cartel. J.R. has maneuvered it all to please Jock.

The family is divided about Bobby running for Dave Culver's senate seat. Jock is certain that Bobby will go his own way. Miss Ellie hopes that her son will be sensitive to environmental issues. Cliff still seethes about losing the nomination.

"It seems the whole purpose I was put on earth was to have the Ewings dump on me," he tells Pam.

Ray Krebbs takes Donna Culver to dinner to persuade her to use her influence to get the Daughters of the Alamo—including Miss Ellie—to back off their ecological stand. Donna is furious at being wooed for political reasons, but ends up in Ray's arms as their passion for each other erupts. They decide to marry.

Bobby James Ewing is elected state senator.

Meanwhile, Sue Ellen deals with the shock of discovering that it was Dusty who had her followed. He really is alive but has been reluctant to resume their affair because he survived the plane crash only as an invalid. It seems that a ranch hand's body was identified as his. Dusty has been in and out of hospitals for months and will never walk again. Furthermore, as his father, Clayton, reveals to Sue Ellen in a private moment, Dusty is now impotent.

THE NEW MRS. EWING
by Linda B. Elstad

Donna Culver becomes the newest Mrs. Ewing when she marries Ray Krebbs. Ellie rails at Jock, who has changed the trust to accommodate his new-found son. Ray has no Southworth blood in him, and the ranch was Ellie's family prize. To make matters worse, Jock hadn't even consulted her.

"The time to talk was before you changed the trust," Ellie tells him coldly.

The elder Ewings aren't the only couple with marital problems. Bobby confronts Pam's would-be lover, Alex Ward; Lucy takes a job on Alex's new magazine—*Miss Young Dallas*—which makes Mitch feel even more inferior: now Lucy's earning money on her own.

Bobby wins Dave Culver's old state senate seat.

MARK OF CAIN
by Leah Markus

J.R. becomes more involved with Leslie Stewart, but it remains unclear who is using whom. Leslie places a powerful ad for J.R. in the *Wall Street Journal*, thereby alienating his friends in the cartel, and then throws him a challenge. She tells J.R. that she is leaving town, and that if he wants her to stay, he must divorce Sue Ellen.

Meanwhile, Bobby is caught between his parents on the issue of the Takapa land development. Ellie sides with the ecologists to stop the multimillion dollar project, even though Jock is one of the investors. Bobby is pressured to step down from the Takapa senate committee by his peers, who fear a conflict of interest, but he won't let himself be pushed out that easily.

"I gave a lot of thought to what you said earlier, but I promised the people in my district that I was going to represent them and I'm not going to back off from something unpleasant. So, Senators, I'm in!"

THE GATHERING STORM
by Robert J. Shaw

Miss Ellie threatens to divorce Jock. Their marriage has been variously strained over their son Gary, the discovery that Ray is Jock's illegitimate son, and now over the Takapa business. Bobby's role as a member of the senate committee investigating the Takapa development divides the family even more. No one knows which way he will vote.

J.R. isn't certain which way to manipulate his family. "Daddy, have you thought about the fact that this is a community property state? If it goes as far as a divorce for you and Mama, Ewing Oil would be divided up. Mama would get her share. That'd be the end of it!"

"Over my dead body, boy!" rages Jock. "I'd sell it first, yessir. I'd sell it out from under her—lock, stock, and barrel!"

Just in case, J.R. begins private negotiations to make sure he's got a job if his parents do divorce. Weststar Oil could take very good care of him.

EWING VS. EWING
by Leah Markus

Miss Ellie consults an attorney about divorcing Jock while J.R. schemes to sell Ewing Oil out from under his family.

"If you're really serious about Weststar acquiring Ewing Oil, we'd better move real fast," J.R. tells his would-be boss. "Trust me, we have a deal."

Pam and Bobby help the bride and groom celebrate.

Bobby is also dealing, trying desperately to find a compromise to solve the Takapa problem. Finally he proposes trading some land he bought with the developers so that the state of Texas would get its park, and the developers would get the resort they want. Both parties accept the compromise.

But the solution does not solve Jock and Ellie's marital problems. "This hearing is the only thing that's over," she says in the courtroom as she turns and walks angrily away from Jock.

Then Ray realizes that if it's not Takapa she's angry about, it has to be him. He and Donna invite Jock and Ellie over to their place where Ray presents them with a legal document he has drawn up, renouncing his shares of both the Ewing Trust and Southfork ranch.

"I'd rather give it up . . . leave Southfork rather than see you and Miss Ellie split up, Jock. You're paying too high a price for me to be a Ewing."

Ellie admits that Ray has been correct about her feelings, but asks him to stay. Then she and Jock make up.

Jock and Ellie have one of their few misunderstandings. Ellie is opposed to Jock's stand on Takapa and sides with the environmentalists, who do not want the housing development–resort built.

NEW BEGINNINGS
by Arthur Bernard Lewis

Jock and Ellie's reconciliation puts J.R. on the spot regarding his plans to sell Ewing Oil. Furious, Jeremy Wendell of Weststar plots revenge against J.R. for going back on the deal. He decides to hire Leslie Stewart, and she has her hands full when J.R. comes to her to say he's filing for divorce from Sue Ellen. His parents are out of town on their second honeymoon and he figures it'll be easier with them gone. J.R. tries to consummate their "deal," but Leslie pushes him out the door and retreats to the waiting arms of her ex-husband.

Still trying to get at J.R., Wendell sides with Cliff to try to tie J.R. to the Asian revolution. But they aren't the only ones after the elder Ewing son. Donna feels that J.R. is setting Ray up for a fall by pushing him to handle a project in Lubbock.

"If Ray gets into trouble over this, I'll find a way to pay you back," Donna vows after a nasty chat with J.R.

Sue Ellen realizes that she has to give up her renewed affair with Clint, her teen-aged lover, and devotes herself to being young John Ross' mother. She tries to work things out with J.R. one more time. For a moment, the two seem headed toward a new understanding, but the calm is broken by the jangle of the telephone.

"It's Kristin calling from California. She's given birth to a boy. You have another son."

What are mothers for? Pam's gives her a supportive hug as Pam leaves the doctor's office after learning she cannot have children.

FULL CIRCLE
by Arthur Bernard Lewis

With the help of his new friends at Weststar, Cliff Barnes may finally be getting his long-sought revenge against J.R. He begins to build evidence to prove that J.R. helped to overthrow a government in the recent coup in Asia. Barnes turns over his evidence to Bobby, whose senate committee he serves as legal counsel. Bobby's group may now be forced to conduct a full-scale investigation, which would once again pit brother against brother—with a little help from a brother-in-law.

Meanwhile, Pam's doctor tells her that she can never have children. Although she shares this painful news with her mother, she does not reveal it to Sue Ellen, especially after the two women have a heart-to-heart talk, and Sue Ellen confesses, "If it weren't for John Ross, I would have left J.R. last night," alluding to the news of Kristin's baby.

After the birth of her child, Kristin comes back to Dallas for a secret meeting with Jordan Lee, a prominent member of the cartel.

"Don't you want to know about your son?" she asks him.

Sue Ellen contemplates giving up her son in order to escape J.R. and Southfork.

EWING-GATE
by Leonard Katzman

When word of J.R.'s alleged conspiracy in Asia reaches the press, Leslie Stewart decides that she is playing on the wrong team. She reveals that she has tape recordings of J.R. telling her of his involvement in Asia—evidence that puts J.R. in jeopardy of losing Ewing Oil and going to jail as well.

Sue Ellen and Dusty are reunited, they hope for good. Sue Ellen plans to steal John Ross from Southfork while J.R. is in Austin asking some politicians to help him out of his bind. But J.R. walks in just as Sue Ellen is about to walk out with John Ross in her arms.

"I'm leaving you and I'm taking him with me."

J.R. seizes the child and orders Sue Ellen to be thrown out.

Sue Ellen is forcibly removed from her child and her home.

Kristin tells Jordan Lee (Don Starr) that he is
the father of her child and cashes in
on her pregnancy . . . again.

Sue Ellen rejoices when she discovers that Dusty
survived the plane crash. She tells him she doesn't
care that he's confined to a wheelchair, may never
walk again, and cannot have children—or anything.

He then has a showdown with Kristin, who wants more
money from him, ostensibly for his son.

As the tension increases at the senate hearings, J.R.
saves himself and the company by turning up a government witness who explains his expenditures in the Far
East. J.R. comes out looking like a humanitarian, not a
power broker.

"I don't know how you did it, J.R., how the hell you
bribed him to appear, but it's not over yet . . . not by a
long shot. I'm still going to get you," vows Cliff.

Later that evening, a body is seen floating, face down,
in the Southfork swimming pool.

Cliff Barnes feels that he is being framed for Kristin's death—another one of J.R.'s dirty little schemes.

MISSING HEIR
by Arthur Bernard Lewis

Cliff Barnes arrives at Southfork for a meeting with Bobby but ends up in the swimming pool instead—fishing out Kristin Shepard's body.

"I jumped into the pool and found she was dead. I looked up and he was standing there with that grin of his...I've seen it before—just after he's stuck a knife in somebody's back."

As far as Cliff is concerned, J.R. is a murderer. But J.R. turns accuser and tells Bobby that it was Cliff who drowned Kristin. He hardly has time for his mudslinging, however, for he discovers that Pam has kidnapped John Ross in order to turn him over to Sue Ellen.

Pam takes the child to Abilene, where Dusty and Sue Ellen pick him up for the drive to the Farlow ranch, the Southern Cross, outside San Angelo. When J.R. gets there to demand his son back, both Dusty and Sue Ellen stand up to him. "Not this time," says a newly brave Sue Ellen. "John Ross stays with me. I'm suing you for divorce."

Furious that Sue Ellen has won the first round, J.R. returns to Southfork and unleashes his anger at Pam. His abuse is so strong that Bobby finally takes a swing at him. And J.R.'s problems don't end with a fight. A few hours later he's booked for the murder of Kristin Shepard. The D.A.'s office has apparently discovered a motive.

Southern Cross, the Farlow spread, ostensibly located in San Angelo. The real ranch is located down the road a piece from Southfork, in Forney, Texas.

Ellie arrives by Southfork helicopter to visit her grandson while Sue Ellen remains estranged from J.R. and under the protection of the Farlows.

GONE BUT NOT FORGOTTEN
by Arthur Bernard Lewis

J.R. and Cliff Barnes confront each other again at the inquest held to establish the facts behind Kristin's death. J.R. tells his version of the story, pointing out that he has taken a lie detector test. Even though this information has to be struck from the record, J.R. shows that he knows how to make points in a courtroom.

The coroner further supports J.R. by announcing that Kristin has been found to have in her system a drug that often proves fatal because of its depressant powers.

"In my opinion, Kristin Shepard walked through that railing and straight off the balcony all by herself."

Once cleared, J.R. begins a custody fight to regain his son. He decides to kidnap the boy back when Sue Ellen is away at Kristin's funeral. But his plot is foiled by Dusty Farlow, who knows how to anticipate J.R.'s thinking.

boy in her hands and can complete the kidnapping, but relents at the last minute.

"He may belong at Southfork, but not this way."

Sue Ellen and Dusty are having their share of problems. Besides having to deal with J.R., Sue Ellen is reminded of Dusty's impotence. Although she claims it doesn't matter, it does.

Bobby suggests to Pam that they adopt a baby since after learning she can't have children she is having severe psychological problems. Bobby feels she has become too involved with John Ross because she doesn't have a child of her own.

SHOWDOWN AT SAN ANGELO
by Leonard Katzman

J.R. uses his mother to gain entry to the Southern Cross. In order to see John Ross, J.R. talks his mother into letting him accompany her to the Southern Cross and then uses her as a shield to snatch back his son. Ellie has the

LITTLE BOY LOST
by Leonard Katzman

Even Ellie has lost patience with J.R., which means he could find himself in a real custody fight for his son. He plans to buy a judge to make sure the hearing for custody goes his way, but suddenly the hearing is pushed up to the next day and all his plans backfire.

J.R.'s argument for custody is based on the fact that Sue Ellen is now living an adulterous and immoral life with her lover. He gets a big shock when Sue Ellen's attorneys provide medical affidavits that prove that Mrs. Ewing and Steven "Dusty" Farlow could not possibly be lovers.

"Mrs. Ewing did not leave her husband for reasons of the flesh . . . instead she renounced them. She is dedicating her life to living with and caring for a man with whom she will never have sexual relations. Far from subjecting her son to an unfit environment, Mrs. Ewing is showing him the purest of all emotions." Naturally the court awards Sue Ellen custody.

Pam's depression deepens to the point that the family doctor suggests she get psychiatric help.

THE SWEET SMELL OF REVENGE
by Linda Elstad

J.R. uses his power to try to force the Farlows to stop protecting Sue Ellen and John Ross. He buys $50 million worth of Farlow oil, and plans on buying more, to freeze out the Farlow distributors, but Clayton and Dusty have proven themselves worthy adversaries.

Pam's emotional condition leads her to the edge of Reunion Tower—a tall building in Dallas—where she stands on a ledge in a catatonic state. Bobby rushes to her

Bobby rescues his troubled bride.

side to try to persuade her not to jump. When talk doesn't work, he grabs her and brings her to safety.

Pam agrees to go to Brooktree for further psychiatric counseling.

THE BIG SHUTDOWN
by Arthur Bernard Lewis

To further tie up the Farlow distributors, J.R. has to increase the stakes from $50 million to $200 million. He's certain that once he ruins the Farlows financially, Sue Ellen will no longer be attracted to Dusty, and in any event the Farlows will no longer have the power to protect her.

The risk of sitting on all that crude without releasing it to market is dangerous. If the price of oil drops, J.R. can lose his shirt.

"Look at it this way, you won't have to foreclose. If I default on the loan, which I won't, your bank will own Ewing Oil and I'd end up working for you," J.R. tells his banker with his fatal smile.

Bobby buys information from Kristin's recent lover in California and discovers that Jordan Lee may be her baby's real father.

BLOCKED
by Arthur Bernard Lewis

Holding onto all that crude puts Ewing Oil in a tight situation financially. Ewing Oil is hurting almost as much as the Farlow refineries.

Sue Ellen realizes that it is J.R. who has put the squeeze on the Farlows and goes to his office to confront him. She decides to leave the Southern Cross before her presence further jeopardizes the Farlow family fortune.

"Farlow can have his oil," says J.R., "as soon as he sends back my son."

But Dusty and Clayton refuse to be blackmailed. Clayton agrees to sit down with J.R. and talk it over.

"It's no deal," Clayton says after J.R. outlines his offer.

"I'll break you," J.R. vows in return.

"Better men have tried," Clayton warns him. "No, J.R. you're the one who's going broke. I'm late for our little meeting, because I stopped for the latest report on oil prices...down two dollars a barrel and falling...and you're sitting on five million barrels. Your bankers won't be patient forever. You know, when your daddy gets back from South America, there just might not be a Ewing Oil."

Rebecca and Cliff visit Pam at Brooktree sanitarium, where she is recovering from her breakdown.

Pam visits Sue Ellen and John Ross at Southern Cross.

Bobby checks out the birth certificate for Christopher Shepard, Kristin's son, as he negotiates to acquire the baby after Kristin is killed. Christopher is legally adopted by Bobby and Pam months later.

(above right)
Ellie bikes down to the mail box, anxious for Jock's letter from South America.

THE SPLIT
by Leonard Katzman

Ellie receives a bulky envelope from Jock containing a legal document instituting a new plan for Ewing Oil. The new setup will severely curtail the free rein J.R. has had as head of the company. Jock, in South America for the last several months doing special work for the U.S. government, is not sure when he will return and his fears of J.R.'s headstrong ways make him reorganize the company. Each family member now controls a certain amount of the Ewing Oil stock.

Clayton watches Sue Ellen romp with John Ross in the pool while keeping an eye on the news. To get his wife back, J.R. has been buying up oil to try to force Farlow into bankruptcy.

This will naturally put a severe crimp in J.R.'s style. Now even his brother Gary has a voting interest. Because John Ross also has a voting share it becomes even more imperative for J.R. to regain custody of his son. He flies to San Angelo to meet with Dusty.

"How long do you think my wife can stay with a sexual washout?" J.R. asks.

FIVE DOLLARS A BARREL
by Leonard Katzman

Cliff Barnes puts together a group of J.R.'s enemies to buy up his bank notes at a discount.

"Not only is it secured by the oil J.R. has stockpiled, but it's backed by $50 million in Ewing assets. When he forfeits on those notes," Barnes asks his partners, "how long do you think he'll last?"

J.R. is too busy doing plotting of his own; he needs to influence several family members to get control of the company. Gary gives a proxy on his votes to Lucy; little John Ross's share is with Miss Ellie as long as the boy is off Southfork; Ray is having financial difficulties with a development and may need J.R. to co-sign a loan for him—which J.R. will do to get control of Ray's vote.

As oil prices continue to fall, Cliff then pushes J.R. to give him part of Ewing #6—the field over which their fathers broke up their partnership.

"You're a dead man, J.R., and I'm the head pall-bearer," Cliff gloats.

STARTING OVER
by Leonard Katzman

Ellie decides to help Ray out of his financial bind. She goes to the bank, only to discover she's got her own financial problems caused by J.R.

J.R., doing his best to rectify that situation, flies to New York to make arrangements for Ewing Oil to go public.

While he's out of town, Bobby checks into the company health records to ascertain J.R.'s blood type, which matches up with that of Kristin Shepard's infant son.

"J.R.," he mutters to himself, "you are about as low as they come. You're the father of Kristin's baby."

WATERLOO AT SOUTHFORK
by Linda Elstad

Ellie calls a family meeting at Southfork to demand an explanation for the Ewing financial difficulties.

Dusty finds swimming therapeutic.

"J.R., the notes on those loans are due and payable in four days. Our cash reserves are practically depleted. I want to know what's going on."

After hearing J.R.'s explanation his mother takes matters into her own hands—by flying to the Southern Cross and personally selling Clayton back his oil. The two enjoy each other's company—Clayton is every bit as strong as Jock.

Then she calls another family pow-wow to let everyone vote on whether or not J.R. should stay on as head of Ewing Oil.

Ellie casts the deciding votes herself—in favor of J.R., but with the provision that Bobby go back into the oil business to be his watchdog.

She then goes to J.R.'s divorce hearing to make sure he doesn't drag Sue Ellen's name through the mud. Her arrival puts a damper on J.R.'s plans; the judge awards permanent custody to Sue Ellen and sets alimony and child support payments at $6,000 a month.

BARBECUE TWO
by *Arthur Bernard Lewis*

Miss Ellie plans the annual Ewing barbecue to coincide with Jock's return from South America. The party, in typical Southfork style, is filled with color and excitement. J.R. and Sue Ellen find renewed interest in each other; Cliff discovers that he too is still interested in Sue Ellen; Ray gets drunk and embarrasses Donna; Clayton and Rebecca Wentworth renew their friendship; Katherine Wentworth—Pam's half-sister—demonstrates quite an attraction to Bobby.

After a slow but miraculous recovery, Dusty proves that he's the man he used to be—at least with a horse. He tells his dad and Sue Ellen that he's going back on the rodeo circuit.

Guests arrive for one of the famous Ewing barbecues. This one was held to coincide with Jock's homecoming from South America. Rolls Royces are parked along the driveway while a "Texas Taxi" drives other guests to the front door.

The minor family intrigues are put aside when Ellie relates a phone call to J.R.: "Jock was flying in from the interior by helicopter...it crashed...they've been searching all day...nothing. The locals have given up...they say that Jock is dead!"

THE SEARCH
by Arthur Bernard Lewis

All the Ewings are unable to accept the fact that Jock is dead. J.R., Bobby, and Ray fly immediately to South America to ascertain the truth. There they find an injured man, who tells them his small plane collided with a helicopter. The helicopter, he continued, had fallen into the lake. Ray and Bobby dive below the surface of the lake; they find pieces of the helicopter—and Jock's medallion, evidence that their father was on board.

DENIAL
by Linda Elstad

Jock's death is devastating to the whole family. J.R.'s grief is so overwhelming that he is unable to deal with the simplest business arrangements; Bobby must do both their jobs.

At first amazed at the strength Ellie has shown throughout the ordeal, the family soon realize that Ellie is suffering from denial.

"He's alive, Bobby," Ellie tells her youngest son. "As long as I believe—he's alive!"

When Harvey Smithfield, the family lawyer, brings up the subject of Jock's will, Ellie tells him that it's premature to talk about a will at this time.

Bobby is working on an even more active case of denial; he has never told Pam whose baby Christopher really is. Now he decides to doctor the baby's birth certificate so that Pam will never discover the truth. He fears the news that Christopher is really Kristin and J.R.'s son will tip the balance of her already fragile emotional state.

HEAD OF THE FAMILY
by Howard Lakin

Bobby asks Miss Ellie for the authority to run the family business, as J.R. continues to grieve for Jock. Bobby is forced to keep one eye on ranch management as well, for Ray is suffering, too, and is also torn by his failure as a businessman and his dissatisfaction with merely running the ranch. On top of all that, there's Pam and the new baby.

Afton began her adventures in Dallas as one of J.R.'s tootsies.

Bobby tells J.R. that if he doesn't pull himself together the Ewings could be in danger of losing everything Jock stood for.

"If this family quits just because Daddy's gone," Bobby tells J.R. angrily, "he didn't leave us much of a legacy, did he? Maybe someday you might want to tell John Ross what his granddaddy spent his life building. How are you going to do that? You better get off your butt, J.R.; we've got work to do."

THE PHOENIX
by David Paulsen

When J.R. discovers that Jock left Ewing Oil divided among all the Ewing heirs, he sides with Ellie about the postponement of the reading of Jock's will. According to the terms of the will J.R. may very well have another power struggle on his hands.

"As far as I'm concerned," he tells Bobby in a patronizing way, "if Mama won't believe that Daddy's dead, then for her sake, neither will I!"

His old fighting spirit returns, and he uses Marilee Stone to try to regain his standing with the cartel. Marilee toasts J.R. with champagne and purrs: "It was worth the wait." But when Marilee wants more pillow talk, J.R. begins oil talk. Marilee promises to help him.

MY FATHER, MY SON
by Will Lorin

J.R. makes another deal with the cartel, thanks to Marilee Stone, but his delight is eclipsed by anger when he discovers that Cliff has spent the night at Sue Ellen's apartment. Even though they have not become lovers again, J.R. assumes that they are—and is furious.

J.R. tells Afton Cooper about it, hoping to make her jealous, but she soon realizes that J.R. is the jealous one.

"I thought you and Sue Ellen hated each other. I figured neither one of you gave a damn what the other did. But you sound like a man carrying a torch for his ex-wife. What really surprises me is that you care about anyone but J.R. Ewing! I really love it. You're really jealous of Cliff—right out of your cotton-pickin' gourd!"

But when Afton asks Cliff to tell her the truth about Sue Ellen, Cliff is all too honest. He admits that he loves her and wants her.

"You'll never get her," Afton warns him bitterly. "J.R. will crucify you first."

Donna Culver Krebbs pens the biography of her former husband, Sam Culver (D-Texas). The book becomes a regional bestseller, and Donna appears at a Dallas bookstore to autograph copies.

ANNIVERSARY
by David Paulsen

Sue Ellen is astounded when J.R. remembers the anniversary of their first meeting and begins to believe that the man has changed. She's lonely and miserable as a single and is very receptive when J.R. tries to woo her back.

"I understand how you feel, Sue Ellen. It's just that I get so depressed every time I drop John Ross off. I thought maybe I could stretch out the day a little longer if we all have dinner together. I'll go after dinner."

Is this a new J.R.? Clayton doesn't think so and tries to warn Sue Ellen, but she is blind to reality. It suits her to believe that J.R. will be a different man and that the Ewing family belongs together back at Southfork.

"I miss you Sue Ellen . . . my life just isn't the same without you."

Bobby and Christopher—named for his mother, Kristin.

ADOPTION
by Howard Lakin

Bobby sets up Pam in her own exercise business so that she can work better hours than she did at The Store. Now that she's a mother, Pam wants a more limited work schedule. Bobby's fears that something could go wrong at the adoption hearing prove unfounded, and Christopher becomes legally their son.

Brotherly love strains past the breaking point after J.R. has the police jail his half-brother for being drunk. All J.R. wants from Ray is control of his 10 percent vote in Ewing Oil.

Yet, to Sue Ellen, J.R. is still a changed man. Pam warns her to be careful, but Sue Ellen admits, "The trouble is, J.R. still gets to me."

But not enough for Sue Ellen to not come through for Pam and Bobby. Bobby explains that Christopher is really J.R.'s son, but that he needs Sue Ellen's deposition to proceed with the adoption. Sue Ellen willingly lies and claims she has no idea who the baby's true father is.

J.R. continues trying to buy her with expensive jewelry, but Sue Ellen is finally onto him. "Everything's the same as it's always been between us. Sick, sick, sick!"

THE MAELSTROM
by Will Lorin

When J.R. observes how happy Pam and Bobby are with their new son, his pain at not being with John Ross full-time worsens. He decides to find out what happened to his other son—the one Kristin gave birth to in California.

Because Sue Ellen already knows the secret of that baby, she is boiling mad and hurt all over again. She vows to Clayton that she will hurt J.R. as much as he has hurt her.

She knows just how to do it—by running to Cliff's ever-waiting arms. J.R. responds in a fury.

"I'm going to destroy you!" he vows to Cliff.

"You tried that," Cliff says. "It didn't work."

"You don't understand. I don't want to wipe you out. Not any more. When I'm finished with you, there will be no more Cliff Barnes in Dallas, in Texas, or in any place. You will cease to exist—and that's a promise."

J.R. bumps into Katherine Wentworth on the street in Dallas and convinces her that they have a common enemy or two—namely Pam and Cliff.

THE PRODIGAL
by David Paulsen

A glance at Pam and Bobby on the sofa with Christopher one night makes J.R. think that the baby may be his son by Kristin. It's not the baby that J.R. wants as much as he wants a club to hold over Bobby's head.

Seeing the original birth certificate convinces J.R. that there are too many coincidences for his hunch not to be true. Pam's baby is named Christopher, so is Kristin's; Pam's baby was born in August, so was Kristin's. J.R.'s snake smile grows bigger and bigger—he's gathering information on all fronts.

Katherine Wentworth becomes his next target. The beautiful, dark-haired daughter of Rebecca is now in Dal-las working on a local television news program. After they meet on the street, they make a lunch date. Katherine shows her sibling rivalry rather quickly, and J.R. is certain that Cliff and Pam's half-sister can lead him to some interesting inside information.

VENGEANCE
by Howard Lakin

Cliff Barnes falls for the trap that J.R. and Marilee Stone have set for him. Their phony geological reports make a piece of worthless land look like a gold mine. Barnes takes $4 million out of Wentworth Tool and Die to invest in the scheme—putting him on the brink of destroying the Wentworth family fortune—just as Katherine had predicted.

J.R. is having so much fun that he then decides to go after his brother, figuring he can force Bobby to turn over his voting power in Ewing Oil to him in order to keep Christopher.

"Little brother," J.R. says in a mock conversation with Bobby, "I almost lost John Ross because of you, but now I can turn everything around. I've got my twenty shares in Ewing Oil and Ray's ten, and Bobby, if you want to keep Christopher as your very own, you're going to have to fork over your twenty shares. With those fifty shares, nothing and no one can stop me."

BLACKMAIL
by Leonard Katzman

Jeff Farraday—Bobby's contact to Christopher's papers—is murdered before he can turn over to Bobby all the evidence he had promised. Blackmail from Farraday was a lot easier to deal with than from J.R., the baby's real father.

"I'm delighted that you're adopting my son. I know that you and Pam love the boy, and he turned her life round. I don't mind his calling me Uncle J.R."

"And how much will this cost me?"

"Not much. I'll never say a word about Christopher as long as I know you'll vote your twenty shares of Ewing Oil the way I want, whenever I want. Simple isn't it?—you help me and I'll help you."

Things get even worse when the police ask Bobby to come in for questioning in connection with Farraday's death.

THE INVESTIGATION
by Bruce Shelly

Lucy's disappearance is beginning to be taken seriously. J.R. thinks she's on another of her escapades, but the rest of the family are convinced there's more of a problem.

Indeed, Lucy has been kidnapped by photographer Roger Larsen, her former lover, who keeps her gagged and tied to a chair when he's not with her. Pam remembers that Lucy was becoming afraid of Roger's recent turn of temper. She had already warned him to stay away from her niece, and now suggests that she and Bobby go to his studio to investigate. Roger tries to send them to another address, but Lucy's cries for help are heard and she is rescued.

While Pam and Bobby are with Lucy, J.R. is with Marilee—toasting the demise of Cliff. "Here's to the only

eight-thousand-foot grave in Texas," J.R. announces gleefully, thinking of the dry well that Barnes has spent $5 million on.

J.R. tells his good news all over town—especially to Katherine Wentworth. Cliff tells the bad news to Sue Ellen and then asks to borrow $4 million dollars from her. Sue Ellen is horrified.

"You don't love anything but power," she tells him, "how could I have been so stupid?"

Barnes has been just as stupid. To recover the $4 million he needs to pay back his mother, he sells his share of the Ewing–Barnes field back to J.R.

"Well, Cliff," snarls J.R., "how does it feel? A couple of days ago, you owned my oil field, you were going to marry my wife, and you were going to hit the big gusher. Barnes, now you've succeeded at becoming the perfect failure."

ACCEPTANCE
by Will Lorin

J.R. is in top form and on top of the world. He has ruined Cliff, who has been asked to resign from Wentworth Tool & Die; he's got Bobby under his thumb over Christopher's true parentage; and Sue Ellen is receiving his roses and attentions.

She is afraid to totally trust him, but keeps leaning more and more in the direction he wants—the Southfork direction.

GOOD-BYE, CLIFF BARNES
by Arthur Bernard Lewis

Sue Ellen agrees to remarry J.R.—leaving Clayton Farlow holding an unused engagement ring and Cliff Barnes even more distraught than ever.

Pam and Bobby's marriage is none too stable when Pam learns that J.R. is Christopher's true father.

"You lied to me, Bobby. You lied to me a lot. Kristin's baby...J.R.'s baby...you brought Christopher home for J.R., not me."

But Pam comes to realize that Bobby did everything out of love for her and that she and Bobby are the only real parents Christopher knows. They go to California to track down leads left behind by Kristin and Jeff Farraday and discover that Kristin miscarried J.R.'s baby.

Cliff is destroyed by the many disasters that have befallen him. He overdoses on pills and alcohol, but is discovered by Afton and, comatose, is rushed to the hospital.

Sue Ellen and J.R. outside the hospital—each feeling somewhat responsible for Cliff's attempted suicide.

J.R. knows a few ways to ruin a man. All he needs is a high-priced hooker to finish off an opponent's career.

CHANGING OF THE GUARD
by Arthur Bernard Lewis

Sue Ellen is torn by guilt over Cliff's suicide attempt and tells J.R. that if Barnes dies, she cannot remarry him.

"Sue Ellen," J.R. says, "I can understand the way you felt—the reason you said the things you said because your heart went out to him. But now it's time for us to go home, back to Southfork."

Sue Ellen feels guilty though, and is not ready to go back to the ranch yet. While she sits vigil at the hospital, J.R. has all of John Ross's toys and things packed up and sent to Southfork. Too bad he doesn't own ice skates: J.R. gets a very chilly reception from his family. Ellie is pained that the Barnes–Ewing feud has gone this far; Bobby is furious that J.R. tried to blackmail him over Christopher and that he is also a part of the reasons behind Cliff's suicide attempt. Bobby calls the family together to vote out J.R. as president of Ewing Oil.

The Ewings move into a period of stress. J.R. tells Miss Ellie that if Sue Ellen won't come back to Southfork, he will be moving out. Lucy discovers that she is pregnant with Roger Larsen's child. And a newly unemployed J.R. agrees to run Harwood Oil from behind the scenes so that he can keep a hand in the power game which is so vital to his self-image.

WHERE THERE'S A WILL
by Leonard Katzman

Cliff comes out of the coma and slowly begins the climb toward better health. Pam tries to cheer him up with the news that he forced J.R. out of the presidency. "Bobby's running the company now," she says, "so we can call an end to the feud."

But you can never call an end to J.R.'s schemes. With Cliff safe and his own job gone, J.R. easily convinces Sue Ellen that he wants to remarry her because he loves her—not because of John Ross's voting stock. Then he asks to peek at Jock's will, just to get a leg up on the rest of the family. He discovers terrible news; Harv Smithfield tells him, "When your Daddy was in South America he added a codicil that changed the terms of his will dramatically, and he included instructions that no one, I repeat, no one, is to see the will before it's read to the whole family."

So J.R. manages, by his usual scheming, to have Smithfield's son-in-law get him the papers, muttering to himself proudly, "As my daddy used to say, where there's a way there's a will."

BILLION DOLLAR QUESTION
by Arthur Bernard Lewis

J.R., having seen the new codicil in his father's will, knows that he is safe and pushes the rest of the family toward the official reading of the will. Yet, when J.R. lobbies to have Jock declared dead legally, Ellie balks: she is still unable to accept the fact that Jock is really dead.

With the Oil Baron's Ball approaching, Ellie decides to make her social debut without Jock. J.R. wants the world to know his news before the ball so that he can wield his new power at the social event of the season.

THE BIG BALL
by Leonard Katzman

J.R. continues to whisper advice to Holly Harwood, who in turn checks on everything he says with Bobby. Although she has signed over 25 percent of her company to J.R., she doesn't completely trust him, and won't go to bed with him.

Lucy has an abortion and decides to divorce Mitch.

Sue Ellen goes to the Southern Cross to have some time to think, and is shocked when Dusty shows up with a wife. It seems that Dusty is only impotent with Sue Ellen.

When Dusty and his bride start talking in front of Sue Ellen about having children; she is obviously hurt. After half a day in their company, Sue Ellen makes her decision and calls Miss Ellie.

"I just realized that I belong at Southfork. I'll see you soon."

Sue Ellen returns for the Oil Baron's Ball and Punk Anderson's announcement of a memorial scholarship fund at SMU in Jock's memory.

JOCK'S WILL
by David Paulsen

By the end of the Oil Baron's Ball, Ellie realizes that it is time to officially lay Jock to rest and have the legalities taken care of. She decides to go ahead with the official hearing and with the reading of the will.

At the inquest into Jock's death, the family face the awful truth when they hear testimony from the pilot of the plane that collided with Jock's.

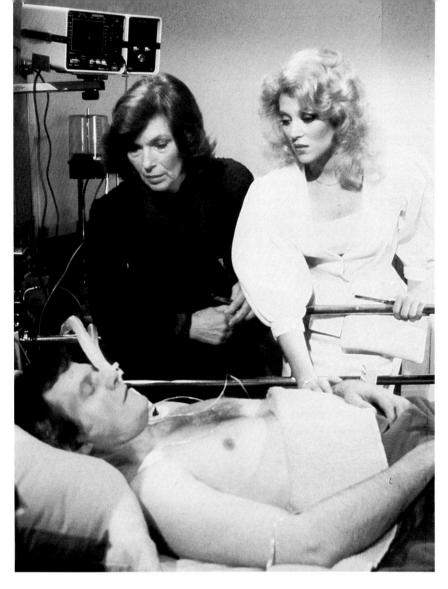

Afton and Rebecca stand vigil at Cliff's bedside after his attempted suicide.

(*right*)
The Oil Baron's Ball, where the Jock Ewing Scholarship Fund is announced.

138

Harv goes ahead with the technicalities; however, since there is no body it may be a little hard to prove a death without waiting the traditional seven-year period. J.R. makes the arrangements for depositions in South America and, at the same time, surprises Sue Ellen with invitations for their remarriage.

After a tension-wracked hearing, the judge makes his decision: "I see no reason to contradict the motion. The judgment of this court is that John Ross Ewing Senior died in a place unknown in the jungles of South America."

Gary and Ray are asked to fly to Dallas for the reading of the will. More tension fills the house, but J.R. is calm.

"They're all worried about the will," Sue Ellen notes. "How come you're not?"

"My Daddy was a fair man," J.R. tells her with a straight face, "I've got a notion he provided for me just fine."

J.R. was right, of course. Jock's will left Southfork to Miss Ellie along with $50 million and assorted community property holdings; $10 million goes to each of the four Ewing sons; Lucy receives $5 million in trust; and a separate trust is set up for all Ewing grandchildren.

Ewing Oil is divided into two equal shares, one to be run by J.R. and one by Bobby; at the end of one year, whichever brother shows the greatest gain for his share will win 51 percent of the company stock. The loser will get 19 percent of the stock, and the remaining shares are to be divided between Ray, Gary, and Miss Ellie.

The final codicil is the most powerful: "In the unfortunate event that, before this year is up, one son predeceases the other, the remaining son will automatically inherit his shares and will take over the company."

AFTERMATH
by David Paulsen

The battle of the brothers is on. Bobby considers a Canadian oil deal while J.R. hires a private detective so he can blackmail a member of the Office of Land Management. But J.R. is certain that he'll be the one to end up triumphant.

"If I can't win against that boy scout," he tells Sue Ellen, "I ought to have my merit badges taken away."

Ellie is at a loss to understand why Jock has pitted his sons against each other. Punk explains it to her:

"I was down there with Jock when he made his decision. It was the hardest thing I ever saw him do. To split his two sons whom he loved so much . . . Miss Ellie, he agonized over that. But he kept coming back to one thing—only the strongest should take Ewing Oil in hand. He had to be sure who the strongest one was."

HIT AND RUN
by Howard Lakin

Once J.R. discovers that Carol Driscoll, the new wife of the OLM's Walt Driscoll, is a terrible driver, he begins to formulate the plan that will put Driscoll in his pocket. He needs approval from Driscoll to allow him to pump more oil so he can win the race against Bobby, but so far, Driscoll has been reluctant to grant permission. Enter the best little blackmail scheme in Texas. J.R. arranges for a fake hit-and-run accident to set up the perfect framework for some nice blackmail.

Meanwhile, Rebecca has bought an oil company for Cliff to run and urges him to join the cartel and avenge himself against J.R. Cliff's presence in the cartel poses more of a threat to J.R. than he had anticipated. As Bobby so aptly puts it, "With Cliff in the cartel now, there are going to be damned few people in this state who'll even deal with you."

THE EWING TOUCH
by Howard Lakin

Walt Driscoll grants J.R. his oil variance in exchange for covering up Carol's hit-and-run accident, and J.R. pumps much more oil out of his land than God ever intended. The variance is granted only to J.R.'s fields, not to Bobby's. The oil cartel does not understand why J.R. is pumping to capacity when there is a glut of oil on the market.

But J.R. knows exactly what he's doing. He cancels orders for parts that would make repairs on Bobby's wells and begins to make new and treacherous deals that will guarantee what he's always wanted—full control of Ewing Oil. He certainly hasn't lost his touch.

FRINGE BENEFITS
by Will Lorin

J.R. and Cliff both want to buy the same refinery, but the owner won't sell out without pressuring both Afton and Sue Ellen for a few kindnesses. Afton decides to compromise herself to help Cliff get the oil refinery. The cartel sides with Cliff in the battle against J.R.

The rest of the Ewings prepare for J.R. and Sue Ellen's upcoming wedding. Clayton Farlow flies in to give away the bride while Ellie makes the point to her would-be beau, Frank Crutcher, that one wedding in the family is enough—she feels pressured by him and thinks they are moving too fast. After all, she's not really ready for such a commitment so soon after Jock's death.

Cliff wears his heart on his sleeve; the bride sports a 13.5-carat diamond ring.

Pam asks Bobby to forget the Ewing war and leave Southfork, but Bobby refuses to give up the fight.

THE WEDDING
by Will Lorin

J.R. also has fighting—or infighting—at home. Even though he and Sue Ellen are remarried at Southfork (with Pam as the matron of honor and Bobby as the best man), tension runs so high between the brothers that Pam is afraid her husband will explode.

Bobby doesn't help matters: "If J.R. says one word to me, just one word, so help me, he'll spend his honeymoon in Dallas Memorial."

The Ewings pack up their troubles and hide them for the public when the guests arrive for the wedding. Although the ceremony is boycotted by the oil industry, other family friends fill out the party. Even Cliff attends, much to the bride's dismay.

POST NUPTIAL
by David Paulsen

When Sue Ellen walks down the aisle and sees Cliff there, she knows there will be trouble. Clayton feels it, too, as the bride's foot falters; J.R. feels it when Cliff takes a swing at him.

When he sees Cliff dancing with Sue Ellen, J.R. pushes them apart menacingly. "You may have botched up killing yourself, but I sure as hell won't."

Clayton is wary. He warns the groom, "I may have given Sue Ellen away, but that doesn't mean I don't care what happens to her. I never want to hear you're making her unhappy again!"

While J.R. is away on his honeymoon, Bobby learns that the excess oil being pumped from J.R.'s wells may well be sold to an embargoed nation. "The only place you can get a price for it these days is from somewhere it can't be bought officially," warns a member of the OLM.

Appalled, Bobby asks J.R. about it. J.R. just plays fox, leaving Bobby even more angry.

Donna sits on the Texas Energy Committee, a political appointment that pits her squarely against J.R.

"J.R., your assurances don't mean much to me, but there's something I can assure you of. Brother or no, whatever it takes, I'll never let you destroy Ewing Oil."

BARBECUE THREE
by Arthur Bernard Lewis

Half the county is invited to the annual Ewing barbecue, so it's no surprise that Cliff shows up. And whenever Cliff and J.R. are in the same area, there's bound to be trouble. Cliff leads a group of oilmen friends in an attack on J.R., which leaves Ellie wondering yet again why her husband created such a problem with his will.

J.R. announces he will open a chain of two hundred cut-rate gas stations, gas stations he bought with the help of Holly Harwood.

"Why'd you do it?" Ellie asks J.R.

"I did it 'cause it's good business."

"You did it," says Pam angrily, "so you could take over Ewing Oil."

Bobby vows that he can fight as dirty as his older brother in order to win control of the company.

Ellie is so furious she decides to go to court to contest Jock's will.

MAMA DEAREST
by Arthur B. Lewis

Bobby reluctantly sides with J.R. when Miss Ellie threatens court action to contest Jock's will. Pam sides with Miss Ellie; she too has had enough of this brother-against-brother business. Pam's decision to support Miss Ellie leads Bobby to wonder just why his wife is not backing him up.

Meanwhile, J.R. has others out to get him. Cliff and the cartel, trying to beat out J.R.'s cut-rate gasoline prices, discuss starting another Texas gas war. J.R.'s business practices get him a lot of positive media attention, so when Donna tries to have J.R.'s variance rescinded she finds a great deal of resistance.

Donna and Ray meet the press.

Sue Ellen, believing J.R. is a changed man, says "I do" one more time.

Cliff Barnes never did know how to keep his mouth shut.

THE EWING BLUES
by David Paulsen

The second time around, Sue Ellen has decided to participate more actively in J.R.'s business. She backs him completely in his gas war and even goes on television with him to defend his position. This serves to further alienate the J.R. Ewings from the rest of the family as Ellie wrestles with the decision of going to court to try to break Jock's will.

The breach between Bobby and Pam worsens when Pam continues in her show of support for Ellie. Bobby is betting that his mother will not go through with the proceedings since to overturn the will means declaring Jock incompetent. But he appears to be wrong when Ellie announces sadly, "However much it hurts, I have to overturn Jock's will."

While Pam and Bobby are estranged, Pam meets millionaire Mark Graison and finds herself very attracted to him.

THE RECKONING
by Will Lorin

The hearing to break Jock's will is very painful for all members of the family—especially Ellie. The complications and implications are deep—if the will is successfully overturned, both Gary and Ray will be left without trust funds. Ellie assures Ray that she will cover him financially, but Ray says he will not accept charity.

Sue Ellen discovers Mark Graison's attachment to Pam and reports it to J.R., who can use the information as a weapon in his battle against brother Bobby.

Rebecca asks Cliff to hold off his action against J.R. until the ruling on Jock's will—the day of reckoning.

A EWING IS A EWING
by Frank Furino

The judge rules against Ellie and decides that Jock's last codicil stands—he was neither incompetent nor suffering from jungle fever.

Now that they know where they stand, Bobby and J.R. are back into the battle for Ewing Oil. Bobby discovers ties between George Hicks, an energy commission member, and J.R., and Holly and J.R. come to a more solid working relationship.

Ellie escapes the tension at Southfork by vacationing in Galveston, where she bumps into Clayton. J.R. has just conned Sue Ellen into setting up Clayton in a business deal, and Farlow is furious. Clayton calls J.R., breathing

fire. "You may have Sue Ellen fooled, and that's a shame. But I never did buy your act—and I don't intend to start now. Don't you ever try using your wife or anyone else to get at me again or I'll break you in two!"

Clayton isn't the only one angry at J.R. Holly pulls a gun on him and then reads him the riot act—her riot act.

"You arrogant pig. Did you really think I'd allow your filthy hands on me again? I could kill you now and never regret it. But this is a new ball game with new rules, J.R. We're business partners and that's all we are. You ever try to force yourself on me again and you're a dead man."

CRASH OF '83
by Howard Lakin

Bobby pulls a J.R. and sets up George Hicks with a hooker named Wendy so he can get the OLM to reverse its stand on J.R.'s variance. Pam is disgusted by the whole thing.

Ellie returns from Galveston obviously taken with Clayton. Although they had bumped into each other by accident, they spent a lot of time together and enjoyed each other. Clayton is hurt by Sue Ellen's attempt to use him and Ellie is just recovering from Jock's death, but the two are beginning to shape up as a couple. "Of all the people in the world for Mama to take up with..." J.R. huffs.

But Ellie isn't taking up with him just yet. Although Clayton sells the Southern Cross so that he can come to Dallas, Ellie wants to make sure that Rebecca Wentworth, who has also been seeing Clayton, doesn't get hurt. Clayton protests that he and Rebecca are "just friends."

Meanwhile Rebecca has her hands full with another man—her son. When Cliff discovers that J.R. is about to buy a refinery, Rebecca is quick to mention that she knows the owner and can influence him not to sell to J.R. "One way or another," she vows to Cliff, "we'll keep J.R. from getting that refinery."

When Cliff can't get on the company plane to make the deal, Rebecca goes in his place. The jet crashes over Dallas.

REQUIEM
by Linda Elstad

Rebecca is taken (with serious internal injuries) to intensive care at Dallas Memorial, where she asks Pam to take care of Cliff and protect him, then she dies.

Cliff blames himself for his mother's death. After all, if he had gone to the meeting, it would have been him—

not her. Cliff can't help but lay the rest of the blame on the Ewings. If it hadn't been for the feud, or for J.R. trying to buy a refinery, his mother would not have had to get on the plane. J.R. knows it, too. "It should have been Cliff Barnes on that plane, not his mother," J.R. tells Sue Ellen. "But no . . . he was probably off somewhere crying in his beer as usual."

Clayton sees Rebecca's death as J.R.'s responsibility not Cliff's. "All Rebecca was trying to do was stop you, and she paid for it with her life!" Clayton yells.

Katherine flies to Dallas from New York to join Pam and Cliff in their sorrow, but lashes out at Cliff for having let their mother fight his battles. "You weren't content to embezzle from my father's company. You weren't content to drag the whole family into your endless losing battle with the Ewings. No, you had to drag Mama into it while you hid behind her skirts. You're the one who caused Mama's death, and I'm going to make you pay for it if it's the last thing I do!"

When the funeral is over and Pam has had time to think, she tells Bobby that she's leaving Southfork—without him.

LEGACY
by Robert Sherman

Pam and Christopher leave Southfork. J.R. is absolutely delighted. He has wanted Pam and Bobby to split up since they first got married; and perhaps now Bobby will be so distracted that his business will fall behind. Katherine is also thrilled by the split; she's had her eye on Bobby since the day they met.

Indeed, Katherine proves that she fits in at Southfork. She has a good bit of J.R. in her. Outraged at the terms of her mother's will—Barnes–Wentworth went to Cliff alone, Wentworth Industries was split between her and Pam, and Wentworth Tool & Die was equally divided among all three of Rebecca's children—and certain that the Wentworth fortune should be hers alone, Katherine begins to plot her revenge against Pam and Cliff. She's not ready for all-out war yet, though, so she covers up her anger.

J.R. is worried that Bobby is gaining on him and suggests that they end the race and compromise—but Bobby will have none of it. He's out to prove something to himself.

"Just save it, J.R., will you? There was a time when I might have taken your offer but certainly not now. I'm pulling ahead of you in the fight, and I'm going to whip you. And I'm going to take Ewing Oil right out of your hands."

Holly Harwood discusses her business empire with Bobby, although J.R. is her secret partner.

BROTHERS AND SISTERS
by Will Lorin

Pam begins plotting with Cliff, which puts her on the opposite side of the fence from Bobby and creates even more strain on their relationship. J.R. is pleased at this development and schemes to make the separation permanent by encouraging Mark Graison in his pursuit of Pam. Katherine makes no secret of her interest in Bobby—she even sets him up to see Pam and Mark together. Then she plays it real sweet and loving, as if she were dying to do anything to help out.

Clayton finalizes the sale of the Southern Cross and moves to Dallas, making a subtle claim on Ellie—much to J.R.'s dismay.

Cliff (with girlfriend Mandy Winger) faces an angry Katherine Wentworth after their mother's will has been read.

The fight between J.R. and Bobby intensifies. Bobby becomes almost obsessive about winning the contest. His back to the wall, J.R. decides to chance making a killing in one big deal; he plans to sell one million barrels of oil to Cuba for $40 million. It's the deal of his life; he'll either win Ewing Oil or go to jail.

CARIBBEAN CONNECTION
by Will Lorin

Bobby's secretary reports to him a conversation that she overheard. From this evidence Bobby is able to discover that J.R. is indeed shipping oil to Cuba.

As the deal progresses, J.R. quietly puts all the paperwork in Holly Harwood's name, so that if anything goes wrong, he looks clean. Holly is too new to the oil business to understand this, so she accepts J.R.'s arguments about why the deal has to be done his way.

"For a lady who has made nothing but money from my advice, I'm getting sick of you looking suspicious every time I come to you with a deal," he tells her angrily as he tries to force her into signing the papers.

When Holly takes her problem to Bobby, the younger Ewing has all the proof he needs. Even Ray joins him to help pin down J.R.

"If we don't stop what he's doing," Ray tells Bobby, "it could be the end of Ewing Oil."

THE STING
by David Paulsen

Bobby and Ray set up Walt Driscoll—J.R.'s partner in the Cuba deal—by causing a small automobile accident that makes Driscoll have to rush to catch his plane to Puerto Rico, where he is to deliver the money for the final transaction in the big million-barrel deal. In the confusion, Ray swaps briefcases on Driscoll.

"Wait 'til he opens his case," Bobby says with some glee to Ray. "The rest of Driscoll's hair will fall out!"

When he goes through security at the airport, Driscoll gets a big surprise—his attaché case has two loaded guns in it. Driscoll is sent to the Dallas County jail. J.R. is livid at the possibility of the Cuba deal being stymied.

Meanwhile, Pam and Mark Graison guide Cliff into buying a small company from Mark that makes drilling-related equipment. Cliff returns to the business world and begins to pull himself together.

HELL HATH NO FURY
by Arthur Bernard Lewis

J.R. decides to do business with Cuba legally in order to get his money back, and the Ewing brothers fall victim to the women they know. Katherine chases Bobby aggressively and urges Mark Graison to take Pam to Europe, while Holly Harwood, who vows revenge on J.R. for her loss in the Cuban deal, has decided to poison his marriage. When the ladies meet at the beauty parlor she whispers a few well-chosen insinuations to Sue Ellen. Then Holly lays it on thicker and thicker, slowly convincing Sue Ellen that J.R. is cheating on her again.

Cliff explains to Pam that Bobby's Canadian deal is worth a fortune but probably won't pay off in time for Bobby to get the money he needs to win Ewing Oil.

"Why is this supposed to make me happy?" Pam asks her brother.

"Bobby will lose Ewing Oil to J.R. and you'll have him back."

Katherine overhears this conversation and realizes that if she's ever going to get Bobby, she has to win him before the J.R.–Bobby fight is over. "Here's to winners," she says in a toast with J.R., her new ally.

Holly wins her round. Sue Ellen finds Holly's lipstick on one of J.R.'s shirts. She is shattered.

CUBA LIBRE
by Leonard Katzman

The State Department allows J.R. to go to Cuba legally—although they are puzzled by his sudden interest. First J.R. flies to Puerto Rico to make contact with the man who set it all up. He is surprised to discover his name is meaningless there and he does not wield the kind of power he is used to.

Bobby gives Holly Harwood some brotherly advice.

Holly and J.R. toast their new relationship.

But he still knows how to play the game. "I understand it all, señor. When I have the upper hand, I play it to the hilt myself."

While J.R. is gone, Sue Ellen goes to the office to chat with Bobby about her husband. "Is there some kind of connection between J.R. and Holly Harwood?"

When Bobby explains about the Cuban deal, Sue Ellen begins to understand: Holly lost $17 million so she tried to get back at J.R. by telling lies to Sue Ellen. Just to make sure, Sue Ellen goes for a chat with Holly. Leaving Holly's home, she's not so certain at all.

J.R. finally enters Cuba to get the money but is taken prisoner right after he lands.

TANGLED WEB
by David Paulsen

J.R. is soon freed; his night in jail was just meant to teach him a lesson in risk-taking. His jailer, Ignacio Perez, takes from J.R. a check for $1 million as a finder's fee and gives J.R. in return a check for $40 million drawn on a Swiss bank.

When he returns to Dallas, J.R. offers Bobby a box of Cuban cigars and some advice. "Your assets are frozen in the middle of Canada, Bob. You took the high road and I took the low road... but I got the company before you."

Meanwhile, in France on business, Pam and Mark bump into friends of Bobby's from Dallas. Pam feels very awkward and embarrassed. "The truth is there is an enormous attraction between us," Mark tells her after their friends leave, "and it is truth that you are purposely ignoring. If you were really married, you'd be with Bobby. But you're not single either. Being caught in the middle is driving both of us a little bit crazy."

Their affair is put on hold when Afton calls Pam to warn her about Katherine.

"There can't be anything between us, Mark, until I take care of what's waiting for me back in Dallas. I can't close my eyes to those problems."

Pam and Bobby aren't the only ones with matrimonial problems. Holly continues to bait Sue Ellen and finally springs the trap. She tells Sue Ellen exactly when J.R. will be in her arms and Sue Ellen goes for the bait. She walks into Holly's home right in time to find J.R. and Holly in bed.

THINGS AIN'T GOIN' TOO GOOD AT SOUTHFORK
by Leonard Katzman

When Sue Ellen walks into Holly's bedroom, J.R. doesn't even see her. How can he? He's too busy nuzzling Holly's

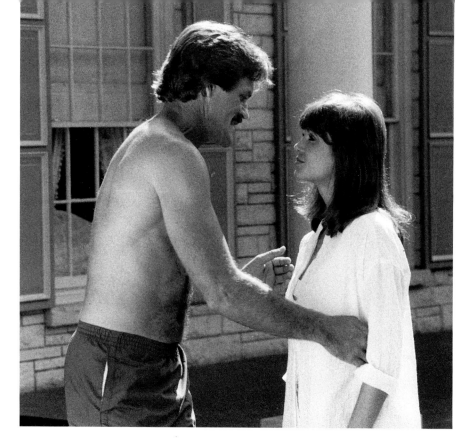

Mark and Pam get serious.

gorgeous neck. Sue Ellen turns, leaves, and drives straight to a bar. When J.R. returns to Southfork and Sue Ellen is not there, he begins to piece together the scenario.

"You must have heard her wrong, Bobby. I was with Holly settling details of the Cuban triumph—the one that's going to win me Ewing Oil. I didn't see her there so she must not have gone to Holly's after all."

Drunk, Sue Ellen gives Clayton's hotel as her address and is taken to his room. Clayton is quite shocked to return home from Southfork and find Sue Ellen there—and drunk, to boot.

"You gave me quite a surprise last night," he tells her the next morning. "It's been quite a while since I caught a lady in my bed."

Pam returns from France and confronts her sister, but Katherine just sweet-talks her, and then puts her in the middle of a business problem that will go either Cliff's way or Bobby's depending upon Pam's vote.

Miss Ellie discovers Sue Ellen at Clayton's. Although Clayton explains that nothing is going on between them, the meeting is painful for her. Even more painful is the showdown that occurs when a drunken Sue Ellen tells J.R. what she has seen at Holly's, then rushes out of the house and tears off down the road in J.R.'s car. Lucy's boyfriend, Ray's cousin Mickey Trotter, tries to stop her, but both of them end up in the car, tires squealing down the gravel drive. As she pulls recklessly into the main road, another car sideswipes Sue Ellen, and she and Mickey end up overturned in a ditch.

Sue Ellen still carries bruises from the accident, in which Mickey was injured more severely.

PENULTIMATE
by Howard Lakin

Lucy blames Sue Ellen for the accident that has seriously injured Mickey. Ray blames himself for having his cousin come from Kansas to Southfork in the first place and for getting him involved in such a foreign lifestyle. Clayton blames J.R. for the whole thing, and Bobby thinks it's Holly's fault that Sue Ellen fell off the wagon and ended up in a car accident.

"You drove her back to the bottle, J.R.," Clayton states matter of factly. "You might just as well have put it in her hand. I warned you before you two married—hurt her and you answer to me. I'm not going to stand by and let you abuse her."

Holly accepts some of the guilt herself. "I swear, I never meant for things to go this far. I thought Sue Ellen would show up, see us in bed together, and go into some kind of rampage. I didn't know she was an alcoholic."

"Sue Ellen lives in a fantasy world," Bobby explains. "There everything is perfect. She runs away from reality. She'd crawl into a bottle rather than face it."

Blood tests confirm that Sue Ellen was driving with three times the legal limit of alcohol in her blood. The police notify J.R. that if Mickey dies, Sue Ellen will be arrested for manslaughter.

EWING INFERNO
by Arthur Bernard Lewis

Ray is unable to contain his feelings of guilt about Mickey—if the boy survives, he will be paralyzed from the neck down. Sue Ellen really can't remember the details of the accident, so Ray offers a $50,000 reward for information leading to the identity of the driver of the car that sideswiped Sue Ellen's.

"Ray's been living out a fantasy," explains Donna. "He sees Mickey as a young Ray and himself as Jock. He was going to try to do for Mickey all the things that Jock did for him when he was growing up. He thinks that Jock would have never let this sort of thing happen to young Ray, so in his mind he not only let Mickey down, but he let Jock down."

J.R. is so upset by all the family turmoil that he confesses to Bobby that he doesn't even care about the fight to win Ewing Oil. For a moment, Bobby considers a truce . . . until the phone rings and Pam announces that she will side with Katherine at Wentworth Tool & Die—the bit that Bobby needs to bring in the Canadian wells is his. Pam also asks Bobby for a divorce.

The police discover that it was Walt Driscoll who was driving the other car. Driscoll thought J.R. was in the car

and purposely rammed it. When he discovered what had happened to Mickey, he killed himself.

"Driscoll may have been driving the car, but the guy who destroyed Mickey's life is J.R.," says Ray as he storms out.

Still smoldering, Ray confronts J.R. "I'm cold sober, and I'm going to kill you," he announces—with a fire poker in his hand.

The poker misses J.R. but knocks over a candle, igniting some painter's supplies in the front hall. The entryway is set ablaze.

Brothers will be brothers—even half-brothers.

J.R. reaches for a brass candlestick as his fight with Ray heats up.

Ray lies unconscious as the paint and wallpaper supplies in the front hall ignite.

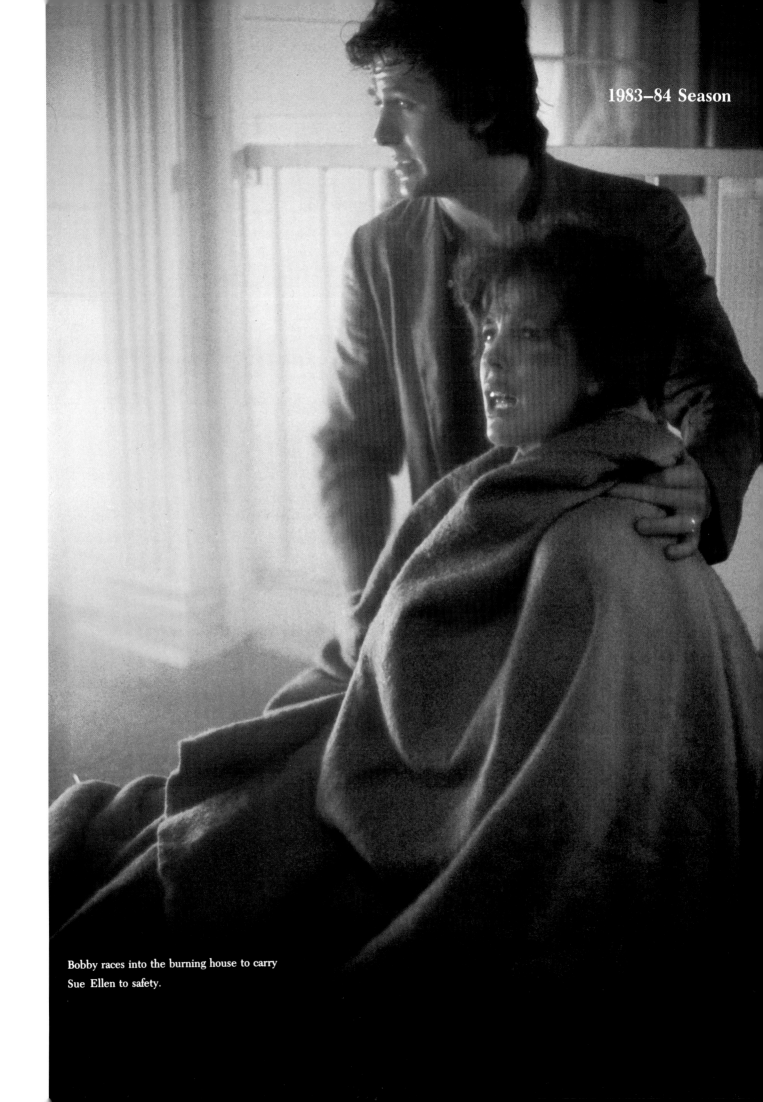

Bobby races into the burning house to carry
Sue Ellen to safety.

The Brothers Ewing survive.

THE ROAD BACK
by Arthur Bernard Lewis

Bobby drives up to Southfork in time to see the smoke and flames and rushes inside. He finds the semi-conscious Ray and together they rescue the unconscious J.R. and pull Sue Ellen and John Ross to safety. Firemen soon arrive to put out the blaze. "What happened?" Donna asks as everyone begins to recover.

"Ask your husband," J.R. tells her. "He tried to kill me. The fire started during the fight. If smoke detectors hadn't been wired into the fire station, the whole house would have burned down."

Clayton, on vacation with Ellie, reads about the fire in the newspaper but decides to keep it a secret from her, fearing that another disaster would be too much for her to bear. J.R. realizes that the fight to control the company has been a strain on the whole family and suggests to Bobby that the two brothers run it together.

"Together—the way Daddy wanted when he was alive. Share and share alike. I really mean it, Bob."

Bobby tries to patch things up with Ray as well, but Ray still holds J.R. directly responsible for Mickey's accident. J.R. points out that Ray helped Bobby with the sting operation that trapped Driscoll in the first place. "None of us has clean hands . . . none of us!"

John Ross is caught again in his parents' emotional tug-of-war.

Sue Ellen discovers that Driscoll caused the accident on purpose. "J.R., I've been walking around with all this guilt. I thought I was responsible for the accident. Why didn't you have the decency to tell me? You would have let me go on thinking I had destroyed Mickey Trotter's life, but I didn't. I didn't!"

The realization gives Sue Ellen the strength she needs to quit drinking.

Bobby and J.R. agree to end the feud and go to Harv Smithfield to sign the appropriate papers. To their horror, Smithfield says they can't.

"My hands are tied. The contest had a year to run. That year is up a month from now. Any other agreement would not stand up in court; it would violate the terms of Jock's will. One month from now, the contest will be up; at that time, I will declare a winner, and one of you will own 51 percent of Ewing Oil."

THE LONG GOOD-BYE
by Leonard Katzman

Sue Ellen tells J.R. that she won't leave him but wants an "open marriage" with separate bedrooms at Southfork. "You and I will not live as man and wife. From now on, it's separate bedrooms and separate lives." Pam wants her marriage back but with one bedroom outside of Southfork.

Bobby is torn between wanting to work it out with Pam and not wanting to upset his mother further by moving away from Southfork. Meanwhile J.R. and Katherine are downright furious at the idea that Pam and Bobby might make their marriage work again.

"If you want Bobby," J.R. advises Katherine, "and you do, you're going to have to work to get him. Together we have to keep the two of them from getting back together."

J.R. goes so far as to warn Pam that he will do everything in his power to hurt Bobby and destroy Cliff if Pam comes back into the Ewing family.

"If you return to Bobby, all hell will break loose. I'll call off the truce that exists between us. We'll end up in a dogfight that will make everything you've seen before look like a love match. And as for Cliff, whatever it takes, using every penny that Ewing Oil has, I will destroy him. Once and for all I will put an end to Mr. Cliff Barnes, and whoever else goes down with him, so be it."

THE LETTER
by David Paulsen

J.R. plants the seed of Pam's destruction with Katherine, who will go to any lengths to try to win Bobby. When Katherine can't talk Pam out of going back to Bobby, she decides to fake a letter—from Pam about Mark—which would throw a new light on a reconciliation.

"I don't read Pam's mail," Bobby says when offered the letter.

"I didn't want to read it either, I found it accidentally. But you have to hear part of it. 'Six years of marriage cannot easily be dismissed. Therefore if that means remaining with my husband when it no longer makes me happy, in order to avoid causing him pain, then perhaps that is what I have to do. I know I would be better off if Bobby just let me go, but if he doesn't, I may have to give in and return to him. His happiness should be as important to me as my own.'"

The letter has the effect Katherine intends. Pam meets Bobby for a date—only to discover that Bobby now wants out.

"I want you to know that I'm letting you go. It's not fair to either of us like this. It's for the best. I think it's time we both finally realized it's over."

MY BROTHER'S KEEPER
by Arthur Bernard Lewis

Katherine plays "sister dearest" to perfection and has Pam in her grasp. She has successfully busted up Pam and Bobby's reconciliation while acting as if she were Pam's best friend.

J.R. acts like Bobby's best friend, too, never letting on that he has sabotaged the drilling in Canada to ensure that Bobby's well won't come in until the contest is over.

"Listen, Bobby," J.R. says with all sincerity, "you and I have fought like hell at times, but we're still brothers and I care about you. Take care of yourself, and when this divorce is over, we'll knock 'em dead at the office. The Ewing brothers working together will just make this little old town sit up and take notice."

The lawyers work out the divorce, although Katherine and J.R. are the only ones who are really happy about it. Afton tries to tell Pam that she's been set up by her own sister, but Pam refuses to believe it.

THE QUALITY OF MERCY
by Leonard Katzman

Pam moves into the big house her mother left and begins to entertain Mark Graison on a more serious basis. She is still unable to believe what Katherine did to her. Katherine is taking it slowly and tries to work her way into Bobby's heart by the back door. She invites him to dinner to console him after the divorce.

Bobby meets his old love, Jenna Wade, at Billy Bob's.

Mickey needs more than consoling. He's lost his will to live and has entered a very angry stage. Although Lucy has told him she will marry him and take care of him forever, Mickey realizes that their plan will never work.

"Can't you understand? There's not going to be any house or any wedding. We're never going to get married. I'm useless. You can't tie yourself to me. I'm never going to get out of this bed."

Mickey's depression worsens and he confides to Ray and Lil, his mother, that he wishes his life was over. His wish is not far off; he suffers cardiac arrest and then falls back into a second coma. Unable to stand the suffering, Ray helps out in the only way he knows how. He unplugs Mickey's life-support system.

CHECK AND MATE
by David Paulsen

Ray Krebbs is arrested for murdering his cousin, Mickey Trotter. Lil and Lucy are in a state of shock. Donna wants to hire a good attorney for her husband, but Ray says he doesn't need an attorney—he's guilty. Donna prevails, though, and brings in Paul Morgan, a leading attorney.

Meanwhile J.R. and Katherine are still plotting. Katherine learns that J.R. has never meant to end the battle for control of Ewing Oil.

"You *haven't* given up the battle, have you? You just tricked him into thinking you have," Katherine asks J.R.

"That'll be our little secret, won't it," J.R. smiles. "You and Bobby are going to be real happy together—some place far from here. And old J.R. is finally going to have his daddy's company all to himself."

When the final day comes to register the audits, Punk Anderson reads a last letter from Jock to his sons, asking them to work together no matter who wins the contest. J.R. asks for the totals "just for fun" and is pleased to see he has "won" the battle. Just as he is about to weasel out of his agreement with Bobby to share the company, Bobby's friend from the Canadian oil deal walks in with a check for some $26 million. The additional money makes Bobby the winner. Now J.R. is panicked that his brother will do to him what he had already planned to do to Bobby.

But Bobby wouldn't do a thing like that. He gracefully agrees to the share since that's what his daddy really wanted all along, and he has already given his word. "You and me together—brothers," says J.R. gleefully as he hugs Bobby.

RAY'S TRIAL
by Arthur Bernard Lewis

Bobby bumps into Jenna Wade again. Jenna refuses his many invitations, because she doesn't want to get hurt. She is now waiting on tables at Billy Bob's.

"Being an ex-rich girl doesn't pay the bills. I even thought I was underqualified for waitressing, but they hired me anyway. It pays the association fees on the condo and keeps Charlie in clothes."

Bobby is so preoccupied with having rediscovered Jenna that he forgets a date with Katherine. An angry Katherine calls J.R.

"This is a problem you're going to have to solve yourself. I have my own problems," says J.R.

Ray also has problems—he's about to be tried for Mickey's murder.

Ray's lawyer tells him the best defense is to make Ray look like a saint. But the state's attorney claims Krebbs "took it upon himself to play God with an innocent who couldn't defend himself."

To make Ray's case better, his attorney decides to call Lil to the stand. Ray leaps to his feet.

"No," he screams, "no! You can't do that!"

Pam becomes the ex–Mrs. Bobby Ewing, and it hurts.

Donna visits Ray in jail.

Donna comforts the distraught Lucy.

THE OIL BARON'S BALL
by Leonard Katzman

Once on the stand, Lil Trotter admits that she asked Ray to pull the plug on Mickey. But the judge still declares Ray guilty of manslaughter and passes sentence—five years of imprisonment, suspended.

Everyone else attends the Oil Baron's Ball, where Cliff is named Oil Man of the Year. Katherine fuels the fire between Jenna and Pam and stands back to enjoy the flames. The two women have a nasty go at each other in the ladies' room during the ball.

As Cliff steps up to accept his award, he tells J.R. that he plans to tell the true story about Jock and Digger.

MORNING AFTER
by David Paulsen

In accepting his award from the Oil Barons, Cliff says that Digger deserved as much acclaim as Jock since it was Digger who found the original oil sites. Cliff's words are toxin to the Ewings, and a fight ensues with Bobby, Mark, Ray, Cliff, and J.R. all going at it.

When the boys report the fight to their mother at her vacation spot in Jamaica, Ellie relates to J.R. the whole background to the Barnes–Ewing feud and how she ended up marrying Jock rather than Digger.

Cliff Barnes is named Oil Man of the Year.

156

Jenna treats Bobby's wounds after the fight and they spend the night together. Katherine wishes she was the one.

"Bobby," she smiles, "I was very disappointed when you didn't ask me to the Oil Baron's Ball."

"It never occurred to me; you're Pam's sister."

Bobby slowly begins to realize that Afton was right about Katherine, but he also realizes that he's much more interested in Jenna.

THE BUCK STOPS HERE
by Arthur Bernard Lewis

Although Sue Ellen and John Ross's camp counselor, Peter Richards, are very attracted to each other, Sue Ellen has kept some distance. After all, Peter is hardly more than a teenager, almost twenty years younger than she. But he's madly in love with Sue Ellen. Sue Ellen has slowly found herself more and more responsive to him,

partly owing to the loving care he has given John Ross. J.R., who wants what he can't have and has wanted Sue Ellen since she moved into her own bedroom, fears that Sue Ellen and Peter have become lovers.

"John Ross told me everything," he tells his wife. "You were carrying on with that counselor so the whole camp and your son could see it."

"I am not carrying on," retorts Sue Ellen, "and Peter is not my lover. And if you do anything to hurt that young man, you are going to wake up one morning and find out you no longer have a wife, even in name only . . . and you will no longer have a son. So no threats, J.R., or I will end this mockery we call a marriage once and for all."

Sue Ellen and J.R. aren't the only couple around Southfork with problems. During the big rodeo in town and the parties after it, Pam and Bobby dance together and realize they still have some unfinished business; Katherine tries to run Jenna and Charlie out of town; and another woman makes a play for Mark Graison. Everyone rides the mechanical bull; Jenna goes for style over speed, forfeiting the competition, but then slides into Bobby's arms. Pam leaves with Mark as their relationship escalates.

The annual brawl at the Oil Baron's Ball.

This time the Ewings react to remarks Cliff made about Jock.

Katherine dupes Bobby into a tête-à-tête over a picnic lunch and confesses her love for him.

The Wentworth-Barnes clan dines al fresco as the family gets to know Mark Graison. (Stanley Marcus once owned the house rented for Pam.)

Sue Ellen drops off John Ross at camp, leaving him with his counselor, Peter Richards, played by Christopher Atkins.

Clayton and Ellie announce their engagement.

Peter and Sue Ellen have their first meeting alone.

J.R. starts the day in hot water— compliments of Donna.

Jenna shows her stuff on the mechanical bull.

TO CATCH A SLY
by David Paulsen

Cliff has blackmailed J.R.'s secretary, Sly, into doing some spying on his archrival. Although Sly doesn't want to do it, she is pressured into it by the threat that her convict brother will serve his full term without parole. J.R. realizes that something is going on when he loses one deal too many—his first one—to Cliff's one-upmanship.

"J.R. is furious about losing that Kesey company to you," Sly reports to Cliff.

"Let's hope it gives him ulcers," says Cliff earnestly.

J.R. is more than furious. He's curious. He decides to bug Cliff's phone and soon discovers that Sly is his source. Rather than fire her or prosecute her, he decides to turn her into a double agent against Cliff. "Cliff set himself up," says J.R. with his famous smile. "What I'm planning to do is bring him down and bring him down very, very hard."

BARBECUE FOUR
by Arthur Bernard Lewis

J.R. creates a fictitious deal—the Travis Boyd deal—to trap Cliff and passes on the information through Sly.

"Good," says J.R. "If he closes that deal, we know he's stuck his head in the noose."

Sly discovers that Cliff has no influence at all on her brother's parole and really feels used. Cliff agrees to support Sly financially while she takes care of her brother.

Jenna refuses to give up her waitressing job, despite Bobby's request that she do so. He takes her to dinner at Southfork, and Jenna giddily confesses, "You're going to make me feel like part of the family."

"I'm willing to risk it if you are," Bobby smiles back.

Meanwhile, Katherine is still trying to get rid of Jenna. She even goes to Rome to find out the real identity of Charlie's father. When Katherine finally gets Charlie's birth certificate in her hands, she is dismayed to find that Bobby has a stronger tie to Jenna than she had guessed: Charlie is his daughter.

Ellie and Clayton return from their vacation in time for the annual Ewing family barbecue, during which they announce their engagement.

Not everyone is pleased.

PAST IMPERFECT
by David Paulsen

Clayton's announcement throws Miss Ellie's sons into turmoil and fury: J.R. even hires a detective to dig into Clayton's past. Ellie refuses to wear the huge engagement ring Clayton has bought for her until things settle down and the family problems can be worked out. Clayton suggests that he and Ellie move off Southfork, but Ellie would never seriously consider that.

Bobby buys a boutique for Jenna so that she can have her own financial independence but at the same time not have to work the long, hard hours at Billy Bob's. Instead of being thrilled, Jenna is furious and storms out.

"I will not be a kept woman!" she shouts. "I won't take handouts from you or anybody else. I am my own person,

Cliff beds Marilee Stone (played by Fern Fitzgerald), another of the many women he and J.R. have shared.

I make my own decisions, and that's the way I'm going to stay."

J.R. pretends to be friendly with Clayton and orders champagne to seal their truce. When Farlow discovers that J.R. has been snooping into his past, the man erupts in fury.

"I was a fool to fall for that line of yours. You're as devious as you ever were!"

PETER'S PRINCIPLES
by Arthur Bernard Lewis

Although Sue Ellen has tried to put a stop to her growing involvement with Peter, he leaves college and leases an apartment to be their love nest. Sue Ellen is distraught, but she finally agrees to see him if he will stay in school.

J.R.'s detectives have discovered that Clayton has a sister and he casually mentions her at a family gathering to see if he can get a reaction. Clayton is so annoyed with J.R.'s snooping that he complains to Ellie about it. Ellie cautions J.R. to lay off and not interfere with her plans to marry Clayton.

OFFSHORE CRUDE
by David Paulsen

Pam asks her ex-husband to help her prevent a reopening of the feud, so Bobby and J.R. discuss Cliff. J.R., as usual, plays it very coy and says he has no interest in competing with Cliff.

"If that idiot wants to keep the feud going, that's his business," J.R. tells Bobby. "We couldn't have any kind of edge on him in this deal because they're all government bids and they're sealed."

Then he slips Cliff some information through Sly that will tighten the noose on the trap he has been building

about an offshore drilling operation. Cliff is so excited about the news that he tries to convince Marilee Stone to invest with him. But J.R. has bribed someone to give him information about the sealed bids, so he can tumble Cliff once and for all.

SOME DO...SOME DON'T
by Leonard Katzman

Peter has been able to talk Sue Ellen out of breaking off their affair—until she is mistaken for his mother. Then she decides the affair has to stop. J.R. agrees. He wants Sue Ellen back as a real wife and suggests they have a second child. Sue Ellen refuses.

Sly continues to set up Cliff for J.R., but Pam warns her brother about Marilee and he backs out of the offshore drilling deal.

J.R. hopes that his scheming can catch all the Barneses in one blow. "Can you imagine, having all the Barnes clan out of my life for good?" he sneers to Sly.

Katherine returns to Dallas and offers Bobby a reasonable explanation for her behavior.

"I finally realized I was just lonely and confused. I guess I transferred Pam's feelings for you to myself. I really don't know how to describe it except it was foolish of me. I don't want to throw our friendship away because of my being impetuous."

Bobby tells Katherine that they will always be friends. Then Katherine goes running to J.R. for help in breaking up Jenna and Bobby. J.R. refuses. "I think Bobby and Jenna are a match made in heaven. Besides, he's the father of her little girl."

"You don't know that for sure," says Katherine.

"I do know it. A friend of mine in Rome got me a copy of the birth certificate years ago."

Katherine is flabbergasted.

Mark tells Pam he is going out of town on a business trip, but actually he is staying at the Texas Medical Center.

EYE OF THE BEHOLDER
by Leonard Katzman

Ellie decides against marrying Clayton after all. J.R. is of course thrilled; things are really going his way. Although he is shocked to see that Bobby has become involved in the Boyd deal with Cliff, he signs the papers.

"Everything is moving in the right direction," he tells Sly. "Bobby is replacing some of our old and dying fields with the Boyd deal, and Cliff Barnes will set himself up for the biggest fall in the history of independent oil companies."

Peter agrees to go to a party with Lucy, who explains to him that she hasn't been dating since Mickey died but needs an escort for her girlfriend's party. She doesn't know about Sue Ellen, of course. Peter shyly accepts on a "just friends" basis. When he comes to pick her up, he runs into Sue Ellen, which creates an inner turmoil for her. After all, her lover is now off with her niece, for whom he is a much more appropriate beau. This point is not lost on J.R., who comments, "I'm glad he finally settled on someone his own age. For a while there I thought I was going to have to challenge him to a duel."

At Donna's urging, Ellie sits down to explain herself to Clayton. He thought she had called off the wedding because of problems with the family; instead, he is shocked to discover that she has a personal problem she has not been able to share with him and is terrified he won't understand.

"Clayton, I had surgery. I've had a mastectomy. The doctor found cancer . . . they cut off my breast. It affects the way I feel about myself so I know it will be harder on you."

"It doesn't change anything," Clayton gently assures Ellie.

TWELVE MILE LIMIT
by David Paulsen

J.R. arranges to sell his geologist's reports on offshore tracts to Cliff, who has finally convinced Marilee Stone to go into business with him. Sly gives Cliff the reports, made to look like J.R. had them done just so he too could plunge into the dangerous waters of offshore drilling.

J.R. is having much more fun fishing in the waters of Clayton's past. His investigator finally comes up with something that interests J.R. It seems there's an old rumor that Clayton Farlow killed his wife to get to her money.

WHERE IS POPPA
by Arthur Bernard Lewis

While on a secret rendezvous at a hotel in Houston, Marilee agrees to a partnership with Cliff as long as the other members of the cartel don't know about it.

Cliff soon discovers that J.R. has blackmailed Edgar Randolph into giving him secret information about the offshore tracts. Meanwhile, Bobby tries to get Clayton to be his partner on the offshore deal.

Sue Ellen has a minor accident in front of Jenna's boutique and is sent to the hospital, where J.R. rushes to see her. He gets quite a shock from the doctor.

"I just wanted to tell you that Mrs. Ewing is going to be fine—no broken bones, just a few scratches and a mild concussion. She doesn't even look like she's been in an accident, but she did lose a considerable amount of blood when she miscarried. The accident apparently caused her to lose the baby. I'm sorry."

WHEN THE BOUGH BREAKS
by Leonard Katzman

J.R. is certain he fathered Sue Ellen's child during a one-time reconciliation they had, but Peter is certain that he is the father. Bobby has paternity problems of his own, wondering about Charlie's real identity. Jenna has always been vague about who was Charlie's father, and Bobby now understands that this issue has to be resolved.

"I was just kind of thinking," Bobby tells Jenna, "that since Christopher's adopted, it'd be kind of funny if Charlie really were mine; she'd be my only blood child. The more you won't talk about who her father is, the more I really believe I am."

TRUE CONFESSIONS
by David Paulsen

In her relentless pursuit to find out who Charlie's real father is, Katherine has finally tracked down Renaldo Marchetta in California. Naldo then flies to Dallas to see Jenna. He asks to meet with her and Bobby while Charlie is out of the house.

Before Sue Ellen left the hospital, she explained to Peter that they never could have had a life together whether he was the baby's father or not. She ends their relationship tartly, but Peter ends up returning to Southfork as a model for Lucy.

Bobby picks up Christopher
for his regular visit to Southfork.

Clayton's sister Jessica (Alexis Smith)
arrives from London for the wedding.

Naldo explains that he wanted to bring Charlie to Italy to see her grandparents and got her birth certificate for a passport. When he saw her birth certificate, he saw Bobby Ewing's name on it. Bobby is delighted, until Naldo points out that the dates don't match up. A year and a half had passed between Charlie's birth and the last time Jenna and Bobby had seen each other.

"You should be honest with him," Naldo tells Jenna. "Admit to him who the girl's father is."

"One of these things is a lie," Bobby tells Jenna. "Which is it? The name or the date?"

After the confrontation, Naldo meets up with Katherine for his payoff.

AND THE WINNER IS...
by Arthur Bernard Lewis

The sealed government bids for the offshore drilling are finally opened and Cliff discovers that he has been hoodwinked by J.R. into bidding far too much.

Bobby tells Pam that he has stopped seeing Jenna. Pam has not been able to give Mark an answer to his marriage proposal, because she still really loves Bobby. The two of them take Christopher out for ice cream and have a great time. Pam is ambivalent about Mark and asks Bobby's advice.

"Don't expect advice from me," Bobby tells her sadly.

Pam makes up her mind while talking to her sister.

"Katherine, I now know why it's taken me so long to give Mark an answer to his proposal. Bobby is still part of my life. I can't marry another man while I feel this way."

FOOLS RUSH IN
by David Paulsen

Because of J.R.'s deception, Barnes must now raise $260-million to complete the offshore drilling he won the rights to. Cliff goes to Vaughn Leland for a loan, not knowing that Leland too is scheming with J.R.

Ellie and Clayton proceed with their wedding plans. Clayton's sister, Jessica, is invited to come from England, where she lives now. Charlie asks Bobby what's going on with him and her mother, and Katherine makes yet another play for Bobby, hoping that maybe Clayton and Ellie won't be the only ones getting hitched at Southfork. She has more than one reason to want Bobby; J.R. informs her that he made a tape that he will use to finish her off if Bobby and Pam get together again.

"Katherine," he tells her, "do your best because if your best isn't good enough, I'll play Bobby that tape I made.

Remember? You and me in the sack together? And he'll never look at you again."

After overhearing a conversation between Sue Ellen and Peter, J.R. decides to investigate the young man's past.

Pam goes to Houston for a Wentworth board meeting and runs into Mark's doctor, who is desperately trying to reach him. Pam sees the concern in the doctor's face and begs for some information.

"Mark's going to need all the love you can possibly give him in the next few months. I had some tests done . . . he's got a rare disease . . . a form of leukemia. There's nothing we can do. It's irreversible."

THE UNEXPECTED
by Arthur Bernard Lewis

Pam keeps Mark's illness a secret. Katherine pressures her into marrying Mark. "You can't walk out on a dying man," she says.

Pam agrees to marry Mark, more out of pity than out of love. Katherine doesn't care about the reasons; she is thrilled and demands the incriminating tape from J.R., feeling she has fulfilled her half of the deal with J.R. by getting Pam out of his life.

"Today may be the second happiest day of my life," J.R. tells Katherine when he hears her good news about the upcoming Graison nuptials.

Bobby is terribly saddened when he hears of Pam's decision and admits to Jenna that he is torn between his love for Pam and his love for her and Charlie.

Jessica arrives at Southfork for the wedding but does not get along well with Ellie. There's no actual fight, but when Ellie welcomes Jessica to the family, Lady Montford makes her thoughts painfully clear: "Family? I don't think so, Ellie. I wouldn't count on your marrying my brother Clayton. No, I wouldn't count on it at all."

STRANGE ALLIANCES
by Leonard Katzman

J.R. and Jessica get along great and are delighted to find many mutual interests, including the prevention of the marriage of Ellie and Clayton Farlow. Of course, J.R. acts like the perfect son, but Sue Ellen at least knows he's not sincere. Meanwhile, when Jessie, Clayton, and Ellie go out, Jessie does all the talking, mostly offering subtle digs at either her brother or Miss Ellie. Beneath her pleasant exterior she is very similar to J.R. In fact, the two finally get together to form an informal alliance with one plan in mind—to stop the wedding.

Pam is not stopping her wedding. In fact, she begs the doctor not to tell Mark the truth until after the wedding. She thinks Mark won't marry her if he finds out he's dying. Yet, part of her is afraid that her marriage to Mark will end her relationship with Bobby, that she will lose him forever.

"You have to face it, Pam," Katherine reminds her all too quickly, "Bobby is out of your life now."

But that may not really be true.

BLOW UP
by David Paulsen

Mark makes festive plans for the wedding, totally unaware of any health problems. Clayton and Miss Ellie also make wedding plans. J.R. volunteers to be the best man, but Clayton tells him that he's already chosen someone else—Ray. Even Cliff's talking about weddings—he promises Afton a big diamond just like the one Mark gave Pam as soon as his wells come in.

J.R. and Sue Ellen make final preparations for the party they have been planning in Jessica's honor. J.R. decides to invite Peter as Lucy's unofficial date. "I've got a feeling it'll be a night you'll remember," he tells the boy.

Indeed it is. J.R. sets up Sue Ellen and Peter while Lucy is watching. In one glance she understands the whole thing.

"You're interested in girls all right," Lucy says to Peter. "I found that out tonight—and I found out which one you're interested in! How long have you two been having this little affair?"

J.R. jumps to Sue Ellen's defense and reprimands Lucy for her assumptions, labeling her as drunk and sending her to her room. Then he tries to make up to Sue Ellen and asks her to come back to him as his wife.

"I can't, J.R."

Meanwhile, Donna has been observing Jessica and has a bad feeling about her. She talks to Ray and Bobby about it, but they reach no conclusions. J.R., on the other hand, talks to Jessica about her conclusions, and Jessica convinces him that she can yet come up with a way to prevent the wedding.

"Are we thinking along the same lines?" J.R. asks her.

"I doubt it," replies Jessica mysteriously.

TURNING POINT
by Arthur Bernard Lewis

Cliff still doesn't realize that Sly and J.R. have set him up, and that each well he drills is just an effort in futility. He's signed loans at the bank that jeopardize his entire fortune and is in so much trouble he even tries to rifle Afton's bank account.

J.R. is having fun not only with Cliff, but also with Peter and Jessica. First he has the boy busted for possession of cocaine, then he begs Jessica to tell him a secret that can prevent the marriage.

"J.R., I want the marriage stopped as much as you do," Jessica tells him, "but digging into Clayton's past won't do it. He's always been an honorable man."

Clayton senses trouble brewing when Jessica and J.R. become so friendly. He warns his sister to stay away from the eldest Ewing son.

"He's a dangerous man," Clayton informs her. "He's had a private detective checking out my past."

"He won't find out anything," Jessica says smugly. "You don't think I'd be stupid enough to tell J.R. our little secret, do you?"

J.R. overhears their conversation and gets his detective working double time. He desperately wants that secret to stop the wedding.

LOVE STORIES
by Leonard Katzman

To cover herself about the tapes, Katherine confesses to Bobby that she slept with J.R. Bobby tells her that he doesn't care whom she slept with because he thinks of her only as a friend. Rejected and dejected, Katherine gets so drunk that Mark Graison has to take her home. In her pain, Katherine alludes to the "real" reason why Pam is marrying him; although she tries to cover up her indiscretion, she has alerted Mark to a problem.

Mark asks his doctor about it and discovers that he has only a short time left to live. He decides not to marry Pam but to go out like a man, before he can become too ill and feeble and be a burden to anyone.

Later, his plane is reported lost over the Gulf of Mexico.

HUSH, HUSH, SWEET JESSIE
by David Paulsen

Jenna and Bobby are on the verge of announcing their engagement when they find out about Mark's death. They decide to wait with their news until a happier time, although Jenna now fears that Pam will come back into Bobby's life and ruin her chances of ever becoming Mrs. Bobby James Ewing.

J.R. continues his investigation of Clayton and begins putting together a theory that Clayton murdered his wife

Sue Ellen and Peter get to know each other better.

One of Afton's most endearing qualities
is her uncanny ability to size up another
person's true thoughts.

for her fortune in order to save his failing ranch. He goes into Jessica's room to snoop around further. He discovers that Jessie is really Dusty's mother, and that *she* was the one who murdered Clayton's first wife and set fire to the Southern Cross. Realizing that his mother could be in grave danger, J.R. mobilizes Bobby and the rest of the family to find Ellie, Jessie, and Donna.

They discover Donna unconscious in her home. Jessie knocked her out with the telephone before escaping with Ellie to the other side of midnight.

"We've just got to find them. Jessica's already killed once. Who knows what she'll do with Mama!" J.R. says frantically.

END GAME
by Arthur Bernard Lewis

Jessica is tracked down in a motel in Comanche, Texas. Totally out of touch with reality, she is driving to the Southern Cross, where she thinks she still lives with her brother and her son. She gives herself up peacefully to Clayton, and Bobby and J.R. discover Miss Ellie in Jessica's trunk—bound and gagged, but otherwise unharmed.

Cliff is in such desperate financial ruin that he agrees to sell his share of Wentworth Tool & Die to Katherine. Although it's valued at $25 million, Katherine will pay only $18 million, just enough to cover one loan payment to the bank and one week's drilling in the offshore tract. Afton points out to Cliff that there's something wrong with his crew, because everyone else has hit oil in their adjoining tracts. Cliff turns on her, telling her she doesn't know what she's talking about. Cliff finally realizes that Afton's notion that J.R. has sabotaged the crew is a possibility. He changes crews and begs the bank for more time, using Mark Graison's death as an excuse.

Cliff comes to believe that he has lost everything, that J.R. has finally totally ruined him. Just then his well comes in—with a big one, a real gusher. But no one can find Cliff to tell him the good news. He has passed out drunk in his car, unable to cope with his mistakes and failures. He has no idea that he is now one of the richest oilmen in Dallas.

KILLER AT LARGE
by Arthur Bernard Lewis

Afton is shocked to discover Bobby's body on the floor of J.R.'s office. Bobby was in J.R.'s office to see if his telephone had been bugged, like all the other phones in the office. While Bobby lies unconscious in the hospital, J.R. realizes that he was the gunman's target.

Cliff finally finds out about his new-found riches. He also finds out that he might have shot Bobby. He certainly had every reason in the world to want to shoot J.R., and he doesn't really know where he was the night before.

"I think you went to the Ewing offices to kill J.R. and you shot Bobby by mistake," Afton tells Cliff.

"That's ridiculous," Cliff responds. "Is that why you went there? To stop me? I hope you didn't tell the police this crazy story, I could be in a lot of trouble."

Bobby comes to, but he is left blind. The doctors do not know if he will be permanently blind, or if he will regain his sight in a matter of time.

BATTLE LINES
by Arthur Bernard Lewis

Bobby confesses to Donna and Ray that he was in J.R.'s office to check out the phones, and, further, that he doesn't trust his brother while he is blind and in the hospital. Donna agrees to take over Bobby's share of the workload at Ewing Oil; she's qualified to step in and is more than anxious to keep a watchful eye on J.R. J.R. is outraged that Bobby would do such a thing.

"Don't get too comfortable in Bobby's chair," J.R. tells Donna, "you're not going to be there long, darlin'."

Jenna's worst fears come true as she sees her chances of marrying Bobby becoming as dim as his eyesight. Despite her protests, Bobby refuses to marry her while he is blind. "Jenna," he tells her, "unless I can see again, we can't get married."

The question of who fired the shot is still not solved. J.R. thinks maybe it was Sue Ellen, still angry at the way he framed Peter. When the gun that was used is found in Cliff's townhouse, Cliff Barnes is arrested for attempted murder.

IF AT FIRST YOU DON'T SUCCEED
by David Paulsen

Bobby decides to undergo risky surgery that could restore his eyesight. Before the operation, J.R. comes to his room for some brotherly confessions.

(left)

Lucy gets a job as a waitress at the same greasy spoon where her mom used to work—but with less success.

"Guilt has never been one of my strong emotions," the older brother tells the younger, "you probably know that better than anybody. But since Barnes shot you, I've been feeling a lot of guilt and if I could, Bobby, I'd change places with you in a minute. I was responsible for the whole thing. The night before you were shot I went to his office and told him how big a fool I'd been playing him for. Oh Bobby, I can't tell you how sorry I am."

Not as sorry as the police, who are forced to release Cliff after a lady of the evening provides his needed alibi. Once Cliff is off the hook, it's obvious the killer is still at large.

A maniacal Katherine enters Bobby's room dressed as a nurse.

JAMIE
by David Paulsen

Just as Katherine is about to give Bobby a fatal injection, he wakes up and begins to scream. The noise brings J.R. back into Bobby's room, where he is able to stop Katherine. "Call the Dallas police," he shouts to a hospital guard. "I think she tried to kill my brother. I also think she's the one who took those shots at me and hit Bobby by mistake."

Katherine becomes hysterical and confesses.

"Mistake? There was no mistake! I love him, don't you understand that? I love him! He doesn't want me. He wants Jenna and, before that, he wanted Pam. Sweet, darling Pam, whom everybody adores. Well they're not going to have him—neither one of them. Don't you see? They poisoned his mind against me to keep me away but they're not going to have him. I'll see to it because if I can't have him, nobody can."

Bobby's eyesight returns, and Jenna feels relieved to think she will finally be marrying him. Bobby returns to work and Southfork.

Just as life is returning to normal, Southfork gets a new visitor.

"This is the Ewing ranch? You must be J.R. Ewing."

"That's right, and who are you?"

"Jamie Ewing. Jason's daughter. My daddy and your daddy were brothers."

FAMILY
by Leonard Katzman

Jamie arrives at Southfork with news that her father, Jason, was Jock's estranged brother who just died in Alaska. She is penniless and had nowhere else to go. Miss Ellie

Bobby is shot, but J.R. thinks he was the target.

The Ewing extended family look
with amazement and dismay
as ragamuffin cousin Jamie Ewing
comes up the drive at Southfork.

gives Jamie a guest room and welcomes her to the family; J.R. wants proof that Jamie isn't a fraud. He drills her over the dinner table, trying to find out if she really knows anything about the oil business. But Jamie one-ups J.R.

"How many producing wells are at the Kenai right now?" she asks him sweetly.

J.R. guesses wrong; Jamie wins a toast from the rest of the family for standing up to him.

Later J.R. tries to buy Jamie away from the ranch. "How much will it take for you to drop this stupid act and get out of here?" he asks her.

But Jamie refuses him.

J.R. suggests to Sue Ellen that she spy on Jamie and try to draw her out so J.R. can check up on her background.

SHADOW OF A DOUBT
by Leonard Katzman

Pam is shocked when she sees Mark's car being driven in Dallas. She goes to his house and discovers that his will provides for the total maintenance of his home and possessions—polo ponies and all—for two years after his death. Pam decides that Mark must be alive. Her renewed interest in finding Mark leaves Bobby convinced that he doesn't have a chance with her, so he finally makes wedding plans with Jenna. Jenna wants to get married immediately, lest something go wrong, but Bobby asks her to wait until Ellie returns from her honeymoon so that she can help plan a big Southfork wedding.

Jamie and J.R. continue their feud, fueled by the fact that Sue Ellen has taken such an interest in the girl. Sue Ellen buys her a new wardrobe at Jenna's boutique; J.R. is not pleased.

"What are we going to do next? Cap the girl's teeth?"

J.R. tells Sue Ellen that he'll never consider the girl a Ewing.

HOMECOMING
by Arthur Bernard Lewis

J.R. tells Bobby that he is concerned about Pam's new power and wealth and the fact that Barnes–Wentworth has been hiring away his executives. The man is downright worried about Cliff becoming a worthy adversary.

"Mark Graison's will hasn't been probated yet; when it is, Pam could come into a substantial fortune, which she'd add to the fortune she got when her Mama died. I tell you, that woman has a knack for piling up unearned dollars."

But the only thing on Pam's mind is the fact that Mark could be alive, seeking medical help somewhere, and

planning to come back. To further convince her, she talks to Mark's doctor, who was also his best friend; she comes away convinced that Mark did not have the kind of personality that would allow him to kill himself.

Clayton and Ellie return from their honeymoon. Bobby thinks that Jock's portrait should be moved out of the house and into the office but J.R. is very sensitive about anything of his father's being touched. Clayton comes to realize that living at Southfork, he is living with Jock's wife, Jock's sons, and Jock's ghost.

OIL BARON'S BALL III
by David Paulsen

Ellie recognizes the pressure that Clayton is under by living in Jock's shadow and makes a few moves to put him more at ease. She treats him to a night out at a hotel and later surprises him with a new bedroom suite.

The family attends the annual Oil Baron's Ball and J.R. meets the very attractive Mandy Winger, who he can't believe is Cliff's date.

Although Jenna and Bobby are in the throes of their wedding plans, no specific date has been set, and J.R. worries that Pam might still have a chance. To make sure the wedding goes on, J.R. takes things into his own hands. He takes the microphone at the ball and announces, "Ladies and Gentlemen, may I have your attention please. This is the happiest night of my life, and I want to share this with you. A long time ago, my brother Bobby was going to announce his engagement right here at the Oil Baron's Ball. Unfortunately, that announcement never occurred. But tonight . . . tonight is a different story. I am delighted to tell you that, one month from today, my brother Bobby is going to marry his childhood sweetheart—the one girl that he has loved all his life—and that's Jenna Wade!"

SHADOWS
by David Paulsen

Bobby is angry at J.R. for taking matters into his own hands. "If I wanted to announce my wedding plans, I'd have done it myself," he tells J.R. "It was a lousy and insensitive thing to do and you did it to embarrass Pam in front of all those people at the ball."

Jamie tells Sue Ellen that she appreciates everything that's been done for her; however, she can't spend her life shopping and going to the hairdresser. She really wants to get a job.

Pam continues her relentless pursuit of information on Mark, especially now that Bobby has made his marriage plans official. "I know everyone thinks I'm crazy to go on looking for Mark. Well, I'm not. He may be alive out there somewhere, and if he is and he's sick and alone, he needs me more than ever. I don't care what anybody thinks! I'm going to go on looking. And if he *is* alive, I'm going to find him."

Naldo surfaces again and makes an appointment to see Jenna. He confesses that it was Katherine Wentworth who paid him to do what he did to help break up Bobby and Jenna a year ago. "No matter how unpleasant that birth certificate business was, I'm not completely sorry it happened. It brought us together again, and it made me realize how much I have missed the daughter I had never seen. I intend to see her. I will do anything I have to do to make that happen."

CHARLIE
by Leonard Katzman

Jenna tells Bobby that she saw Naldo and explains the part that Katherine played in the birth certificate mess. Then she confesses that she is really worried that Naldo will make trouble.

Bobby confronts Naldo and tries to buy him a one-way ticket out of their lives. "I will not leave without my daughter and you cannot stop me," Naldo tells Bobby.

Jenna decides to tell Charlie that Naldo is her real father.

When Charlie disappears, Jenna is certain that Naldo has kidnapped their daughter. But it turns out that Charlie is in the stable with her horse. She ran away because she was upset by Jenna's news.

"I always wanted you to be my daddy, Bobby," Charlie tells him.

"Well, I will be, honey. Your mama and I are going to be married, and the three of us will be a family; then you'll be the daughter I always wanted to have. I love you very much."

BARBECUE FIVE
by Arthur Bernard Lewis

Sue Ellen gets Jamie a job at Ewing Oil as a receptionist. J.R. isn't thrilled, but at least he can keep his eye on the girl now.

J.R. also wants to keep an eye on Mandy Winger, so he brings her flowers and begins the famous J.R. seduction. J.R. is especially interested in the woman because of her relationship to Cliff.

Jenna takes Charlie to meet Naldo, who is intent on charming his daughter back into his life. Jenna still thinks it's a big mistake. Naldo continues to see Charlie, and he

announces to Jenna that he plans on marrying her to re-unite his family.

Meanwhile, J.R. is doing everything to un-reunite his family. He kicks Jamie out: "Pack your stuff and get the hell out," he tells her menacingly. But Jamie has one more ace. She reveals a document that divides Ewing Oil between the original partners—Jock, Digger, and Jason.

DO YOU TAKE THIS WOMAN...
by Leonard Katzman

J.R. is astounded by the papers that Jamie has unveiled and hopes to prove them forgeries. Jamie hadn't shown them before because she wasn't planning on cashing in on them; it was only when J.R. got so nasty that she thought it was time to go into action. Jamie goes to Cliff to help her prove the document is legal. Cliff, of course, couldn't be more pleased. J.R. is not thrilled, but doesn't want anyone to know he's nervous.

"I don't know what came over that poor girl," he tells Jeremy Wendell with mock sincerity. "I brought her into my home, bought her a lot of nice clothes . . . I even gave her a job at my office, and then she embarrasses me like that. But I saw through it right away. It was just a little prank, that's all."

Naldo continues seeing Charlie and gives her a cameo that has been in his family for several generations. He talks of one day taking her back to Italy to see his family, but Jenna protests to his "filling the girl's head with all that nonsense."

Sensing that something could go wrong with Naldo, Jenna begins driving Charlie to and from school. But Naldo kidnaps Charlie before Jenna can pick her up from school one day. Jenna's worst fears are realized. On the day of the wedding, she stands Bobby up for the second time, leaving behind a note:

"Bobby, I'm sorry. I know you can't understand why I'm doing this, but I hope you somehow can forgive me. I can't marry you. As much as I love you, I love someone else more . . . and I'm doing what I must."

DÉJÀ VU
by David Paulsen

J.R. calls Southfork from Jenna's condo to tell Sue Ellen that there won't be a wedding. Ray makes the announcement: "Folks, we don't have all the details yet, but there seems to be some kind of problem. I'm afraid the wedding's going to have to be postponed."

J.R. and Bobby head out after Marchetta, certain that Jenna has run off with him again. They don't know that

(*right*)
Charlie is found hiding in the barn;
she later confesses that she wishes
Bobby was her real father.

Pam runs full-page newspaper ads trying to find
the missing Mark Graison, who may or may not
have been killed in a plane crash.

J.R. is tickled pink at Jenna and Bobby's lovin'. He'll finally be rid of Pam.

Jenna moves into Southfork as a permanent fixture in Bobby's life.

Charlie has been kidnapped. Jenna realizes that the only way she can see her daughter again is to play along with Naldo.

Naldo finally contacts Bobby and gives him instructions for a meeting. When Bobby shows up, he discovers that Jenna has just remarried Naldo.

ODD MAN OUT
by Arthur Bernard Lewis

Naldo rapes Jenna on their wedding night, with Jenna screaming at him, "Stay away from me or I'll kill you!" Unfortunately, the motel manager hears her threats, so when Naldo is found dead, Jenna is in a lot of trouble.

J.R. tries to convince Pam that Bobby is as broken up over Jenna's disappearance as Pam has been over Mark's. "Bobby has vowed to find her just like you've vowed to find Mark Graison," J.R. tells her. "I just think it's ironic that you're both searching for people you love."

In fact, Bobby is more hurt over Jenna's action than distraught. He proposes a toast that no one in the family mention Jenna's name again and then toasts "the life she's chosen for herself . . . wherever she is . . . whomever she's with."

He doesn't know that at that moment, she's with a dead man.

LOCKUP IN LAREDO
by David Paulsen

Jenna is arrested for Naldo's murder and sent to jail in Laredo. With her one phone call, she calls the Ewings for help. They rally to her side.

Jenna's attorney, Scott Demerest, thinks that Jenna might have been chloroformed, which is why she doesn't remember what really happened. Scotty also thinks that on the other hand it is just possible that his client did murder her husband.

But Jenna's main concern is to find her daughter. Worried that she will skip town to find Charlie, the judge refuses to set bail. Bobby volunteers to put up one or two million dollars, but the judge feels the Ewings can easily take that kind of loss and that therefore Jenna must remain in jail without bail.

Meanwhile, Donna and Ray go to Austin to dig through Sam Culver's papers. They find a diary notation that supports Jamie's claim to part of Ewing Oil.

WINDS OF WAR
by Leonard Katzman

Jenna's attorney informs Bobby that the police have discovered a complete set of Jenna's fingerprints on the murder weapon. Then Marchetta's accomplice, Veronica, calls Bobby to ransom off Charlie. Bobby agrees to meet her in California with $50,000 in cash for the safe return of the girl.

J.R. tries to shove Jamie around a little more, but she fights back by telling him, in front of Sue Ellen, that she saw him snuggling with another woman. Sue Ellen is so upset that she goes off the wagon again.

Cliff realizes that J.R. has been wooing Mandy in order to transmit false information to him, just as he used to with Sly. But Cliff finds a better ally—Jamie—who is willing to help him destroy J.R.

BAIL OUT
by David Paulsen

Jenna is finally released on bail and moves into the Southfork guest house. Bobby wants to get married quietly, but Jenna says she can't think of marriage until her trial is over.

Pam discovers that she has been sent on a wild goose chase by J.R., who left a trail of tips indicating that Mark was alive and in a Caribbean clinic.

Pam confesses to Bobby that the only reason she was going to marry Mark was that she didn't want him to have to face the end of his life alone. Bobby reminds Pam that because of the murder charge she faces, Jenna really needs him now.

Cliff tells Mandy that he and Jamie are going into partnership to work out a strategy so they can claim their shares of Ewing Oil.

LEGACY OF HATE
by Arthur Bernard Lewis

Furious that J.R.'s meddling in her life has again successfully kept her and Bobby from getting back together, Pam joins forces with Jamie and Cliff to take their two-thirds of Ewing Oil away from J.R.

She pays a call on J.R. at the office and tells him just what she thinks:

"Cliff and your cousin Jamie want to split up Ewing Oil and they asked me to join their fight, but I said I wouldn't because of Bobby. Well, that won't stop me anymore. You have no heart—you have no feelings. You can't be hurt like other people. But you do have one soft spot, one weakness, and that's Ewing Oil. I'm going to join Cliff and I'm going to back him up all the way; Cliff and Jamie and I are going to take your company away from you. And then I'm going to watch you hurt."

Mandy feels guilty and unhappy about herself and her position—she's slept with J.R. and continues to spy on Cliff for him even though she realizes they're both using her.

SINS OF THE FATHERS
by Leonard Katzman

Cliff, Jamie, and Pam serve injunction papers on Ewing Oil and try to freeze Ewing assets until a judge can rule on the validity of Jamie's document. J.R. is beside himself. "Cliff Barnes and that little traitor he's working with don't stand one chance in a million of getting a hold of my company," he fumes.

When the judge at the injunction hearing rules in favor of the plaintiff, J.R. decides to try secretly to remove some of the assets out of the company in order to invest money in a dummy corporation.

To try to sort out who really owns Ewing Oil, J.R. locates Alf Brindle, a man who worked the discovery rig with Jock, Jason, and Digger. He brings him up to Dallas and invites Pam, Jamie, and Cliff to a meeting. Alf reports that Jason tried to steal everything from Digger but that Jock sorted it all out and always stood by Digger. J.R. proposes that Brindle testify in court so the world knows that Jock never cheated Digger out of anything. Then Brindle pulls out an old document that he's kept for Digger all these years—a match to Jamie's.

"Jock was always saying he was afraid something might happen to him and that Jason would take over. He made out this paper so that nobody could cheat Digger out of his third of the company."

"Would you swear to that in court?" Cliff asks Brindle.

"Of course I would."

THE BROTHERS EWING
by David Paulsen

Clayton is angry at the way J.R. handled Brindle. "If you had been more careful, this wouldn't have happened," he tells his stepson.

J.R. does not want to hear criticism from Clayton or anyone else and makes it clear that he'll tolerate no lectures. He continues to transfer Ewing assets into dummy corporations, and then swaps them with worthless tracts of land. He asks Clayton to help by trading in some of his land. Clayton refuses, considering the scheme too dirty and unethical. Ellie backs up her husband, much to the dismay of the boys.

J.R. turns to Sue Ellen for comfort, but she rejects him outright. He then turns to Mandy: "The truth is, I miss you," he tells her.

Her attorney works to get Jenna a change of venue because of all the pre-trial publicity. "I'm not saying I can get you off," he tells Jenna, "but I'd feel much better arguing the case in front of a Dallas jury than one from Laredo."

Donna goes to Miss Ellie to tell her how upset she is that Ray has been siding against Clayton. Suddenly he's become very involved in the oil company and Donna feels terrible about it, especially since Ray has now made it clear that he's on J.R.'s team.

"Look Donna, I'm not naive," Ellie says. "I know J.R. very well. And I know that he's capable of doing all sorts of things. And somehow this time I'm hoping that because of what's at stake, he'll act differently."

Pam leaves Dallas for Hong Kong to follow a lead that Mark Graison had been seen in a clinic there. Sue Ellen, who has wanted to see the Orient since childhood, decides to go along. Before she leaves, she tells J.R. that if he's set up another wild goose chase he'll soon regret it.

SHATTERED DREAMS
by Arthur Bernard Lewis

Donna and Ray continue to squabble over his involvement with J.R. and J.R.'s unethical schemes to save Ewing Oil from any possible split. Clayton, who until now had been so close to Ray, advises him to get out of the struggle.

"It's really Bobby and J.R.'s fight. You never had anything to do with that company. What happens if you lose the case? Are you ready to deal with that kind of defeat? Right now you and Bobby and J.R. are real close. Just how long do you think J.R. is going to consider you a real full-fledged Ewing brother when this case is over? About twenty seconds!"

The judge grants a change of venue for Jenna's trial, and Veronica Robinson, Naldo's accomplice in Charlie's kidnapping, agrees to testify for Jenna. With her testimony, Jenna might get off. Then Veronica is found dead in the airplane lavatory.

DEAD ENDS
by Leonard Katzman

An autopsy reveals that Veronica was a heavy drug user. Bobby thinks that perhaps whoever killed Naldo and Veronica was a drug dealer. Jenna sinks into depression. "Veronica was my last hope," she sighs.

J.R. hires a detective to look into Jason's background. He finds out just about everything he can about Jason, including information about Jamie and her brother, Jack, who had a falling out with his father five years earlier and disappeared.

Pam and Sue Ellen tour Hong Kong, where Pam goes to a clinic to see a man named Swanson who is supposed to be Mark; he refuses to see her.

Jenna Wade stands trial for the murder of her ex-husband, Renaldo Marchetta.

Jack Ewing shows up in Dallas after he discovers his sister Jamie has found family there.

Bobby and Pam know it will never really be over between them.

(left)

Alf Brindle (played by Eddie Firestone) reveals a whole new version of the back story—so new that David Jacobs had to readjust his own script so the threads would match up in the televised prequel, called *The Early Years*.

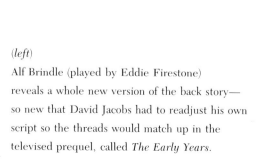

"Mr. Swanson has told me that he does not want to see you or anyone. He did not tell me his reasons. He is now in remission; his condition has not worsened since he came to visit us," says a clinic spokesman. "Mrs. Ewing, there is no guarantee that this man, whoever he is, is ever going to get any better. I've explained everything to him but he still insists that he will not see you. I think you should go back to the United States. This is a long way to come for no results, and I am sorry, but I will honor Mr. Swanson's wishes."

Pam disguises herself as a nurse and bribes someone to take her to see Mr. Swanson. It is not a pretty sight.

TRIAL AND ERROR
by David Paulsen

Pam tells Sue Ellen that the man she found at the clinic wasn't Mark, and she's ready to give up the search. But after returning to Dallas, she suspects that once again J.R. is behind her misery. Sadly, she accepts the fact that Mark must be dead.

Mandy tells J.R. she is becoming more and more emotionally involved with him and wants out of their relationship. J.R. says, "Mandy, I don't think you realize how much you mean to me. I'd do almost anything to keep from losing you. Just give me a little time. It'll work out."

Donna strikes oil on her small tract, but the news only increases the tension between her and Ray. Eventually, she decides to move out.

"I don't need her success," Ray tells Clayton bitterly, "I need a wife."

Cliff is having more success in the romance department. Since going to work at Barnes–Wentworth as an expert in cold-weather drilling, Jamie has made herself more than helpful to Cliff. She even provides him with a constant supply of Chinese take-out. "I get the feeling I have spent my entire life with the wrong women," he tells her. "You're what I'm looking for. You know what's important in life. You know what a man needs."

The case of Jenna Wade, 85-19478, is tried in criminal court. The district attorney tells the jury, "Jenna Wade did indeed commit murder, and I shall ask that she be punished to the fullest extent of the law."

Bobby is unexpectedly called as a witness against Jenna, and Veronica's sister reveals that she has information that will clear Jenna, but she will not come forward with it because she fears that she too will be murdered.

THE VERDICT
by David Paulsen

Bobby tracks down Ann McFadden, Veronica's sister.

Ann says she destroyed the information, a letter that her sister wrote her. Bobby doesn't believe it.

"Ann, I know that you are afraid. But I also know that you're a decent person and you wouldn't let an innocent woman go to jail. Call me."

Ann finally agrees to give the letter to Bobby.

The letter is read in court; it reports that whoever killed Naldo is now after Veronica. The prosecution tries to discredit the evidence because Veronica has already been proven to be a kidnapper and an extortionist.

The jury finds Jenna not guilty of murder but guilty of voluntary manslaughter.

SENTENCES
by Arthur Bernard Lewis

Jenna is sentenced to seven years in jail. Bobby announces that he is Charlie's real father—after all, her birth certificate says so—to prevent her from becoming a ward of the state while her mother is in prison. J.R. uses this technicality to hurt Pam even more and drive yet another wedge between the couple; he is afraid that with Jenna in jail Bobby may return to Pam.

Sue Ellen returns from the Orient and makes it clear to J.R. that although he can sleep with anyone he wants, she is outraged at the public stand he takes with Mandy. She threatens to divorce him again.

Other couples at Southfork are having their troubles too: Ray wants Donna to come back; Lucy has Mitch on her mind again. Things are going better for Cliff and Jamie, who admit they are very interested in each other. Another Ewing–Barnes romance, it's almost a Bobby and Pam story in reverse.

TERMS OF ESTRANGEMENT
by Peter Dunne

When J.R. realizes how dangerous Jamie and Cliff would be as a team, he decides to get Pam and Bobby back together again. He now thinks Pam can be more useful as a sister-in-law than ever before.

Bobby discovers enough new information about Veronica's death to get Jenna's case reopened.

Jamie has a heart-to-heart talk with Sue Ellen. She tells her it's time for Sue Ellen to stop blaming J.R. for her problems. "As long as J.R. Ewing is your husband, it's your problem. Burying your head in the sand is no solution. Blaming other women is not fair. You have to do something for yourself, and when you realize that, you can count on me for help."

Sue Ellen acknowledges the truth in Jamie's argument

and takes a class in self-awareness. She has a lot to learn, since J.R. has become especially abusive. He tells her plainly that he thinks she's a loser.

Jamie agrees to marry Cliff; soon thereafter, her brother, Jack, comes to town.

"Why don't you just crawl back to where you came from?" Jamie asks him.

"I'm sorry you feel that way," Jack says with his easy smile, "because I kind of like it here in Dallas. I'll see you around, Sis."

THE EWING CONNECTION
by Arthur Bernard Lewis

Jamie confides to Pam and Cliff that her brother has surfaced. "I haven't seen him in years, and while I was packing up my things, he just walked into my apartment. He's a natural-born con artist and I don't put anything past him."

Jamie is right on target. Without fully identifying himself, Jack has already been to J.R. to make a deal—offering information in exchange for 10 percent of Ewing Oil. As they are in the middle of negotiations, J.R. tells him that no one but a Ewing will ever own part of the company. Jack agrees with him, then introduces himself.

"I tell you," J.R. marvels, "there's nothing like the smell of money to get the relatives out of the woodwork. Why didn't you tell me who you were the other night? Do you have any way of proving who you are?"

Jack shows his passport, then tells his tale. He claims to have proof that neither Jason nor Digger has any claim at all to Ewing Oil. This proof he'll only give after 10 percent of the company is signed over to him.

Harv Smithfield draws up the papers. Bobby and J.R. agree that since they own the biggest shares of Ewing, they should each kick in 5 percent. Jack promises to produce a man who will solve everyone's problems.

"This better not be a con job," J.R. warns.

DEEDS AND MISDEEDS
by David Paulsen

Sue Ellen is out of the house when John Ross has to be rushed to the hospital for an emergency appendectomy. J.R. turns vicious and claims she is an unfit mother. His verbal attack sends her back to the bottle. Secretly, J.R. is thrilled he was able to push Sue Ellen to drink. He sees it as a way to get her out of his life permanently so that he can finally have Mandy.

Jack assures Bobby, J.R., and Ray that Jamie doesn't know her papers won't hold up in court. He takes everyone to California to meet a man named Windham.

Donna tries to tell Ray that she is pregnant but his anger over her oil wells gets in the way and he abruptly tells her he has no time to talk—he's off to California with his brothers.

Cliff and Jamie are married in an impromptu ceremony inspired by Cliff's need to be able to cut Jack out of the family inheritance. "It's very sudden," Pam notes. "Are you sure about this, Cliff?"

"I'm tired of being single," Cliff assures her with a twinkle in his eye.

Lucy flies to Atlanta to see Mitch and is very impressed by what he has become. She hopes her new maturity impresses him too. Meanwhile, in California the Ewings are meeting with Windham, who tells them that the legal documents they need to prove Digger and Jason were out of the partnership are probably with Jock's first wife, Amanda.

Amanda, who has been in a mental institution for the past forty years, is convinced that Bobby is Jock and that time has stood still, so she readily produces the papers she has been safekeeping.

"I think Cliff Barnes and Jamie Ewing are up the creek without a paddle," J.R. announces after looking over the documents.

DELIVERANCE
by Peter Dunne

Clayton suggests that J.R. tell Cliff about the documents so that Barnes will drop the suit. But J.R. isn't so chivalrous. In fact, he aggravates the feud to make sure they will see their day in court. J.R. is anxious to once again make a fool of Barnes.

J.R. realizes that to ask Cliff to drop the suit is one sure way to ensure that Barnes will continue the fight with vigor.

"Drop the suit?" Cliff asks the eldest Ewing incredulously. "Are you kidding? Not on your life. I've got proof that two-thirds of Ewing Oil doesn't even belong to you. I've got you by the throat. And I'm not going to let go. I want this to go on public record. I want everybody to know how Jock Ewing did my Daddy in. And I'm going to sit there and watch you squirm while I do it."

Jenna languishes in jail while Bobby works to find the real killer. He successfully sets a trap, and the right man confesses, but Bob also has a confession to make: he knows that his heart really belongs to Pamela.

Mitch and Lucy find their love has held up over the years as well. Mitch asks Lucy to move to Atlanta to live with him so they can try it again on a less legal basis.

The Barneses and Ewings go to court. Windham testifies that when Ewing Oil was suffering financial setbacks in the 1930s, Digger and Jason wanted out, so Windham bought their shares. Then Windham sold them back to Jock. He shows the documents that back up his statements. The Ewings move for dismissal of the case.

SWAN SONG
by Leonard Katzman

The Ewings throw a celebration for the whole family. Even Jenna, who has finally been cleared and released from jail, is there, as well as Lucy and Mitch. But the celebrating proves to be too much for Sue Ellen, who passes out dead drunk. J.R. rushes to Mandy's arms.

"I gave Sue Ellen every chance in the world to be a good wife. The die is cast now. There's no going back. You and I are going to have the kind of relationship that you've always wanted," he tells her.

Pam worries that Jenna's being out of jail and back at Southfork will ruin her relationship with Bobby. "One of the things I love about you," she tells him, "is your sense of honor. I mean, how could you not marry her? You're really obligated."

Lucy and Mitch's wedding at Southfork reminds Bobby that it's sort of a Ewing tradition to remarry. Both J.R. and Lucy have married the same person twice. Bobby suggests that he and Pam follow this pattern.

"I think Jenna knows how I feel. She's just going to have to understand. It'll be better for her than being married to a man who's in love with someone else. If you still love me, if you'll have me, I want to marry you. We don't have to live at Southfork. It can be anywhere you want to . . . as long as we're together. Will you marry me again?"

"Oh yes, yes. I want you so much. I thought I'd lost you forever."

Bobby spends the night, and he and Pam begin making plans to remarry and reunite their family. In the morning, Bobby leaves Pam's to head back to Southfork. A car comes careening across the driveway toward Pam with deadly intent. Bobby leaps across the gravel to knock Pam to safety. The driver hits him instead. He rolls across the top of the car and onto the driveway. Pam cradles him in her arms while screaming in agony a silent "Noooooo!"

The car crashes; the driver, Katherine, is killed instantly.

Bobby James Ewing dies a few hours later at Dallas Memorial Hospital.

"All that wasted time," he whispered to Pam before he died, "we should have been married."

THE FAMILY EWING
by Leonard Katzman

The Ewings gather at Southfork to bury Bobby. At Pam's house, Cliff and Jamie try to comfort her. Pam blames herself. Only Miss Ellie seems able to cope—she draws up lists of things to be done and begins to plan the funeral.

"Don't bury the pain inside, Ellie," Clayton tells her.

Gary returns to Southfork and provides a shoulder for Ellie to lean on. After all these years, Gary has found himself and is able to provide solace to his mother.

She decides to bury Bobby on a beautiful green hill overlooking Southfork, near a tree house where the Ewing boys played as children.

Bobby James Ewing, 1948–1985. Rest in peace.
After the funeral J.R. would lament that he never got to tell his brother how much he really loved him.

"Of all the places on Southfork where he used to play, this was his favorite," she tells Clayton. "Gary used to come out here with him. When the other boys were playing, J.R. was learning from Jock, but I think he would have traded everything if he could have been the one that Jock built the tree house for."

Sue Ellen, who learned of Bobby's death after everyone else, goes on a bender. Dusty wants to take care of her, and J.R. seems more than happy to get Sue Ellen out of his life. "You just go in the house, throw Sue Ellen over your shoulder, and carry her the hell out of Southfork," he tells Dusty. Ellie tries to explain to Sue Ellen that she is an alcoholic, and Dusty cannot offer her the kind of help she needs, but Sue Ellen takes offense at the speech. She leaves the ranch and goes right to a bar. Dusty follows her there and drags her away.

Dusty explains to Sue Ellen that he still loves her, that he will help her dry out. His main goal is to get her in shape for Bobby's funeral.

The funeral is a small family event. The ceremony is short and simple. Most of the family members move away and return to the house, leaving J.R. alone with the casket. He speaks to Bobby.

"Never really told you how much you meant to me. All the fights, all that time buttin' heads with one another... I'm sorry we were never friends. I wish I'd taken time to tell you that I loved you... I do... and you tell Daddy I love him too. Good-bye, Bobby. I miss you!"

ROCK BOTTOM
by Joel J. Feigenbaum

Sue Ellen has a sudden change of heart as she and Dusty leave the ranch. She tells him it was a mistake for her to walk out and that she plans to go back. J.R. is not impressed with her return. His harsh rejection turns her, once again, to alcohol. She jumps in her car and roars off to the nearest bar. After downing too much vodka, Sue Ellen is too drunk to drive. She attracts a man who volunteers to take her home and then robs her of her Mercedes. The next morning, without purse, identification, or any sense of herself, Sue Ellen wanders through an unfamiliar part of town. A bag lady offers her a drink, but Sue Ellen disdainfully rejects the offer.

Clayton and Ellie worry about Sue Ellen and go off to look for her.

"Every time she drinks, her chances only get worse," Ellie tells Clayton.

"We don't know that she's been drinking."

"Don't we?"

But Ellie can't devote herself entirely to Sue Ellen's problems—Bobby's will must be read. The family is shocked to discover that Bobby has left his share of Ewing Oil to Christopher, in Pam's trust. J.R. can't believe he may have to be in partnership with Pam, while Cliff wants nothing more than to arrange for Pam to sell her shares—to him.

Only Mandy gives J.R. the understanding he needs. But Mandy does worry about the fact that J.R. is still a married man.

"I have a feeling," J.R. says to her, "a very strong feeling, that the Sue Ellen problem is going to take care of itself."

Indeed, Sue Ellen has returned to the bag lady she once shunned and now greedily shares her bottle of cheap wine.

THOSE EYES
by Peter Dunne

Clayton and Ellie intensify their search for Sue Ellen, who Ellie feels very strongly must be in trouble.

Meanwhile, J.R. considers his own troubles. He can't believe that he may end up in business with the person he hates the most—his former sister-in-law, Pam. J.R. offers to buy Christopher's shares of Ewing Oil, and Jeremy Wendell of Weststar works with Cliff to convince his sister to sell her Ewing Oil shares to them. Pam is truly torn between wanting to do the right thing for Christopher and wondering what Bobby would want her to do.

Clayton and Ellie finally find Sue Ellen. She has been moved from the city drunk tank to a detoxification unit. Dusty comes to the "detox" ward and gives Sue Ellen some gentle assurance. "I'm here because I love you, Sue Ellen. I'm here to keep my promise to help you. I want you healthy again. Because I want you."

But Sue Ellen can only beg him for a drink.

As Dusty tries to comfort Sue Ellen, J.R. comes in and finds his wife in her lover's arms. He and Dusty exchange punches while Sue Ellen, traumatized, begins to shake and quake all over. J.R. decides to commit Sue Ellen to a sanitarium.

"It's all right, J.R.," Ellie tells him after he signs the papers. "You've done what had to be done. Someday Sue Ellen will thank you for this."

RESURRECTION
by Hollace White and Stephanie Garman

Ellie begins to wonder if she too should sell her shares of Ewing Oil to Weststar. Although she doesn't want to see the family business come to an end, she also does not want a repeat of the struggle for control that tore Bobby and J.R. apart after Jock's death.

Sue Ellen discovers that she has no choice but to join an alcoholics program at the clinic. When Dusty tries to visit Sue Ellen at the sanitarium he discovers she isn't allowed to have visitors, so he bribes an attendant to let him in. Clayton warns him that his involvement with Sue Ellen is poorly timed, but Dusty seems very determined to make the love affair work out this time.

When her attendant pulls out a flask and offers Sue Ellen a drink—for a price, of course—Sue Ellen is sorely tempted. Then something inside her gives her the strength to turn away. Ferociously, she presses the "call" button and rings for a doctor. The action surprises and enlightens her.

"I can do it!" she says to herself. "I can do it. I just need help."

Cliff continues to pressure his sister to sell to Jeremy Wendell at Weststar, and Pam gets more and more confused. Unable to deal with the business or the decisions she needs to make, Pam runs from the house—and gets quite a shock.

SAVING GRACE
by Joel J. Feigenbaum

Pam runs out of her house and smack into Mark Graison, who she was certain was dead. Trying to recover from her shock, Pam can only tell him, "I don't know whether to laugh or cry."

Mark sweeps Pam away, taking her away from the pressures of having to make a decision and off to try to explain his sudden resurrection. Mark reveals that he was in Hong Kong when Pam went there to search for him, but that he paid someone else to be in his bed—he didn't want her to go on believing that he was alive.

Meanwhile, the other Ewings are trying to sort out what they will do. Weststar has made offers to Ray and to Jack for their shares of Ewing Oil, and Ray warns Jack about J.R. Cliff is also actively courting Jack, who storms out and tells Cliff that he is still uncommitted.

Cliff tries to get Mark behind him in his efforts to convince Pam to sell to Weststar. But Graison does not want to tell Pam what to do. To try to persuade him to take sides, Cliff tells Mark J.R. sent Pam on a wild goose chase from place to place, searching for Mark.

Mark goes to Ewing Oil and punches J.R., then gives him something to think about. "You'll regret the day you sent Pam looking for me. Because she found me. And I'm going to do everything I can to make you suffer the way she suffered. Take a good look around you. This place is going to be nothing but memories before I'm through."

MOTHERS
by Hollace White and Stephanie Garman

Patricia Shepard arrives at Southfork to try to patch things up between J.R. and Sue Ellen and to take control of Sue Ellen's shattered life. Miss Ellie, who doesn't much like Patricia, tells her that she doubts there is anything that the two mothers can do; J.R. and Sue Ellen have had their troubles for a long time now, and it's time that they resolved them on their own. Patricia is even more upset when J.R. tells her straight out that he considers his marriage with Sue Ellen over. Patricia buys a house in nearby Turtle Creek and comes back into her daughter's life.

Sue Ellen is still at the sanitarium, but she has become quite determined to conquer her alcoholism. Through work with a therapist, talking about her childhood and her marriage, she is beginning to understand her dependency problems and the need to take control of her own life.

The other members of the family are going through their own private hells trying to decide whether they should back J.R. or sell their shares of Ewing Oil to Jeremy Wendell at Weststar. Ray suggests to Jack that a third option would be for everyone to vote their shares to Ellie and let her make the big decision. J.R. is so upset with the possibility of losing Ewing Oil that he pleads with Mark Graison to intercede on his behalf, saying that Bobby never meant the company to fall from family hands. But Pam decides to sell to Wendell, telling J.R. that it is a business decision, not a personal one, to protect Christopher's assets. When Ellie learns of Pam's decision, she too makes up her mind to throw in with Weststar.

She goes to the office to tell J.R., but overhears him talking aloud to Bobby. He tells Bobby of his predicament, how much he cares about Ewing Oil, and that perhaps now he will just take John Ross and leave Dallas.

Devastated by the thought of losing J.R. too, Ellie retreats to rethink her stand.

THE WIND OF CHANGE
by Peter Dunne

Ellie tells Clayton of J.R.'s plans to leave Dallas and start life over somewhere else.

"We left him no choice," she says. "He already feels everyone's abandoned him, abandoned Ewing Oil. And without Ewing Oil, there's no reason for him to stay. That's why, for better or worse, I can't sell to Wendell now. I need to save my son, not lose him."

Sue Ellen, who has lost her car, her purse, and her self-possession,
is offered some cheap wine by a bag lady.

J.R. and Dusty fight it out over a hysterical Sue Ellen.

Pam tells Mark that she's not completely certain about her decision anymore. Mark assures her that she can still change her mind.

Sue Ellen is released from the sanitarium to her mother's care, and the two women appear at the Oil Baron's Ball, where they are invited to sit with Ellie and Clayton. Mandy, who had disappeared and left J.R. brokenhearted, reappears at the ball and tells J.R. she'll be there for him. Jack pursues his courtship of Jenna, although some small disturbances have interrupted his life lately—his apartment was broken into and his passport was stolen. Furthermore, unbeknownst to Jack, a woman named Angelica Nero has taken interest in his photograph and identity.

The ball proceeds much like other balls in previous years, with Cliff and J.R. at each other's throats. Jamie is so outraged at learning that Cliff pushed Pam into dealing with Wendell for his own personal gain that she hits him in the face with a pie. She then arranges to leave Cliff and move in with Jack.

The Oil Man of the Year award is made posthumously to Bobby Ewing. As Ellie approaches the podium to accept the award, the crowd rises in a standing ovation. Giving her acceptance speech, Ellie talks about Bobby's uncompromising love of his family and his hopes for his son, Christopher. Then she calls Pam to the podium to accept the award for Christopher. Pam makes her own speech, explaining that she cannot sell Christopher's heritage to Weststar.

"With apologies to those who may not understand my sudden change of heart, I cannot . . . will not sell my son's share of Ewing Oil to Weststar."

Pam then privately tells J.R., "I'm not selling the shares at all. From now on, it's you and me. I'll be seeing you in the office, partner."

QUANDARY
by Joel J. Feigenbaum

Ray and Donna did not attend the ball because they have discovered that their unborn child suffers from Down's Syndrome. They are torn and confused as to their next course of action—Ray is in favor of abortion, Donna is not. Finally Donna is able to persuade Ray to join her in investigating what kind of life their child will have if they go ahead.

Cliff tries to get Jamie to come back; she is almost swayed until she discovers that what Cliff really wants is a date for a dinner engagement with shipping magnate Angelica Nero. Jamie refuses and Cliff is forced to meet with Angelica alone. He is shocked when she begins to pitch to him a very exciting deal.

Angelica has used Cliff as bait to attract J.R. J.R. is happy to woo her and win the deal away from Barnes, never suspecting that she has already chosen Ewing Oil because of her interest in Jack. Angelica arranges the meeting with J.R. at a restaurant where she knows Jack and Jenna will dine so that she can get a good look at her target. Afterward, she confides to her assistant, Grace, that Jack is indeed the man she has been looking for.

Donna and Ray visit a school for handicapped children and come away very impressed. They decide to have the baby, despite the problems ahead.

CLOSE ENCOUNTERS
by Hollace White and Stephanie Garman

Things begin to lighten up at Southfork as the Ewings plan a rodeo. Miss Ellie has decided the annual barbecue would be too painful so soon after Bobby's death, but gives the go-ahead for a rodeo to be held on the ranch. J.R., back into the swing of things at the office, anxiously tries to impress Angelica Nero to swing the deal away from Barnes–Wentworth. When Angelica intimates that she is very interested in Jack, J.R. asks Jack to come into the oil business.

Dusty, who has been trying to press Sue Ellen into marrying him, comes to the rodeo, where Sue Ellen makes it clear that she isn't ready to commit herself. Mandy appears at the rodeo at J.R.'s invitation and is openly flaunted as J.R.'s girlfriend.

While watching the various family members compete in different events, Donna falls from the rail and must be rushed to the hospital.

SUFFER THE LITTLE CHILDREN
by Leonard Katzman

Ray, Ellie, Clayton, and Jenna stand by at the Braddock Emergency Hospital, awaiting medical reports on Donna's condition. The doctor asks Ray if he has to make a choice of which life to save, which one it should be.

"Save my baby if you can," Ray tells him, "but don't let Donna die."

Sue Ellen fights for her own territory with her mother and with Dusty, explaining to Dusty that she loves him but she's not ready to live with him. Patricia is unusually supportive of Sue Ellen's separation from J.R. but does push her daughter to bring John Ross to live with them.

Sue Ellen hires an attorney and begins to fight for custody. J.R. is far from pleased.

"Divorce me . . . go marry that cowboy. Do anything you want," he tells her, "but don't even dream of trying to take my son away from me. Because if you should somehow succeed, there's not enough room in this world to keep you safe from me."

THE PRIZE
by Hollace White and Stephanie Garman

J.R. has hired a detective to check out Angelica Nero and her boss, shipping tycoon Dimitri Marinos, as he becomes more involved in a business deal with Marinos Shipping. When Angelica's associate Nicholas reports that the detective has been snooping around Athens, Angelica decides to close the deal with J.R. as quickly as possible and to move ahead with her plans. The detective appears to be onto something, because he calls J.R. from Athens and suggests that the Ewings go slow on the deal. Before flying to a meeting with J.R., the man drops a manila envelope in the mail. When he goes to meet the detective in person, J.R. discovers that his detective has disappeared.

John Ross runs away from home because of his fears of a custody battle. The judge speaks to John Ross and each of his parents separately before making his ruling.

"I must say that while your abilities and qualifications are distinctly different, I'm convinced that both of you love your son. My decision is no reflection on the depth of feeling you each have for him, or he for you. But it falls to me to award custody of John Ross to only one parent . . . and I have therefore made my decision to award that to Mrs. Ewing."

EN PASSANT
by Peter Dunne and Joel J. Feigenbaum

Angelica instructs Nicholas to hold J.R.'s detective in Greece and sets Grace up working temporarily in the man's Dallas office. There she is able to intercept the envelope he sent from Greece; meanwhile Nicholas forces the detective to call his partner and instruct J.R. to go ahead with the Marinos deal.

J.R. begins to build a case for custody on appeal and hires the judge's son at Ewing Oil in order to grease the wheels. Sue Ellen continues to worry about J.R.'s tactics, even though Dusty reassures her that she will again win if J.R. appeals.

Donna breaks away from the silence and anguish she went through after losing the baby and reconnects to Ray, who was so distraught over Donna's behavior and the loss of the baby that he tore down the dream house he was building for them. Donna tells Ellie that she will not have another child—the risks are just too great.

Sue Ellen and her mother go to Southfork to pick up John Ross, but while she's there, Sue Ellen realizes it would be a mistake to take her son from his home. To everyone's total shock, she announces that she's not taking John Ross after all.

GOODBYE, FAREWELL, AND AMEN
by Will Lorin

Harv Smithfield, the family attorney, advises J.R. that even though Sue Ellen is allowing John Ross to stay at Southfork, she still has custody of the boy and can claim him at any time. If, however, Sue Ellen were to move back to the ranch, she would forfeit custody. J.R. then asks Sue Ellen to come back to Southfork, for John Ross's sake.

Sue Ellen tells Patricia that she is not going to try to control John Ross's life the way Patricia did hers. She confides to her mother that she is considering moving back to Southfork, because John Ross keeps telling her in nonverbal ways that he needs her there. Patricia begins to pack her things to leave Dallas. The two women work out their differences and Patricia begins to understand that she can no longer manipulate her daughter.

Jenna tells Jack that they should stop seeing each other. Jack, dismayed, asks Ray for advice; Ray suggests that he just slow down a bit, that perhaps Jenna isn't ready for romance so soon after Bobby's death.

Sue Ellen moves back to Southfork. Mandy, upset by the news, seeks out Cliff Barnes for Chinese food and a chat. Barnes suggests revenge.

CURIOSITY KILLED THE CAT
by Deanne Barkley

When a ruptured water main floods their house, Ray and Donna move into Southfork. Clayton tells his lawyer that he's having financial problems and needs to sell off some of his smaller companies to keep his refinery going, but he doesn't want Ellie to know about his problems. Everyone in the family has noticed how distracted Clayton has been, but he is not aware of any difference in his behavior.

Pam opens a package addressed to Bobby from his friend Matt Cantrell and is surprised to see it holds a huge uncut emerald and the promise that there's more to come from his South American mine. When Pam tells J.R. about the emerald, he scoffs and tells her that it must be fake, since Cantrell is a loser.

J.R. and Angelica continue to do business. Cliff has been telling Mandy that the two are involved in more than business, but Mandy has refused to believe it. Cliff

Pam tries to explain to Christopher that his daddy has gone forever.

Cliff tells Pam that for her own good—and for Christopher's—she should sell their 30 percent of Ewing Oil to Weststar. He doesn't tell Pam how much he will personally benefit from such a sale.

"I thought you were dead,"
Pam tells Mark.

Ellie refuses to give herself permission
to grieve for Bobby. Except for a few
private moments, she pushes onward
for the sake of the family.

gives her a tip-off that sends her to Angelica's hotel, from which she sees J.R. emerge in the early morning, thus confirming Cliff's accusation and her own suspicions. Furious at J.R.'s betrayal, Mandy flushes the diamond bracelet he gave her down the toilet.

Jack, upset by Jenna's jilting him, takes off for places unknown so that he can clear his head. J.R. is annoyed when Jamie says even she doesn't know how to locate her brother.

THE MISSING LINK
by Bill Taub

Angelica is concerned about Jack's disappearance because she has an opportunity to put her secret plan into action in Caracas shortly. J.R. assures her that Jack will be back when needed, but both he and Angelica are anxious.

Matt comes to Dallas to meet with Bobby and is shocked to discover his friend has died. He and Pam chat about Bobby's dreams and how Matt has lived out all their boyhood fantasies, and Pam decides to back Matt in the mine. J.R. agrees to sell his interest in Cantrell's mine since he thinks the whole thing is a waste of time. Mark Graison is not thrilled at Pam's enthusiasm for the mine; he feels that Pam is becoming too involved with Bobby and his ghost.

Mandy leaks information about Ewing Oil to Cliff, which results in his cancellation of all equipment orders to make sure that J.R. doesn't get the items he needs for his drilling with Marinos Shipping. J.R. can't understand how this has happened to him, but soon discovers that Mandy is the spy. He sadly vows revenge.

Jamie, who has been working with Cliff at Wentworth–Barnes since they got back together, goes on a site inspection and is crushed by an avalanche of oil barrels. She's rushed to the hospital, where blood tests reveal that she has a very rare type of blood. The doctor urges the family to locate Jack, who might make a suitable blood donor. Without the right blood, Jamie will die.

TWENTY-FOUR HOURS
by Hollace White and Stephanie Garman

As Jamie lies unconscious, the doctor stresses the urgency of finding a compatible blood donor. While Mark Graison and Sue Ellen try to find other possible donors, J.R. offers a $25,000 reward to anyone who can locate Jack Ewing. J.R. claims to be acting out of concern for his cousin, but the truth is that he needs Jack for Angelica to produce in Caracas in a matter of days.

Jack has gone to an isolated fishing lodge to be alone to think about his problems with Jenna and has no idea that he is being sought. Jenna, distraught and blaming herself for his disappearance, goes to Jack's apartment to find clues to where he may have gone. Some photographs trigger her memory of his fishing cabin. Jenna and Ray fly out in the Southfork plane to New Mexico and return with Jack.

According to Angelica, Jack was so important to her plans because he was the illegitimate son of Dimitri Marinos. When the doctor announces that Jack's blood is an exact match to Jamie's, J.R. is left with serious doubts.

THE DEADLY GAME
by Bill Taub

J.R. uses Graison Research's computers to analyze Jack's blood and discovers that Jack and Jamie did indeed have the same parents. He realizes that Angelica has been lying to him, but he's not certain why.

Angelica, having missed her chance to use Jack in Caracas, now wants him to appear at an oil conference in Martinique. Smelling a rat, J.R. decides to sell part of his share of the Marinos deal to the cartel.

Matt Cantrell gives Pam a brooch set with emeralds from their mine. Pam decides to go down to Colombia to see the mine for herself, even though Mark is furious at the thought. Pam is saddened by his refusal to understand her need to go to Colombia.

Ellie secretly buys up the companies that Clayton has for sale.

"You can't keep buying everything Clayton is selling," Punk Anderson advises her. "You'll go broke if that keeps up."

BLAME IT ON BOGOTÁ
by Peter Dunne

Matt and J.R. meet secretly to confirm their deal: J.R. has been providing Matt with the money, the loose stones, and the brooch for Pam in order to con her into sinking money into the mine. He plans on using her incompetence in this deal against her in his legal campaign to oust her from Ewing Oil. Then J.R. feeds Cliff some phony information about the mine, enticing him to contribute $2 million of his own money to be Pam's partner.

J.R.'s satisfaction with his progress on the mine and the Marinos deal is marred by his discovery that his mother has put up her 10 percent of Ewing Oil as collateral to buy a business through an unnamed Houston broker. J.R. begins work to find out why.

Pam is so excited about her upcoming jungle adventure that she forgets a dinner date with Mark. Mark confides to Sue Ellen that Pam and Bobby were planning to remarry and his feelings that he and Pam may not have a future together after all.

SHADOW GAMES
by Joel J. Feigenbaum

In Los Gatos, Colombia, Matt scans the post office, desperate to get a package of emeralds that J.R. is sending him for their con. The chief of police, Luis Rueda, reveals to Matt that he has the package and that he considers Matt to be a very suspicious character.

J.R. has noticed that Grace has befriended Jack and that the two are beginning to be an item. J.R. is certain this is a ploy on behalf of Angelica to gain control over Jack, and he is still not certain why Jack is so vital to Angelica's plans.

Sue Ellen, who has blossomed in her position as the fund raiser for Graison Research, has so impressed J.R. that their relationship begins to take a new turn. J.R. asks her if he may escort her to the fund-raising auction she is hostessing for Graison Research.

Clayton discovers that it was Ellie who was behind his buy-outs, and while angry at first, he comes to realize what a loving gesture she made. He decides to sell all of Farlow Industries and devote himself to the ranch, horse breeding, and Miss Ellie.

Matt and Pam leave Los Gatos for the mine, a few days' trek into the jungle. Matt leaves camp to take a swim in the river after everyone goes to bed. Pam's screams bring him racing back to camp, where he is knocked unconscious and left for dead.

MISSING
by Leonard Katzman

When Matt comes to he discovers that the camp is destroyed and that Pam and everyone else are gone. He makes his way back to Los Gatos and calls J.R., who decides to come to Colombia to meet with Matt in person. He tells Matt to wait twelve hours, and then call Cliff and Mark. Once he puts the calls through, Cliff and Mark make plans to head down to Colombia.

J.R. stands in the shadows as they arrive. He has explained to Matt that he never meant any harm to come to Pam—he just wanted to discredit her. He has also bribed the police chief into helping out with the case.

While he is gone, J.R. has instructed Sly to explain his absence by telling everyone he is away on business in Europe. After all, no one must know of his association with Cantrell. Angelica doesn't believe the cover story and worries that he has discovered her plan. She tells Grace to seduce Jack, who is very receptive to her.

Matt, Mark, Cliff, and Rueda are setting up a search party when a native boy arrives with a package for them. It is the emerald brooch Matt gave Pam.

DIRE STRAITS
by Joel Figenbaum and Peter Dunne

In Colombia, Mark and Cliff work anxiously with Rueda in the desperate attempt to gain Pam's release. Cliff is perplexed by the $100,000 ransom demand. "Why did they ask for so little when they could have had so much more?"

Reluctantly, Mark and Cliff agree to let Matt go alone to deliver the money. Mark believes that Matt may have had something to do with the kidnapping and will now skip out with the money. When Matt is late in returning, Mark is sure his worst fears are being confirmed.

Finally, Matt returns. The next day, Pam is released into Mark's hungry arms.

Back in Dallas, Ellie and Donna have fears of their own—that Jenna may be cracking up. Jenna agrees to see a psychiatrist, but when at her first appointment she finds herself opening up to him somewhat, she catches herself, withdraws, and then dismisses him from the ranch.

Mandy confesses to J.R. that she was the spy. J.R. feigns surprise, never revealing that he already knew and used her to take phony information to Cliff. He has his eye on Sue Ellen, in whom he has taken a renewed interest. When Jerry Kenderson brings Sue Ellen home from work and gives her a friendly kiss goodnight, J.R. stands in the shadows, watching.

OVERTURE
by Hollace White and Stephanie Garman

Pam insists that she still be taken to see the mine, much to Matt's dismay. In a panic that she will discover the truth, Matt calls J.R., who tells him to simply explain to Pam that much excavation will be needed before she will see any real evidence of emeralds; she shouldn't expect to see them lying on the surface.

In Dallas, J.R. invites Sue Ellen to accompany him to Martinique, where he is headed for a big oil conference. Sue Ellen rejects his overtures and refuses his offer. Hurt, J.R. calls his private eye with instructions to start digging for dirt on Jerry Kenderson.

After listening to Miss Ellie at the Oil Baron's Ball, Pam reveals that she will not sell Christopher's stock to Jeremy Wendell as planned.

(right, above)
J.R. begins a business venture with Angelica Nero, CEO of Marinos Shipping, when he discovers that Angelica is wooing Barnes for the deal. J.R. will be duped many more times by the resourceful Angelica.

Jenna's deepening affection for Jack frightens her, as she has not yet recovered from Bobby's sudden death.

Jack continues to woo Jenna
by visiting her boutique
and taking her out to lunch.
He also becomes very
attached to Charlie.

Ray, filling in for Donna at the school where she has been doing volunteer work, finds himself particularly taken with one of her students, a young deaf boy living with a foster family.

Only Jenna is not doing well. When her psychiatrist brings up the day before Bobby's death, Lucy's wedding day, she rushes out of his office in a fit of anger.

SITTING DUCKS
by Susan Howard

J.R., who has asked Sly to get him all the available information worldwide on Dimitri Marinos, has begun to smell a rat and is holding back in his dealings with Angelica. He connects with a man named Alex Garrett, a former attorney of Marinos's, who mysteriously warns J.R., "Watch out for Angelica Nero."

J.R. decides to go with Jack to Martinique, but to proceed slowly and to find out more from Garrett once he gets there.

Pam gets back to work with J.R. and finds the situation just as unpleasant as ever. When she discovers J.R.'s latest tricks with the cartel she gets furious, but J.R. tells her that her situation in Colombia just proves how inept a businesswoman she really is. Mark helps Pam realize that she doesn't have to carry on for Bobby just to prove how much she loved him; it's time for Pam to get on with her other commitments. On the way to Martinique J.R. finally asks Jack to impersonate Marinos. Jack is furious, but J.R. assures everyone that Jack will cooperate because it is in Ewing Oil's best interests that he do so. Jack is resentful, but finally agrees. He feels betrayed by Grace—as well he should. Behind his back Angelica, Nicholas, and Grace hatch a terrible scheme—Jack and J.R. are to be blown up on the yacht.

MASQUERADE
by Leonard Katzman

In Dallas, Pam is becoming increasingly concerned about Jenna's deep psychological distress. She tries to help Jenna, but is rejected. Inadvertently, Pam tells Jenna that she and Bobby had planned to remarry right before his death, and that Bobby had told Pam that Jenna had known about his feelings.

In Martinique, J.R. continues to try to connect with Garrett, but with no success. Finally the attorney agrees to see him, but only if there is no chance the two men will not be seen together. They settle on a meeting at the upcoming costume ball, where they will both be in disguise.

Meanwhile, Jack and Grace make up and agree to start their relationship over. Angelica witnesses the scene, and although Grace assures her she was just doing her job, no longer trusts her assistant. Grace warns Jack and J.R. that their lives will be endangered on the yacht the next day.

At the ball, Garrett tells J.R. that three years ago, when Dimitri Marinos was near death, he had added a codicil to his will cutting Angelica off from Marinos Shipping. Just after that, Marinos went into seclusion. J.R. begins to understand the clever scheme Angelica has been running.

Just as Angelica introduces Jack as Dimitri, pandemonium breaks loose. The assassination attempt has begun.

JUST DESSERTS
by Peter Dunne and Joel J. Fiegenbaum

In the aftermath of the ball, J.R. and Jack are relieved to find themselves still alive. Grace and Nicholas both turn state's witness, explaining the elaborate plan Angelica had made to prove Dimitri was alive in order to have "him" assassinated publicly. Alex Garrett takes charge of the Marinos affairs and explains to J.R. that although he must temporarily halt the Ewing–Marinos deal, once things are straightened out, he will resume the deal as planned.

Back in Dallas, Pam worries about Jenna. She explains to Mark that she let slip the truth about Bobby and that Jenna hadn't believed her. Mark later confronts Jenna, assuring her that it really is true: Bobby and Pam did plan to remarry. Still Jenna does not believe it. Finally Jenna breaks through to a blocked memory of Lucy's wedding and remembers that she did release Bobby. Jenna decides to move away from Southfork with Charlie.

Donna agrees to adopt Tony, much to Ray's delight.

Pam realizes that she has gone as far as she can with Bobby's dreams and that she should get out of Ewing Oil. She decides to sell Christopher's Ewing shares to J.R.

NOTHING'S EVER PERFECT
by Leonard Katzman

J.R. is jubilant as he prepares to buy Christopher's shares of Ewing Oil and finally take over as undisputed head of the company. He is further thrilled with the deal he made with the cartel, to buy them out of the Marinos deal at fifty cents on the dollar. The cartel members have no way of knowing that Garrett will make good on the deal, so they are more than happy to sell out to J.R. J.R. takes out a $1 billion loan so that he can pursue his two projects at the same time.

Jenna apologizes to Jack and goes to Bobby's grave to say good-bye to him. Having straightened out her problems with Bobby's death, Jenna decides to stay on at Southfork. Perhaps she and Jack can work it out.

Angelica, now hiding in Europe, buys fake documents and begins her plot for revenge. She finds Nicholas in Zurich, and kills him with a well-placed hat pin.

J.R. discovers that there's nothing in Kenderson's background that can be used against him but stumbles on some interesting tidbits about Mark Graison in the process. He decides to speed up investigation into Graison's past. Sue Ellen tells Jerry that she cannot leave Southfork for him. When she bumps into Mandy she is shocked to learn that she and J.R. have broken up. Mandy tells her the cause was another woman—Sue Ellen. .

Convinced that Pam has finally put Bobby's death behind her, Mark asks her to marry him, and she says, "yes," one more time.

J.R. RISING
by Joel J. Fiegenbaum and Peter Dunne

Sue Ellen tries to get J.R. to admit that he broke up with Mandy for her, but he won't commit. He does seek out Kenderson and plants more seeds of discontent.

Cliff throws in his hand with the cartel, in the hopes that together they will have the power to beat J.R. at his own game. J.R. discovers that if he defaults on any of his loan payments, he will lose Ewing Oil. He's not too worried, though, and gives Garrett the go-ahead on the Marinos wells.

Donna and Ray begin the adoption proceedings, but fear that Ray's manslaughter conviction for Mickey Trotter's death will stand in the way. They overcome that obstacle, but find that Tony doesn't want to be adopted by them.

Matt discovers emeralds in Colombia and decides to go back to Dallas to show Pam. .

Angelica, still undercover, enters the United States, intent on revenge.

SERENDIPITY
by Leonard Katzman

The drop in the price of oil forces J.R. to shut down his stripper wells, those wells that only pump fifteen barrels of oil a day. Since he is anticipating five-thousand barrels a day from the Marinos deal, he's not worried.

Ray and Donna discover that Tony has been hurt emotionally by another family he loved and is therefore reluctant to be adopted because he thinks the same thing will happen. They resolve to keep working on it.

Mark tells Sue Ellen that J.R. has been snooping around into his and Jerry's past lives, looking for dirt. Sue Ellen, furious, confronts J.R., who tells her that he only did what he did because the thought of losing her is so

difficult for him. Mark is so enraged that he finally admits to Pam and Cliff that they were right about J.R. all along. Cliff hopes this means Mark will throw in with him and merge Graisco with Wentworth–Barnes. Jamie is so worried about a new feud that she goes to see J.R. and begs him to leave Cliff alone.

Sue Ellen breaks up with Jerry Kenderson, explaining that she wants to give J.R. another chance.

Angelica is booked for speeding and carrying a gun but is soon released and continues on her way to Dallas.

THRICE IN A LIFETIME
by Peter Dunne and Joel Feigenbaum

J.R. settles in to life being just about perfect: he finally has control of Ewing Oil, Jack has decided to leave Dallas, and Sue Ellen admits that she and J.R. do, indeed, have a special thing between them which she can't find with anyone else. J.R. in turn promises Sue Ellen that he will never take her for granted again.

Marilee is so angry at J.R.'s latest ruthless schemes that she tells Cliff that she and the other members of the cartel are ready to band together with him to go after Ewing Oil. Cliff can't wait to do battle again, but Jamie steps in and takes matters into her own hands, by going to J.R. and personally asking him to promise to leave Cliff alone.

Pam and Mark progress with their wedding plans. When the invitation to their wedding arrives at Southfork, Ellie is misty eyed and pensive. Donna also is pensive when, after finally getting Tony to agree to being adopted by the Krebbses, the application is denied because of Ray's criminal record.

Angelica meets with an explosives expert who does some fancy work in her custom-made briefcase as she prepares to take on J.R.

HELLO, GOODBYE, HELLO
by Leonard Katzman

When he discovers that Garrett has shut down the Marinos wells, J.R. angrily threatens his former friend. Without the wells, J.R. faces financial ruin; but if J.R. has to go down, he'll take others with him. His snooping into Jerry Kenderson's past has revealed a choice secret about Mark Graison. Graison was involved in a college prank that resulted in a student death and can be tried at any time.

The new hired hand, Ben Stivers, alludes to a secret of his own in a life related to the Ewings in previous times. Punk Anderson thinks the man is familiar to him, and Ellie, too, is made uneasy by the memories he brings up.

J.R. and Sue Ellen attend the fund-raiser she has orga-

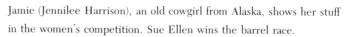
Jamie (Jennilee Harrison), an old cowgirl from Alaska, shows her stuff in the women's competition. Sue Ellen wins the barrel race.

After losing her unborn baby, Donna withdraws from life—and from Ray. In his frustration and pain, Ray destroys the frame of their dream house.

Trooping of the colors—Texas under four flags.

Pam is released by her kidnappers in the Colombian jungle.

nized for Graison Research and get along fine with formerly feuding family members. Sue Ellen is convinced J.R. really has changed. The two have a wonderful time and Sue Ellen moves back into J.R.'s bedroom as a live-in wife. Sue Ellen tells John Ross that his parents are committed to making their marriage work.

But Angelica has other plans.

BLAST FROM THE PAST
by Peter Dunne and Joel Fiegenbaum

Worried that his empire may collapse, J.R. agrees to do business with Angelica Nero, who has returned from her hideout to offer J.R. some papers that will give him power over Alex Garrett. At gunpoint, Angelica forces J.R. to her car and gives him a sample of the documents she is selling. J.R. has them authenticated and is delighted with them and agrees to pay her. They agree to meet at the office on Sunday for the exchange.

Pam and Mark are married at Mark's home. Moments before the ceremony, Ellie tells Pam how much she loves her. All the Ewings and Barneses turn out for the family event. Donna and Ray have finally adopted Tony. Jack refuses to reconsider staying in Dallas, but promises Jamie that she will get to keep his snazzy sportscar while he is off in parts unknown.

J.R. gives Sue Ellen a new engagement ring as the two resume their married life. He postpones a Sunday-morning family outing to go to the office to meet Angelica, who keeps him waiting an extra hour. When Angelica does show, she pulls the pin from her explosive briefcase, thus setting the timer on the detonator. J.R. and Angelica exchange a few angry words, during which Angelica vows to kill Jack and J.R., then J.R. calls in the police, who have listened to the conversation and can now book Angelica. As she is led away, Angelica screams that it's too late for Jack and J.R. anyway.

Worried, J.R. telephones his cousin. Jack and Jamie are in his sportscar, just about to leave for the airport, when Jack hears the phone and runs back to answer it, leaving Jamie waiting in the car. As J.R. asks if Jack is safe, the two men hear an explosion. Jack's car is blown to smithereens. J.R. rushes out of his office to go over to Jack's.

Sue Ellen, who is worried about J.R. being so late, decides to drive to town to find out what's wrong. She knows that J.R. is meeting Angelica and senses danger. J.R. leaves in one elevator just as Sue Ellen enters the office from the other elevator. Seconds later, the briefcase explodes, racking the Ewing Building.

On the morning after her wedding, Pam wakes up to the sound of running water. She walks into the bathroom, opens the shower door, and sees a man who looks exactly like Bobby Ewing.

"Good morning," he says.

"Good morning."

200

Chapter Four

THE MAKING OF DALLAS

As a hit series, *Dallas* is essentially in production fifty-one weeks a year. The writers work all year except for a week at Christmas; the actors have a hiatus between the first of April, when the filming season wraps, and the first of June, when they report to work at MGM-Lorimar studios to shoot interiors for the first six shows of the new season. Then they migrate to Dallas from mid-June to mid-August to shoot exteriors for twelve shows. While in Dallas, cast and crew work six days a week (Sundays are off); key producers and production personnel will throw in an additional half-day on Sunday as required.

A new season unofficially begins the day after the old season, when Capice, Katzman, and the *Dallas* creative staff sit down and say, "All right, this is where we ended, now where do we begin?" The bible is worked out and new actors in supporting roles are signed. (One-shot actors will be cast as each script is developed.) "We differ from some of the other shows in casting," says Capice. "I think that other shows go after a big name and then create a part for that person to play and work it into the story. On *Dallas*, the story always comes first. We shy away from a big name actor who is best known for being himself. We want our audience to accept the actor as the character." When an actor is signed for multiple appearances (a minimum of seven shows), he does not know what will happen to his character in the story or how long he will be around. During the show's developing years, it was not unusual for characters to be tried out. Both Dale Robertson and Howard Keel played suitors to Miss Ellie, but Robertson's character disappeared into the sunset.

After the twelve-show bible is developed, each show will be plotted act by act and scene by scene. There will be approximately twenty-five scenes in each *Dallas* script, divided equally into four acts. The act climaxes are chosen as the story is developed orally. (Each act climax is a mini-cliffhanger that serves to move the story toward a greater climax while allowing commercial breaks.)

Scenes in a *Dallas* script are shorter than in almost every other show. The average scene is about two or two and a half pages of dialogue, whereas in another show, a scene can run from five to eight pages. "There's an emphasis on character and a de-emphasis on plot," says Katzman. Still, a lot more happens on an episode of *Dallas* than on almost any other show on television.

Tracking shots to follow action sequences
require metal tracks laid on plywood planks
so the camera dolly cart can be pulled along
by grips.

(right)
Large white reflectors prevent shadows
from crossing the actors' faces when
shooting on location.

Establishing shots are made to give the
viewer quick visual information, usually
pertaining to time and place.

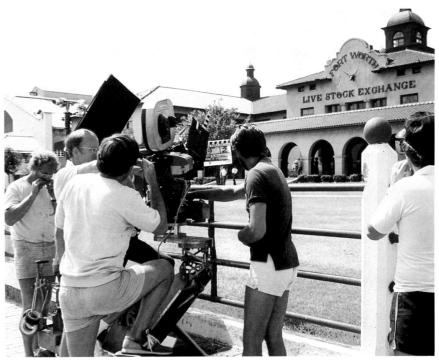

Scripts are mostly written by house writers, but occasionally they are farmed out to free-lancers. Free-lance writers are handed a scene-by-scene outline (called a "step-outline") of the show they are to write. They spend a week "thinking about it," according to the supervising producer, Peter Dunne. "They are encouraged to call me at any time to ask any questions they want." After a week the writers go to the offices on the MGM lot to discuss their thoughts about action and motivation. Then they go home to write for another week, turning in a script that is about fifty-two pages long—approximately one page of dialogue per film minute. Writers earn approximately $16,000 for a script. Sounds easy? It isn't.

The first draft of a script is bound between red paper covers and is called, not surprisingly, a "red cover." The red cover goes to the production people so that they can begin work right away on locations and props. The rewritten version (changed as much as 50 percent) of a script, boasting a yellow cover, is the official shooting script. Yellow covers go to the actors. Pages of subsequent rewrites will be added on various shades of paper, each color coded to the number of rewrites the scene has endured. All copies of all yellow covers contain the same letter, which states, "As you know, our scripts should be treated with the utmost confidentiality, especially those containing sensitive material with regard to the opening and closing sequences of each season. Please do not let your script out of your possession!" High-security pages (such as the ones identifying who shot J.R.) are handed out on a "need to know" basis and may be stamped "For your eyes only."

Actors rarely know what is happening to their characters before they see their scripts. Often an actor will ask producers for help in understanding his character's actions, since without knowing where a character is going or what he is thinking a part can be quite difficult to play. The director or producer will then guide the actor through the crisis. Producers invariably know more about the characters' futures than the actors do.

A show traditionally takes seven "prep" days and seven "shoot" days. Although the prep days actually involve only the director and production personnel, the script has to be finished *before* they begin. Directors are contracted by the producer's office on a show-by-show basis. Several directors have multiple deals (for two to six shows a season), but each episode is still assigned separately. Directors are paid the union minimum of approximately $16,800 for the fifteen days they work. They also receive residuals if the show is rerun or goes into syndication.

At the production meeting before shooting, the director will run through each scene and explain to the heads of departments—props,

Leonard Katzman, writer, producer, and director of many episodes, and known affectionately as "Uncle Lennie," works with Victoria Principal and Patrick Duffy.

costumes, sets, and so forth—just how he envisions each scene. After the meeting, department heads will work up their budgets for the show. The producers and budget director will then decide if the director's version is "doable." The experienced director will ask only for things he knows can be covered in the budget (about $1 million an episode) and knows how to keep cast and crew in good spirits through the pace of the grind. The job is technically, physically, and politically demanding.

"If a writer makes a mistake, we can fix it," says Katzman. "For the director, once you have the film, you don't get another chance. If it's not there, there's nothing we can do."

Because a show takes seven days to shoot, it can become difficult to tell when one show is over and another begins. Every Monday does not bring a new episode. The changing faces of the directors are about all that varies in the grueling schedule. While each show has a title, the title is never broadcast and is merely a reference point for writers. Cast and crew refer to shows by their numbers in the sequence of each year—they do not keep a running tab.

After the Texas shooting, additional episodes are shot on the lot or in the Los Angeles area. The cast and some crew members may return to Dallas for certain night shots or stunt shots. For the show in which Sue Ellen and Mickey Trotter were involved in a car accident in front of Southfork, for example, some of the cast and crew returned to the scene of the crime, and additional local crew were added on. For the excursion to Hong Kong, Len Katzman accompanied Linda Gray and Victoria Principal, and used a local crew for most of the technical work. Some location scenes that are meant to be in Dallas are shot in Los Angeles—Lorimar leases a ranch (J.M.J.) in Hidden Hills, California, that doubles as the back prairie of Southfork. Restaurant scenes can be shot in nearly any area restaurant or on a soundstage. Patricia Shepard's home exists not in the posh Dallas suburb of Turtle Creek, but in Hancock Park, a wealthy residential area of Los Angeles. The Oil Baron's Club is a standing set on Stage 5 at MGM.

Work invariably begins with a 5:30 A.M. makeup call for some of the actors and a 7:18 A.M. call for crew. The first shot usually takes place around 8:00 A.M., as soon as the set is ready. Actors must always be ready and waiting. Since production time is money, actors stand by in their dressing rooms and are brought to the set about two minutes prior to the first walk-through. In addition to rehearsals, the actors will perform at least one walk-through for the camera. They will be already in makeup and wardrobe but draped with large, white, paper napkins at the throat to prevent makeup from ruining their clothes. Additional walk-throughs may be done for lighting or tricky camera shots.

Each scene will be rehearsed once and then filmed, usually twice—unless the first take was astoundingly perfect or the shot is a complicated track shot with a moving camera. After the scene is done, it will be "covered" from several other angles; each angle will favor one of the speaking actors. In editing, the various versions will be cut together so the viewer sees the speaker and one or more reactions. Film shows such as *Dallas* rarely use more than one camera (videotaped shows usually use three cameras) because the look and feel of the film is based upon the quality of the lighting. Two cameras may be used on

Bobby and Jenna film on location at the popular White Water amusement area, while the curious thrill to the real live celebrities in their midst.

(above right)
Locals have come to call the bank building where Dallas exteriors and office scenes are shot "The Ewing Building."

Although a microphone follows the dolly truck, sound will later be added to the scene in a "looping" session at the studio.

an elaborate stunt, but otherwise the lighting will be adjusted to best flatter each situation and actor.

The day's work usually wraps around 6:00–6:30 P.M., but can extend until later depending on the demands of the schedule. The director tries to accomplish all the assigned work on a daily call sheet because there is no room in the schedule to bump over to the next day. Only once, when both Barbara Bel Geddes and Victoria Principal were out ill, was the set closed down and the schedule readjusted accordingly.

Of course, not every actor works every day and not every actor has scenes with all the other actors. Cliff Barnes and Miss Ellie are rarely on camera together. After Pam and Bobby's divorce, Victoria Principal was no longer needed for family living room and dinner scenes. The production office schedules the scenes for each day, the actors needed, and the arrival times for makeup and on set. A "call sheet" is issued around 3:00 P.M. of the day prior to the shoot. Actors must phone in for their "call." If they are not working the next day, the call sheet is marked with an "H" for holding. All actors are paid on a per episode basis, with fees ranging from around $5,000 an episode to

A typical call sheet.

(left)

Larry Hagman gets relief from the heat as he directs a shot from the Southfork pool. Visitors to Southfork uniformly concur that their biggest disappointment with the house is that the swimming pool is so much smaller than it appears to be on screen.

over $100,000, unless they are "day players." Since day players work only one day, they are paid only for that day. Sometimes an actor beginning as a day player becomes a contract player—if his character becomes a series regular.

Actors who direct are paid an additional $16,800 per episode. Only principal actors are considered for directing jobs.

Acts of God

The production moves forward, slowing down or stopping only for natural causes and acts of God. Most natural accidents are finessed.

When the snow that hit Dallas during production of the pilot melted the next day, several tons of gypsum were trucked to the location site to match the snow of the previous day's shoot. When the gypsum read too pink on screen, new gypsum was trucked in. The next day, it snowed again. The weather has always been a formidable factor in the production of *Dallas*. The temperature frequently tops 100 degrees; numerous cast and crew members have been treated for sunstroke. Over the years the production company has learned to deal with the heat—actors are ferried in and out of air conditioning, and Gatorade is in ready abundance. Crew members wear shorts and the men go shirtless, but stars are forced to cope with the heat in wardrobe that includes leather pants, chaps, and three-piece suits.

Weather

There have been several pregnancies on the set. When Charlene Tilton became pregnant her condition was woven into the story line. However, Charlene went on to carry full term while Lucy, her character—who had been raped—chose to have an abortion. After Lucy's "abortion" and before Charlene's delivery, she was photographed so that her changing shape would not be in frame. Morgan Brittany was also pregnant for her last appearance in *Dallas*, so her character, Katherine Wentworth, had to kill Bobby via hit-and-run so that she could be partially concealed inside a car.

Pregnancy

When Barbara Bel Geddes had heart surgery, Miss Ellie was whisked away by Clayton Farlow to Galveston to "rest up." Deciding not to return to the physical strain of a weekly show, Bel Geddes agreed to have her character replaced. Donna Reed played the part for one year, until Bel Geddes was strong enough to return.

Illness

To give Victoria Principal some down time after an old back injury forced her out of work for a week, producers came up with an "ad hoc kidnapping" that was thrown into the plot in case Victoria needed to take more time off. As it worked out, Victoria came back to work quickly and her kidnapping was therefore resolved quickly. Most major characters have now been kidnapped.

Another bright and beautiful working day in Dallas—115°.

After heart surgery, Barbara Bel Geddes retired as Miss Ellie and turned her recipes over to Donna Reed. Bel Geddes subsequently returned to the role a year later; Reed died unexpectedly in 1985.

It was decided that Jock Ewing would not be replaced but would die with dignity, just as actor Jim Davis had done. Davis was in the hospital suffering from cancer for some time, but was not written out of the series until after his death. "His whole life centered around this show," says Katzman. "We kept his character alive so he could read the scripts and have the hope and faith that he would make it back. People couldn't suddenly say, 'Guess what! Daddy died!' It was a very serious, very real situation.

"We felt we were better off keeping alive the character—Ellie and Jock went on a second honeymoon, then Jock went to South America—until we knew what was really going to happen to Jim and could plan an appropriate and fitting death for Jock that would bring honor to them both. Jock Ewing died an oilman who was serving his country. It was a hard time for all of us."

When it came time for Patrick Duffy to leave the show, there was no question that Bobby would die. He could not be replaced and producers did not want him in limbo. Says Katzman, "Patrick just wanted it to be done with dignity." Since it was obvious to producers that Bobby's death would provide a new twist on the cliffhanger for that season, it was easy to build backward and create Bobby's murderer. Katherine had already tried to kill Bobby once—a coincidence that worked handily when Patrick failed to renew his contract.

First Call/Makeup

First call for all actors is for Makeup and Hair. The departments are located on Stage 18, next door to each other and tucked into a corner of the soundstage that also houses Pam's bedroom, Angelica's bedroom, the larger-than-life Southfork foyer, and the dining room.

Makeup and Hair share a common wall but have opposite entrances. Though each room measures only about ten by five feet, two hairstylists and two makeup artists can work on a maximum of three actors without everyone becoming claustrophobic.

While normal makeup for regulars can be finished in about ten minutes, the call sheet allows an hour for women and half an hour for men. Guest actresses may be scheduled for a longer time since the makeup people are not used to doing their faces.

Pam's hairstyles through the years.

Victoria Principal has always been responsible for choosing her own hairstyles. As Pam has become more wealthy, sophisticated, and confident, so have her hairstyles.

Susan Howard takes a powder puff from Sue Cabral. Location shooting in the Texas sun requires twice as much makeup as indoor shooting.

Michael Preece, one of several directors with an ongoing contract, discusses a scene with Victoria Principal. "Directors who tell actors how to play the characters don't last long around here," say crew members.

Makeup men Joe Hailey and Ralph Gulko provide makeup for everyone who goes on camera, including extras—who are referred to as "atmosphere." One of their hardest tasks is to make up an actress to make her look as though she is *not* wearing makeup, or to make a beautiful woman look horrible (Sue Ellen in the drunk tank; Jenna in jail). Derelicts and drunks require more time and effort from the makeup department than diners at a fancy Dallas restaurant. Further aggravating the problem is the summer heat in Dallas, which causes actors to perspire heavily—their makeup runs, streaks, and mottles, and requires constant attendance from makeup personnel. In a typical summer shoot in Texas, Makeup will use twice the amount of makeup they use in the studio in L.A.

"We try to make everyone as perfect as possible," says Hailey, known on the set as Joe Mama. "After all, this isn't real life, it's *Dallas*." Hailey has switched the actresses from traditional stage makeup to Chanel makeup, which is bought over the counter. Victoria Principal has very sensitive skin and quickly builds up a negative reaction to a brand of makeup; while she is currently tolerating Chanel, she will invariably be rotated to another brand when her skin gives the signal. Men are made up with Blasco Ruddy Beige #4. Surprisingly enough, Larry Hagman, Ken Kercheval, Howard Keel, and Steve Kanaly all have the same color skin. Most of the women use Chanel Tawny Beige.

The most difficult job Makeup has is matching makeup shades for sequences. Because scenes are shot out of the order in which they air, Makeup and Hair must ensure that a woman who walks into a courtroom (or whatever the scene requires) with a certain makeup and hairstyle comes out looking exactly the same way. Especially for shows that are shot part in Texas and part in L.A., this matchup can be a tricky one. As many as eight weeks may have passed between two scenes that will be edited together in a back-to-back fashion allowing for no errors.

To keep the matching as simple as possible, the makeup colors for lips and eyes are coordinated to clothing. Makeup then knows that if Pam is wearing a peach blouse her lipstick must be a certain shade, whatever Pam is wearing that year for peach. Each woman also has her own makeup box with the same colors in it. She carries this black, larger-than-a-lunchbox kit with her from her dressing room to the set. Before close-ups, she will call out, "Makeup," or "Joe Mama," and someone will come running with her box to do touch-ups.

Lorimar spends between $5,000 and $7,000 a year on makeup, most of which is bought at Neiman-Marcus, but some of which may come from special suppliers in Paris and Hong Kong. "Lorimar spares

Afton and Pam wear look-alike hairstyles, because the wind was so fierce during this Dallas filming that all women on camera were required to have upswept coiffures.

no expense in how the women look," notes Joe Mama. He is free to buy the latest shades and try out the newest makeup looks on the actresses. Normally, the makeup they wear on camera is also suitable for street wear. Heavier makeup is applied for evening scenes and big ballroom scenes. "The Oil Baron's Ball is when we get into blue eyeshadow and heavy stuff you won't see on the street today. But no matter what the situation, we have one rule here—the women will always look good."

Jerry Gugliemotto dries Susan Howard's hair; an assistant dries out her rented fur coat after an outdoor "rain" scene.

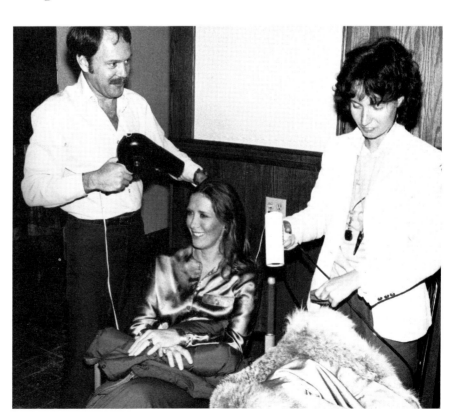

First Call/Hair

Whether the actress has makeup or hair call first is immaterial, since both will be readjusted before the scene is actually shot. Men usually have makeup applied before their hair is combed, because their hair is often fixed in a more rigid style.

Actresses with early morning calls usually tumble out of bed, throw on casual clothes, roll into their cars or limousines, and propel themselves into Hair and Makeup while they are still half asleep. Often they fall back asleep while the hairstylist or makeup man is at work. Some come with freshly shampooed hair wrapped in a towel (even in California it's cold at 5:30 in the morning). If an actress's call is later in the morning or the stylists are very busy, she may just grab a blow dryer or rollers and do her hair herself. The actresses have final say in what style they will actually wear, although only Barbara Carrera wears several styles during the course of a season.

While hair can be washed, dried, set, and styled by hairstylists Jerry Gugliemotto and Diane Pepper, the actresses themselves are responsible for the basic cut that leads to the style. Often an actress does not feel free to change her hairstyle without the producers' permission, but some go ahead and change the style without telling anyone. This must be done between seasons as her style will be kept up throughout the season with a mid-season trim. Female characters on *Dallas* do not go out and cut or color their hair for emotional reasons related to the story line, although both Jenna and Pam have moved from fuller looks to simpler, blunt-cut styles. Actresses are also responsible for their hair color and may be teased unmercifully by other cast and crew members should the merest hint of dark roots appear at the hairline.

It's not uncommon practice on a glamour show for an actress to wear a hair piece to bulk out her hair on camera, but this is not done on *Dallas*. None of the actresses wears any kind of hair appliance, not even a fall, or three-quarter wig.

Wardrobe

Wardrobe is responsible for dressing every actor on screen, from star to extra. Costumer Kathy Monderine attends production meetings and marks her copy of the script with the vital information on wardrobe and costume. Costumes are rarely used in *Dallas*, since the actors generally wear ordinary street or western garb. The producers are very sensitive about the part clothes play in the nighttime soaps and feel that the *Dallas* characters must wear real clothes and look like real people, as opposed to characters on other shows who appear in scenes designed to show off the wardrobe.

Special wardrobe for the stars is handled by designer Bill Travilla, the man best known for creating the famous white halter dress that Marilyn Monroe wore in *The Seven Year Itch*. Travilla joined *Dallas* in 1984 and immediately won an Emmy for costume design. He will do several original designs each season, usually of ball gowns for the Oil Baron's Ball. He also works with the stars in selecting the rest of their ready-to-wear wardrobe. For Angelica Nero, played by Barbara Carrera, the most glamorous person to have appeared on *Dallas*, Travilla has had the opportunity to create the kind of couture that would look ridiculous on almost any other *Dallas* character.

Most of the clothes are bought for the stars in specialty shops such as Lou Lattimore, Loretta Blum, and Marie Leavell in Dallas, although Wardrobe has a house account at Neiman-Marcus so that they can take out several garments, see what works, and return the rest. Because the selection of clothes in Dallas is different from that in Los Angeles, producers prefer that most pieces be purchased in Dallas for a more realistic look. Additional clothing is bought in Los Angeles as needed. In the early years of the show, the actors supplied some of their own clothes. Later, as the show became famous, designers often made arrangements with certain stars to wear their clothes—thus Linda Gray wore designs only by Giorgio Armani at one time. Barbara Bel Geddes had a long-standing arrangement with Jean-Louis, the dean of Hollywood designers, and has her special clothes tailor-made for her by him. The studio, of course, gets the bill.

Each actress gets several new outfits per episode. The retail value of an average ready-to-wear outfit, complete with shoes and accessories, is about $1,000. She does not keep the clothes, even if they are custom-made for her. Everything is returned to a three-tiered pipe-rack closet in Wardrobe beneath the Barrymore Building at MGM, where they hang in areas separated by name tags for the characters. At the end of a season, Wardrobe sells the clothing they won't carry over for another year.

Each character has a specific look that functions as an aspect of his or her personality. Wardrobe changes over the years as the characters grow, mature, and change. When *Dallas* started, Pam wore inexpensive clothes. As she gained in sophistication and became wealthy in her own right, she began wearing quality clothes and a high-fashion look. Sue Ellen's look, which began as very all-American designer sportswear, has also grown much more sophisticated and European. Miss Ellie is so rich she can dress however she pleases, which is what she does. Although viewers often write to complain about Miss Ellie's clothes, few responded positively when Donna Reed dressed up the image with a bouffant hairstyle and Chanel look-alike suits.

The wardrobe department keeps lists for each actor and each episode, showing what is worn by each actor in every scene. Of special concern are the shows that are shot partially in Dallas and then finished in Los Angeles: the same clothes may drape differently on the body because of the heat in Dallas.

Wardrobe buys at least two of everything in order to "double" an outfit in case an accident should damage clothing in the middle of production. For outdoor clothes worn in Dallas, several changes may be needed—especially for men's shirts—because of the problem of perspiration. Seasons, however, do not affect basic wardrobe choices. Sue Ellen is likely to wear leather pants at any time of the year, for example, no matter what the temperature.

Men's wardrobe is determined by Jack Baer, who picks out all the men's clothing and accessories.

Wardrobe is used as a subtle layer of character information and is carefully attuned to the psychological background of each character. At various costume meetings during the year, producers will explain what's in store for certain characters and how their dress should reflect their state of mind. A character would never look awful just because she felt awful, however. Even when a distraught Sue Ellen was dragged away to the confines of a sanitarium, she was ever so roughly grasped by the sleeves of her gorgeous, brightly colored silk blouse.

Miss Ellie dons a twenty-pound beaded gown worth $5,000 for the Oil Baron's Ball.

Changes in Pam's character were revealed in her attire: starting with cheap clothing (below), she worked her way up to working woman suits and then blossomed into designer originals.

Angelica Nero wears a Bill Travilla gown.

Designer Bill Travilla chose this strapless
sequined sheath for Sue Ellen's "coming out"
party at a fund-raiser for Graison Research.

Stage Call

The crew arrive on set punctually, and the assistant director writes down their arrival time—to the second. Actors report to early calls precisely on time, and to later calls with a little more flexibility because work is always slightly behind schedule. Actors are drilled from early in their careers to never be late, so they often arrive early, preferring to spend extra time in their dressing rooms making phone calls or conversing on stage. Curiously, actors often pair off socially in small groups connected by the relationships of their characters. Thus Susan Howard and Steve Kanaly spend time together, as do Dack Rambo and Priscilla Presley. They may "run lines," chat, discuss their characters, or work out ways of playing certain scenes.

The ensemble rotates around a working core of four soundstages—Stage 18 and Stage 19, which are connected by a back path; Stage 23, which houses the outdoor set of Southfork, replete with swimming pool (about 3 feet deep and built to 7/8 scale of the real thing); and Stage 5, where the Oil Baron's Club stands. The daily call sheet tells the actors which stage to report to and even schedules in the amount of time needed to set up the move from one stage to another.

The typical soundstage is fifty feet high and seventy feet long. Aloft are two sets of catwalks for lighting technicians. Each warehouse-sized, corrugated tin and stucco building houses four or five permanent sets, as well as numerous flats that can become various rooms as needed. The essential design of the rooms of Southfork are replicas of the real homes originally used for the interior shooting. Over the years, some have been renovated; the Ewings would naturally redecorate occasionally. The pool furniture, for example, once covered in yellow and white, is now blue and white.

Part of the reason for *Dallas*'s updated look was that a new art director, Matt Jefferies, joined the crew in 1985. Jefferies insisted on the use of real flowers in room settings and spruced up the natural greenery in all shots. The blossoms on trees and shrubbery on Stage 23 are fake if that flower is not in season, but are otherwise the real thing.

Jefferies is responsible for the color and design of new sets, which are worked out with producers so that they coordinate with characters, right down to the color. Sue Ellen's office set, on Stage 23, was designed to be blue-gray, whereas the Hancock Park home that was used as her mother's Dallas home was chosen partly because the living room was peach, and peach seemed to be the perfect color for Patricia Shepard. "But," says Jefferies, "if someone is really conscious of what color the room is, we're doing something wrong. The rooms have to work, and be elegant, but it should be the actors who hold the viewer's attention—not the rooms."

It can take several days to arrange the props or "dress" a set or to set up an "exterior" shot at Southfork inside Stage 23. It may take four men two days just to put all the greenery in place, three hours simply to set up a bedroom. Linens are purchased specially, but most furnishings come from the MGM prop house. The height of the furnishings is adjusted with wooden boxes called apple boxes, which come in three sizes, a "full apple," a "half apple," and a "quarter apple." They are chosen according to the proportions of the room and the relative size of the actors. Charlene Tilton, for example, had to be on apple boxes just to be in the same frame as J.R. in close-ups. Coffee tables, flower carts, everything except beds are balanced on "apples" until the cameraman says the look is right.

Although the usual Southfork set at Lorimar-MGM sits on Stage 23, a new portion had to be built specifically to be burned for the 1983 cliffhanger. The fire burned faster than anticipated, creating nervous panic among cast and crew members but causing no real damage.

Manpower, Texas style.

Pool furniture was once upholstered yellow with white trim, then yellow and white stripes: it's now blue and white stripes.

Livestock

The right look for *Dallas* extends even to the casting of the livestock. Katzman is fond of telling the story of the early days of filming, when *Dallas* was shot at a Frisco, Texas, ranch owned by Mr. and Mrs. Cloyce Box. Sue Ellen was scheduled to play a scene on horseback, and the production crew had dutifully provided a local horse. But rancher Box, watching the proceedings, whispered to Katzman that a woman of Sue Ellen's financial position should be riding a better quality horse. Within minutes, he generously trotted out his own $250,000 quarter horse as a loan. The scene went without a hitch, Sue Ellen looked grand, Box endeared himself to Katzman forever, and the crew learned the lesson of properly casting livestock.

The greatest problem encountered is not the match between horse and rider, but the fact that Texas horses are not Hollywood horses. Hollywood horses are used to cameras and crews, and to walking, trotting, or even galloping a few yards and then stopping so the actor can say his lines. Texas horses are more at home on the range. When the show first began to shoot in Dallas, the active film community now thriving there did not exist. As a result, *Dallas* producers soon realized that they needed someone to train some Texas horses into quasi-Hollywood horses.

Jimmy and Carol Darst, two of the wranglers who worked on the first episodes of *Dallas*, came quickly to the rescue. (All animal handlers are called "wranglers"; if a scene calls for a tarantula, for example, the director will ask the livestock department for a "spider wrangler.") The Darsts had their own ranch and a keen understanding of the film demands for animals. It was Jimmy Darst who suggested that John Ross get a pony after Darst found what he considered a perfect animal for the Ewing heir.

Today the Darsts run a successful business providing livestock to *Dallas* and other productions in the area while still managing their own 2,500-acre cattle ranch, the J Bar C. The Darsts are responsible for the feeding, housing, and exercising of the animals all year round. Although the vast majority of the livestock used in *Dallas* is comprised of horses, cattle appear in some scenes, and occasionally a few goats, ducks, donkeys, or buffalo are called for. The Darsts rent out all these species, both "by the animal" and "by the herd," on a per day or per week basis to the production company, which budgets about a thousand dollars for the livestock in each episode.

John Ross, not quite born in the saddle, learned to ride on a pony provided by Texas animal trainer Jimmy Darst.

The Ranch

Though Southfork is referred to as "the ranch," there have actually been several Southforks, and *Dallas* continues to shoot on two ranches, Southfork in Dallas and J.M.J. Ranch in Hidden Hills, California. The original Southfork, as seen in the first five episodes, was the Box Ranch. The Box home was used for exteriors only; a house on Swiss Avenue, in Dallas, which became known as "the Swiss house," was used for interiors. When the show began life as a series in the summer of 1978, Lorimar switched to Duncan Acres in Plano, Texas. Duncan Acres is now legally named Southfork.

Interiors were shot at the home of Mr. and Mrs. Bruce Calder in Turtle Creek, Texas. The sets on the soundstages at MGM are copies of the Calder home. "They duplicated everything," says Bruce Calder. "Wallpaper, furniture, even the spool headboard I had moved from my mother's house twenty years ago. They also duplicated those awful brocade drapes. It's a strange feeling to see exact reproductions of your home, down to the last detail. The only differences I can observe on television are the placements of a few light switches."

The Duncan home is the current Southfork, although the Duncans no longer own it. Like the Box home, it has a portico, but the Duncan home has four round columns, whereas the Box home has six square

Sue Ellen struts her stuff on Cloyce Box's borrowed quarter horse.

Len Katzman drove hundreds of miles
to find a real house that looked like
Southfork should. He found it twice—
first at the Box Ranch, then later at
Duncan Acres. Duncan Acres is now
legally named Southfork Ranch.

Tourists are allowed only up to the front gate of Southfork on filming days.

ones. The Duncan home is also much newer and has a gabled roof. The Box home has a pitched roof with a widow's walk inside the portico.

The Duncans ran through a roller coaster of emotions with *Dallas* when they owned the ranch. Duncan rented the place to Lorimar the first year, then spent the year in a legal tangle because his neighbors, Mr. and Mrs. John Barber, tried to get an injunction against Lorimar because they felt the commotion was a nuisance and the shooting a threat to the safety of their children. When the courts didn't close the set down, Duncan turned commercial and all but set up a lemonade stand on his front yard. He began to charge gawkers four dollars to set foot on the property and sold off souvenir land deeds at twenty-five dollars a square foot. The Duncans continued to live on the ranch, even during production. They allowed stars indoors to a breath of air conditioning, although Larry Hagman (who will not go near anyone who smokes cigarettes) teasingly called Mrs. Duncan a chimney.

In 1984 the Duncans threw in their spurs and sold Southfork to real estate developer Terry Trippit. Trippit is now in the Southfork business and has begun to seriously merchandise the 164-acre ranch as a party and convention center. Yellow-and-white striped tents huddle beyond the paddock area. They are available for charities, weddings, bar mitzvahs, or any other event you care to create. There are also two enclosed "ballrooms"—large rooms for dances or meetings that can house a thousand people. The Stud Barn, directly behind the big house, is a snack bar.

Behind Jock and Digger is the six-pillar rear facade of the Box Ranch, which resembles the front of Duncan Acres.

Trippit gutted and renovated the 8,500-square-foot, six-bedroom house and now rents it out for $2,500 a night, from 7:00 P.M. to 9:00 A.M. Dinner is extra. "Whatever you want, we can get it for you. It just has a price tag," says Trippit, who rents out to honeymooners and a few corporations. (Tenants usually flip a coin to determine who gets the upstairs master bedroom with its gold-plated bidet and oval Jacuzzi. Trippit provides the bubble bath as part of the deal.) The interior, while tasteful, does not resemble the interiors on the show or anything as lavish as any celebrity home in Bel Air.

Trippit is paid an annual fee by Lorimar for the use of the ranch. He has the right to sell admissions (still four dollars) to the property, to operate two gift shops that sell exclusively Southfork merchandise, and to run the party and convention business and concessions. (Table service for dinner is three dollars per head extra: most folks opt for the buffet.) Approximately three hundred people a day plunk down their money to see where J.R. lives. Some of them even believe that J.R. actually lives there. Although the house is permanently closed to the public, a few tourists have broken windows or jimmied locks to get in—just to say "hi" to J.R.

Because *Dallas* operates as a "closed set" (no visitors during filming), the ranch is not open to the public during shoot days. On those days, tourists must stand by the rail at the gift shop and wait for the limousines to arrive. (Those of less than star status arrive on the set in buses, vans, or station wagons.)

The *Dallas* family in Texas with the local crew members in 1984.

Working in Texas

While working in Texas, Lorimar seasonally hires locals to fill in for cast, crew, and transportation. Locals drive the buses, vans, and station wagons and provide goods and services for the two-month location shoot. While on location, *Dallas* brings in almost $2 million to Texas locals in hard cash and untold millions by ripple effect—tourists who come to Dallas partly because *Dallas* is shot there. Money is paid out by Lorimar to some twenty-three drivers who work on a per day rate, as well as to local crews, actors, camera companies (most of the equipment is rented), and the Marriott Inn, which houses cast (except for the biggest stars, who rent homes or condos), crew, and the production office. As a right-to-work state, Texas offers more flexibility in laws governing the union qualifications of actors, so extras cost less in Texas than they do in Los Angeles. About one-third of the crew comes from Los Angeles; the rest is hired in Dallas. A Texas "family" has evolved, with regulars who can expect the work from summer to summer. "In L.A., we're one of two hundred shows being shot regularly," says Katzman. "In Dallas we're special."

Indeed, the city that was hostile when the film crews first showed up has become more than agreeable now that *Dallas* is a huge hit. Society matrons are usually thrilled to be invited to fill in as "atmosphere" for the Oil Baron's Ball and restaurateurs are not shy about calling the production office and volunteering their restaurants for location shoots. (Lorimar always pays for the use of a restaurant, or, by agreement, makes a contribution to charity in the restaurant's name: absolutely no "freebies" are accepted.) When extras are needed, small feature articles appear in the local newspapers giving phone numbers to call for prospective work. Socialites, many of whom appear at the Oil Baron's Ball, have become friendly with many of the stars and invite them to local parties. Larry and Maj Hagman have taken an active part in raising money for the Cattle Baron's Ball, an event sponsored on behalf of the American Cancer Society. Victoria Principal even chose to be married to Dr. Harry Glassman in Dallas.

Reruns, Repeats, and Syndication

In traditional television practice, a show airs during the regular season and is repeated in the same time slot during the off season, summer. CBS has found that *Dallas* viewers are mainly regulars who are bored watching reruns at the end of the season. Fearing they would lose these viewers entirely, CBS decided to save all its repeats for the syndication business.

"The network made the decision not to play current reruns in the summer months," says Capice. "Shows like ours seem to do poorly in repeats on the network because we have such a loyal core audience. It's unreasonable to think that a few months later they will want to jump back and see an episode they just saw. We like to bring them to the edge with the cliffhanger, and leave them with something to think about until the new season.

"For CBS, there were a variety of reasons to not rerun current shows, including poor ratings. CBS doesn't want to lose its grip on Friday night by allowing viewers to leave *Dallas* during the summer and switch to another show on another network that they might get so involved with that they don't come back in the fall."

The network sometimes programs the preseason warm-up time with a rerun of the cliffhanger, just to get everyone ready for the beginning of the new season, or to attract new viewers who might feel they don't know what's going on and who need the last episode of the last season as an introduction.

Winners from Italy in a contest sponsored by Lux soap
were flown to Los Angeles and given roles as "walk ons"
at the Oil Baron's Ball in 1985.

Debbi Rennard, who plays J.R.'s secretary, Sly, models
one of the Simon Ellis dresses licensed in England
as the Southfork Collection.

Syndication is the selling of reruns as a "package"—the package includes *all* the episodes produced. With *Dallas* the package is sold with an agreement that the stories be broadcast in order, so the audience can follow the story from the beginning. A complete rotation of the package takes approximately ten months, but grows by six weeks as each new season is added. The package may take longer if the station does some preempting, which is common since the independent stations that usually buy syndication packages also air local sporting events.

The stations buy syndication rights at a price fixed by the seller, in this case Lorimar. The price is based on how "hot" the series is and the size of the city where the reruns will air. A bigger city pays a higher price than a smaller city. A large city can expect to pay as high as $300,000 per episode of *Dallas* in syndication.

Syndication works much the same way on an international basis. France has regional programming and national programming but syndication is sold only on a national basis. Therefore all of France gets *Dallas*, not just some cities. French actors dub the voices of the characters. The show has been syndicated in ninety-one different countries but has bombed in two—Japan and Mexico. Other than that, it remains the phenomenon it is in the United States.

The Merchandise

Fans stay in touch with the show through reruns, publications, contests, and merchandise. Novelty merchandise was introduced in the show's second year, and sales of these items peaked just as *Dallas* fever swept the country with the "Who Shot?" cliffhanger. "I Shot J.R." T-shirts were popular, as were campaign-style buttons. Lorimar realized royalties in the low six figures from the sale of novelty buttons alone.

"What we're trying to do at Lorimar now," says Danny Simon, vice-president of merchandising, "is to promote adult licensing. *Dallas* is pretty much out of the novelties business, especially in this country. Our goal now is to create a designer image for the show. So we have created the Southfork Collection. We chose the name of the ranch because the word "Dallas" would have been difficult to protect since it is the name of a city, not to mention a football team. With the Southfork Collection, we are attempting to create products with a quality look and feel. The name "Southfork" represents power, wealth, and prestige. It has all the positive aspects and none of the negatives that individual characters may have. Not all characters, of course, are liked by everyone, and a character's image may suddenly turn sour. By concentrating on the ranch house and its name and image, we have a better chance of bringing long-lasting quality merchandise to the public."

Quality is what *Dallas* merchandise is all about. There's a barbecue grill just like the one at Southfork that can be yours for a mere $1,400; a Southfork hot tub is under consideration. If you live in England or travel there, you might want to buy a dress just like the one J.R.'s secretary Sly was wearing on the show only last week. The collection of ready to wear, by Simon Ellis, is sold in "Southfork Boutiques"—in Selfridge's department store, among others. A gorgeous silk dress costs about $125.

Occasionally, bootleg merchandise appears—like the X-rated video cassette *Dalla-X* that is currently sold in Europe or the T-shirts that said "Cullen killed J.R." printed by a friend of Fort Worth millionaire Cullen Davis.

You don't have to buy *Dallas* merchandise to get in on the fun, however. Numerous European and American companies, including Lux, Revlon, and Betty Crocker, have made product tie-ins. Newspaper or point of purchase coupons ask contestants to enter a random drawing. Winners are flown to MGM Studios, Dallas, or both, to appear as extras in an episode of *Dallas*. Approximately two million people entered the Revlon contest, the most Revlon has ever had in a contest offering.

Sometimes Lorimar will ask a star to help promote a product. Steve Kanaly worked on the *Who Killed Jock Ewing?* publishing project; Ken Kercheval helped publicize the *Dallas* board game. Actors are paid either a fee or a percentage of the revenues from the project.

The Furor and the Phenomena

When *Texas Monthly* magazine named the 150 most important events in the state's 150-year history in January 1986, it pronounced the shooting of J.R. Ewing as one of them. Indeed, on November 21, 1980, 350 million people in 57 different countries tuned in to *Dallas* to see who shot J.R. They were part of an international epidemic that reduced cocktail-party small talk and bookies' hot lines to the simple question, "Who shot J.R.?" Jimmy the Greek laid odds on his favorite: he was right—it was Kristin, Sue Ellen's sister. Abroad, the British went bonkers trying to discover whodunit. Larry Hagman, who was in England during the summer of discontent, confessed that even if the queen herself should ask him, he wouldn't know the answer.

Only a handful of people did know who shot J.R., and the actors were among the last to find out. Revealing pages of dialogue were deleted from their scripts, and although a thief ransacked the offices and stole various *Dallas* scripts, the secret was kept intact. Lorimar executives were themselves at fever pitch, dying to know the secret. The international brouhaha put so much pressure on the studio that they finally invited cast members to a special dinner so they could watch the episode on a big screen and all find out together who the murderer was. (Most thought it was Dusty Farlow, Sue Ellen's lover, who died mysteriously and probably was not seriously dead. Farlow did come back to life later, but not with a gun in his hand.)

Dallas fever took a bit of a dive after that and the show even fell to its all-time low in the 1985–86 season. For the first time in its history, the series finished below number five (it placed sixth in the yearly ratings). Was *Dallas* washed up? Hardly. When word leaked that Patrick Duffy would return to the show, speculation as to exactly what role he would play brought the ratings for the series cliffhanger to an unusual high and left the fans once again gasping for breath in what would prove to be a long, hot summer.

While Lorimar confirmed that Duffy had indeed signed a new contract, no further word was forthcoming. To keep the suspense airtight, Duffy was brought in to shoot his single cliffhanger scene in secret—there was no "Welcome Home Pat" party—and actors who appeared with him in the scene did not know they were working with him until they saw the edited film. Three different versions of the cliffhanger were shot, so even the actors didn't know what was going on. The last Victoria Principal knew of it, her character awakened one morning on her honeymoon to hear water running in the shower, walked to the bathroom, opened the shower door, and lo and behold: Mark Graison is lying dead on the tile floor. He never was a healthy man.

While the traditional nighttime soap format would have the secret of the unmasked stranger, who looked remarkably like Bobby James Ewing, be revealed around the sixth or eighth episode, producers decided not to string out the audience or allow speculation to sink to a ridiculous low (Bobby's evil twin brother? Bobby brain-damaged after the accident?). The first episode of the 1986–87 season therefore was structured to tell all. Even cast and crew were most attentively glued to their small screens. Although they had already shot parts of twelve episodes before the new season opened in September 1986, few of them knew how all the magic pieces would fit together.

Of course, Duffy's return does bring new life to a series that many thought was beginning to get a little rusty around the derrick—Jenna will have new reason to live; Pam has new complications in her life; and J.R., well, J.R. will once again have his alter-ego looking over his shoulder. The tabloids are having a field day with all of it.

"We don't plant the tabloids," says Katzman, "in fact we are alternately irritated and angered by them. Sometimes their stories are basically true but contain errors, other times they are pure fiction. Some of the items make me laugh: we have never approached Diana Ross, Paul McCartney, or Mick Jagger to be on *Dallas*, and we are not discussing a part with Roger Moore." Katzman also denies that Priscilla Beaulieu Presley was told that her next love interest would be a rock and roll singer like Elvis and laughs at the notion that she stormed to the producers' office to say that she wouldn't play out that story line.

That, of course, is the beauty of *Dallas*. You never quite know how much of it you should take seriously:

In Israel, where children wear costumes to school to celebrate the holiday of Purim, little boys now go dressed in Stetsons and cowboy suits and claim to be J.R.;

In West Germany, the Bonn Municipal Theatre produced a forty-five-minute ballet inspired by the show;

In Italy, restaurants report lighter trade on Tuesday and Wednesday evenings during the hours *Dallas* airs;

In Turkey, a parliamentary meeting was reportedly once cut short so members of parliament would not miss the show.

Obviously, people the world over agree with David Jacobs when he shrugs and says, "*Dallas* is just plain fun."

Tune in next week. For even more fun.